A Hand book of Geography : Realms, Regions and Concepts

A Hand book of Geography : Realms, Regions and Concepts

R.V. Prajapati

CYBER TECH PUBLICATIONS
4264/3, Ansari Road, Daryaganj, New Delhi-110002 (India)
Ph.: 011-23244078, 011-43559448 Fax: 011-23280028
E-Mail: cyberpublicationsdelhi@yahoo.com
Website: www.cybertechpublications.com

A HAND BOOK OF GEOGRAPHY : REALMS, REGIONS AND CONCEPTS

R.V.Prajapati

First Edition 2010

Published by :

G.S. Rawat for **Cyber Tech Publications**
4264/3, Ansari Road, Daryaganj, New Delhi-110002 (India)
Ph.: 011-23244078, 011-43559448 Fax: 011-23280028
E-Mail: cyberpublicationsdelhi@yahoo.com
Website: www.cybertechpublications.com

Printed at: Asian Offset Printers, Delhi-53

Preface

Increasing global interests and involvements have demanded the stimulation of a global awareness of the world and this educational need is well served by this latest extensively revised, restructured and thoroughly up-to-date edition. Regional geography is firmly the concept of central importance in this presentation of geographical knowledge on the layout of the world's environments and societies but this is no static descriptive survey. Written in an encouragingly lively style the authors' concern for social, economic and political issues conveys a contemporary realism that is enriched by insights into the processes at work in transforming the world's rapidly changing geography.

The trite statement of intention 'to outline the physical stage on which the human drama is being played out' is deemed to be fulfilled by simple statements on an eclectic selection of topics including tectonic plates, glaciation, global warming, water and world precipitation followed by a summary statement of the climatic regions devised by Koppen and Geiger within which soils and vegetation receive scant attention. The human foundations are laid by a comparable melange of the concepts of cultures and cultural landscapes, highlighting the population distribution, urbanization, patterns of economic development and statements on ethnicity, demographic data and political backgrounds.

The threefold components indicated in the title prove to be of very different proportions and usefulness in their contributions. In the Introduction much ado is made of the concept of the 'geographic realm' adopted as the basic spatial unit in the broad global scheme of world regionalization. Twelve are postulated but without any depth of examination of their rationale. Nor is much enlightenment to be derived from the authors' simple assertion that `each realm is defined in terms of a synthesis of its total human geography, a composite of its leading cultural, economic, historical, political and appropriate environmental features'. By these criteria the Antarctic is deemed not to be a realm but just a continent and is dismissed in a half-page note on national claims to it. Seven of the realms feature as dominated by one major political entity viz. North America (USA), Middle America (Mexico), South America (Brazil), South Asia (India), East Asia (China), Russia and Australia; the other five are organized around many countries but with no dominant state viz. Europe, North Africa and South West Asia, sub-Saharan Africa, South East Asia and the Pacific.

Despite discussion of their political and cultural attributes the realms do not emerge from new thinking but correspond closely, in their role as frameworks within which are contained the regions, to long familiar continental and sub-continental entities. Each of the book's main chapters focuses on one realm. There is little in-depth examination of the concept of regions, but the authors' predilection for social, economic and political geography found an accommodating and rewarding basis for regional studies in the concept of the cultural landscape. Consideration of an immense literature, extensive world travel, and perception in illuminating individual regions have resulted in intellectually satisfying and eminently readable portrayals. The 53 regional units occupy nine-tenths of this book and in them is to be found its special value as a learning and teaching resource. In a common format each chapter is opened by an atlas-style map and a review of the physiography, history and human geography, followed by the regional accounts.

—Author

CONTENTS

1

INTRODUCTION

Geography is the study of the distributions and interrelationships of earth phenomena. Geography is different from other disciplines in that it doesn't have a particular "thing" it studies. Botanists study plants, while geologists are interested in rocks. Geography is defined by its approach or methodology. Geographers describe their discipline as a spatial science. By "space" we aren't talking about celestial space. Geographers are concerned with answering questions about how and why phenomena vary across the surface of the Earth. For instance, geographers investigate patterns of vegetation as they relate to distributions of climate, soils, and topography.

Geographers recognize the dynamic nature of the of Earth's physical systems. The physical geography of Earth changes in response to variations in weather and climate, the shifting of continents, and the sculpting of coastlines by wave action. By recognizing the Earth system is dynamic, geographers take time into consideration when looking at the spatial patterns of Earth phenomena. Therefore, geographers are playing important roles in understanding the effects of climate change on earth systems. The role of geographers in assessing patterns of environmental change is a theme that reoccurs throughout this book.

Geographers study both the form and processes acting at the surface of the earth, the principal domain of geographic study. The Appalachian mountains appear as a series of linear folds in the earth surface. The Cascades on the other hand are much taller than the Appalachians and contain many peaks that are conical in shape, as exemplified by Mt. Saint Helens. If both are mountain systems, why do they differ so greatly in form? Their difference arise from the processes that created them. The Appalachian Mountains were created by folding of the earth's crust. The conical shaped peaks of the Cascades are volcanoes. Many of these form where crustal plates collide, causing rock to melt deep beneath the earth, and finally erupting onto the surface to build the mountains we see today.

Think about what information was required to answer the question as to why these two mountain systems are so different. In order to understand their form we needed to investigate their geologic history in order to determine the processes that created them. Geographers must therefore rely on information provided by other sciences to help understand the form and distribution of Earth phenomena. This is why geography has been called an "integrative science". It draws on the knowledge of many disciplines to understand the natural patterns within the earth system.

Geographers also study how human activities shape, and are shaped by, the natural environment. Geographers are actively engaged in research about the relationship between agriculture practices, water erosion, and flooding. Others are uncovering the impact of air pollution on ecosystems, and how global warming will affect the physical geography of earth. These studies are a part of the "man-land" tradition in geography, which was the precursor to modern environmental studies.

GEOGRAPHY AS A SPATIAL SCIENCE

Earlier we described geography as a spatial science, that is, we are interested in answering questions about some place or location, or looking at distributions of earth phenomena like climate and how climate interacts with other aspects of the earth system. Thus geographers answer four basic questions when studying our environment.

First, geographers are concerned with location. By location we mean physically where something is at. A geographer might ask the question - "Where is a tropical rain forest located?" To answer this, one might simply look at a map and find that a rain forest is located at 5° North, 110° East. The use of latitude and longitude accurately defines where the forest is located.

When geographers investigate place, they describe the environmental conditions that determine the object of study. Now the geographer may pose the question- "What are the environmental conditions that create a tropical rain forest?" To this we can respond by saying that tropical rain forests are found where the average annual temperatures are very high (coolest month averages 64.4°F) and there is ample rainfall in each month (2.4 inches a month). As you can see, our answer said nothing about the location but described what the place is like for a tropical rain forest.

Questions of location and place do not give us much information about the distribution or spatial pattern of earth phenomena. For instance we might want to know - "What is the distribution of tropical rain forests on the Earth?". To this we could answer that tropical rain forests are found in low latitude, rainy, tropical regions such as the Amazon and Congo Basin and throughout much of Indonesia.

Finally, geographers are also interested in spatial interaction, which is how elements of our earth system interact with one another to create spatial patterns. We might ask - "How do mountains interact with weather systems to affect the distribution of vegetation?". By looking at maps of mountain, wind and precipitation patterns and, maps of vegetation we find that mountains oriented perpendicular to the flow of wind create moist conditions on the windward side and dry conditions on the leeward side. Thus forests tend to be located on the moist windward side and vegetation suited to drier conditions on the leeward.

THE CONTINUUM OF GEOGRAPHY

Geography is a wide ranging field that incorporates a number of diverse subject areas. Broadly speaking, geography can be divided into human geography and physical geography. Human geography deals with spatial aspects of human activities and culture. Physical geography, our topic here, focuses on the geographical attributes of the natural environment. The diagram below illustrates the continuum of geography. Though the discipline can be broken down into two separate areas of study, physical geography and human geography, they are actually seen as blending with one another along a geographic continuum.

As we move toward the center of the diagram we enter a zone where the subject matter of the two meet and intermingle. At the center is where the synthesis of the physical environment with the human/cultural environment occurs. In so doing we create a holistic view of earth systems. The study of environmental issues like global warming, response of humans to natural hazards, and deforestation requires this kind of synthesis or examination of relationships between society and the natural environment to understand them.

Each subdiscipline draws on the knowledge provided by a variety of disciplines outside of geography. For instance, to study earth phenomena like the distribution of soils we have to draw on the expertise of such disciplines as soil science, botany, and climatology because soil properties are a function of vegetation, energy, and moisture. Geography, therefore, is a very integrative science.

Physical geography and earth science share much in common. Physical geography places earth science content in a spatial context. This video by the American Geological Institute illustrates why earth science (and by extension physical geography) is important to all of us.

STEPS IN GEOGRAPHIC INQUIRY

Geographers like most other scientists follow a logical order of inquiry when attempting to answer geographic questions. The steps in geographic inquiry are:

- Observation
- Analysis
- Explanation
- Prediction

Some physical geographers are interested in the spatial distribution of weather across the earth. To study such phenomena, the geographer employs many of the same techniques and tools of a meteorologist. Let's look at how a geographer, or meteorologist, studies the pattern of weather across our earth.

Observation

First, observations must be taken of the various weather elements. At particular times each day, hundreds of weather observers make instrument readings either manually or use automated weather instruments to gather data. Here we see an aerovane that measures both wind speed and direction. The data from hundreds of ground-based observations, radiosonde, pilot reports, and satellites are fed to World Meteorological Centers located in Australia, Russia and the United States.

Analysis

From the World Meteorological Centers, worldwide weather data is compiled and sent to a country's national meteorological center. The data is fed into a variety of computer models, equations that relate to atmospheric energy and motion, for analysis and visualization of weather. The output of these models are used explain the present weather and predict future weather.

Explanation

The output of computer analysis, along with many years of observations and training, help geographers and meteorologists explain the weather occurring at a place. A weather map is one of many products created by the National Weather Service. (The brightly colored ones you see on the evening TV weather program are based on these).

Weather maps of present activity and text explanations are issued on a regular basis. Text discussions are provided to help explain what is visualized on the weather map.

Prediction

The ultimate goal of our inquiry is to make predictions. In weather analysis the output of data from our weather models is fed back into the equations, run again increasing the time increment into the future. The results of the run are continually fed back into the computer until the desired time is arrived at (e.g., 24 hour period, 48 hour, etc.) From these computer runs a prediction or forecast is made.

TOOLS OF THE GEOGRAPHER

Maps

A map is the fundamental tool of the geographer. With a map, one can illustrate the spatial distribution (i.e., geographic pattern) of almost any kind of phenomena. Maps provide a wealth of information. The information collected to create a map is called spatial data. Any object or characteristic that has a location can be considered spatial data. The data collected for a map can be qualitative (buildings, rivers, roads) or quantitative (elevation, air temperature, population density). There are many different kinds of maps that serve quite different purposes.

Map Projections

A map projection is a method of portraying the two-dimensional curved surface of the Earth on a flat planar surface. Projections are created to preserve one or several measurements of the following qualities:

- Area
- Shape
- Direction
- Bearing
- Distance
- Scale

Each projection handles the conversion of these metric properties from the curved surface of a globe to the flat surface of map differently.

The purpose of the map is of primary importance in choosing a projection to illustrate spatial patterns of Earth phenomena. For instance, the Mercator projection was long used for navigation or maps of equatorial regions. The cylindrical Mercator projection mathematically projects the globe onto a cylinder tangent to the Equator. Large areas become distorted which increases toward away from the Equator. Distances are true only along the Equator, special scales are provided for other latitudes for measurement.

The Robinson projection uses tabular coordinates rather than mathematical formulas to make earth features look the "right" size and shape. A better balance of size and shape result is a more accurate picture of high-latitude lands like Russia, Soviet and Canada. Greenland is truer to size but compressed.

TYPES OF MAPS

Reference Maps: Topographic

Reference or navigational maps are created to help you navigate over the earth surface. These kinds of maps show you where particular places are located and can be used to navigate you way to them. A street map or the common highway road map falls into this category. Physical geographers use topographic maps to show the locations of landscape features on the earth.

Topographic maps illustrate the horizontal and vertical positions (relief) of land surface features. Topographic maps use contour lines to show elevation (height above sea level). Contour lines connect points of equal elevation above a specified reference, usually as sea level. The heavy brown contour lines with the elevation printed on them are called index contours. Intermediate contours are the lighter brown lines between index contours. Sometimes dashed lines called supplemental contours are used in areas of very low relief. Benchmarks are locations where the elevation has been surveyed. Benchmarks are denoted on a map with the letters "BM", "X" or a triangle with the elevation printed beside.

Not only are natural features like mountains, valleys, streams and glaciers portrayed, but cultural features as well, e.g., houses, schools, streets, urbanized area. Take a look at the topographic symbol sheets provided by the United States Geological Survey to get an idea of the information provided on them.

Colors and shading can also be used to illustrate relief. Shaded relief maps are great at giving us the over all shape of the surface, but can't help us much in determining the elevation of a particular place. The National Geographic Society is noted for its excellent map products (and magazine too). Satellite maps are particularly useful to illustrate relief.

Thematic Maps

Thematic maps are used to communicate geographic concepts like the distribution of densities, spatial relationships, magnitudes, movements etc. World climate or soils maps are notable examples of thematic maps. Graduated circles indicate the area over which the earthquakes were felt. This map was created using a geographic information system which has the capability of overlying different kinds of spatial data to show the relationships between them.

THE ATMOSPHERE

The atmosphere that envelops us reflects the complex interactions between the major spheres that comprise the Earth system. The gaseous composition of the atmosphere is being regulated by the biotic elements of the Earth system as well as the geological processes that have shaped our Earth. Volcanic eruptions release vast quantities of gases and particles into the air causing changes to the composition and heat dynamics of the atmosphere. Human activity has also had a profound impact on the composition of the atmosphere locally, regionally, and globally. In this chapter you will investigate the structure and composition of the atmosphere and its influence on physical systems of the Earth.

Our atmosphere is a dynamic mixture of gases that envelop the Earth. Two gases, nitrogen and oxygen, make up most of the atmosphere by volume. They are indeed important for maintaining life and driving a number of processes near the surface of the Earth. Many of the so called "minor gases" (known here as "variable gases") play an equally important role in the Earth system. These gases include those that have a significant impact on the heat budget and the availability of moisture across the Earth. The atmosphere is not a homogeneous mass of gases, but has a layered structure as defined by vertical temperature changes.

Atmospheric Composition

Two broad regions can be identified using air composition as a means to subdivide the atmosphere. The heterosphere is the outer most sphere where gases are distributed in distinct layers by gravity according to their atomic weight. Extending from an altitude of 80 km (50 mi), the lightest elements (hydrogen and helium) are found at the at the outer margins of the atmosphere. The heavier elements (nitrogen and oxygen) are found at the base of the layer. The homosphere lies between the Earth's surface and the heterosphere. Gases are nearly uniformly mixed through this layer even though density decreases with height above the surface. The only exceptions is the "ozone layer" from 19 to 50 km (12 to 31 mi) and near surface variations in water vapor, carbon dioxide and air pollutants.

Permanent Gases

The permanent gases that make up the atmosphere by volume are nitrogen (78%), oxygen (21%) and argon (.93%). Physical geographers often refer to these gases as the "permanent gases" because their concentration has remained virtually the same for much of recent earth history. Nitrogen is a relatively inert gas produced primarily by volcanic activity. It is an important component of protein in meat, milk, eggs and the tissues of plants, especially grains and members of the pea family. It cannot be ingested directly by organisms but made available to plants, and then to animals, by compounds in the soil. Most atmospheric nitrogen enters the soil by nitrogen-fixing microorganisms. Oxygen is important for plant and animal respiratory processes. It is also important to chemical reactions (oxidation) that breakdown rock materials (chemical weathering). Without oxygen, things cannot burn either. Free oxygen in the atmosphere is a product of plant photosynthesis. Plants take up carbon dioxide and in the process of photosynthesis release oxygen.

Variable Gases

The so called "variable" gases are those present in small and variable amounts. These include carbon dioxide, methane, ozone, water vapor, and particulates among others. Even though they represent a tiny portion of the atmosphere as a whole, they exert a great control over our environment.

Carbon Dioxide

Carbon dioxide(CO_2) makes up only .036% of the atmosphere by volume. Carbon dioxide is essential to photosynthetic processes of plants. Huge quantities of carbon are stored in plant tissue, deposits of coal, peat, oil, and gas. Carbon dioxide is taken in by plants and during photosynthesis is combined with water and energy to form oxygen and carbohydrates. The stored carbohydrates are used to fuel plant respiration and growth.Carbon is also stored in limestone rocks that have formed by the compaction of carbonate-rich shells of ocean life. Because vegetation takes in so much carbon dioxide, we often refer to plants as a "sink" for it.

Carbon dioxide in the atmosphere varies throughout the year, decreasing slightly during the summer as plants leaf out, and then increases during the winter as plants go dormant and photosynthesis decreases.

Methane

Methane (CH_4) is a greenhouse gas contributing to about 18% of global warming and has been on the rise over the last several decades. Though methane makes up far less of the atmosphere (.0002%) than carbon doxide, it is 20 times more potent than CO_2 as a greenhouse gas. Methane is a product of the decomposition of organic matter, with major natural sources being that which occurs from wetlands, termites, the oceans, and hydrates.

A major source of methane is from termites. Termites eat wood and produce methane as a result of the breakdown of cellulose in their digestive tracts. They are thought to be responsible for 11% of the methane in the atmosphere (some estimates are as high as 20% - 40%). The clearing of the rain forests greatly impacts termite populations and in turn the methane content of the atmosphere. When a patch of rain forest is cleared, termite populations explode due to the ample food source that is left behind. Human activities have contributed to the rise of methane in our atmosphere. Landfills, rice paddy agriculture, natural gas systems, and livestock production appear to be significant contributors of anthropogenic sources of methane.

Ozone

Ozone (O_3) is both beneficial and harmful to life on Earth. Much of the ozone in the atmosphere is found in the stratosphere. Here, ozone absorbs UV light from the Sun preventing it from reaching the surface. Without this blanket, humans would be exposed to serious sun burn and potential risk of skin cancer. Ozone is also found in the lowest layer of the atmosphere, the troposphere. Here ozone can act as an eye and respiratory irritant. Ozone also causes cellular damage inside the leaves of plants causing brown splotches, impairing carbon dioxide uptake and disrupting the photosyntheitic apparatus. Such damage can cause economic losses through reduced crop yields. It also damages the carbon "sink" role of vegetation leaving more carbon dioxide in the atmosphere to enhance the greenhouse effect and potential global warming.

Human-produced compounds such as chloroflourocarbons and halides containing chlorine and bromine destroy ozone, and have distrupted the fragile stratospheric ozone layer over Antarctica and the Arctic. Ozone depletion over Antarctica occurs during the spring when sunlight returns to the South Pole and the temperatures are still very cold.

Water Vapor

Water vapor is an extremely important gas found in the atmosphere. It can vary from 4% in the steamy tropics to nearly nonexistent in the cold dry regions of the Antarctic. Water vapor is a good absorber of Earth's outgoing radiation and thus is considered a greenhouse gas. When water vapor is converted to a liquid during condensation, clouds are formed. Clouds are good absorbers of radiation given off by the Earth's surface. The absorption of this energy raises the temperature of the air. But clouds are generally light-colored and hence reflect incoming solar radiation off their tops. The reflected light is sent back to space, never reaching the ground to warm the Earth. Thus clouds can have either a warming or a cooling effect on air temperature. It has been thought that these effects balance one another out but National Public Radio's All Things Considered report suggests that this might not be true, forcing climatologists to rethink the issue.

Particulates

Particulates play several important roles in atmospheric processes. Particulate matter includes dust, dirt, soot, smoke, and tiny particles of pollutants. Major natural sources of particulates are volcanoes, fires, wind-blown soil and sand, sea salt, and pollen. Human sources such as factories, power plants, trash incinerators, motor vehicles, and construction activity also contribute particulates to the atmosphere.

Particulates are very effective at altering the energy and moisture balances of the Earth system. Particulates diffuse sunlight reducing the amount and intensity of solar radiation reaching the Earth's surface. The most spectacular sunrises and sunsets are a result of light being refracted from particulates in the atmosphere. Particulates will also reflect sunlight back out to space, never letting it reach the surface. Decreasing significant amounts of incoming solar radiation can cause global temperatures to decrease. The eruption of Mt. Pinatubo in 1991 caused a .5o C decrease in global temperatures. However, particulates can absorb longwave radiation emitted by the Earth, causing the atmosphere to warm as well. Particulates serve as condensation nuclei for water. In order for water to change from a gas to a liquid, a nucleus upon which water vapor can attach itself is nearly always required. Without particulates, little water would condense to form clouds and precipitation.

NASA scientists using satellite data and computer models found black soot from incomplete combustion may be contributing to changes in sea ice, snow and atmospheric temperatures near the North Pole. They found the timing and location of rising temperatures and loss of sea ice during the end of the 20th century is consistent with a significant rise in human produced aerosols. Their models suggest that one third of the soot comes from South Asia, one third from biomass burning, and the rest from Russia, Europe, and North

America. Soot deposited on snow and sea ice decreases the surface reflectivity causing more sunshine to be absorbed. Airborne soot warms the Arctic atmosphere and affects weather patterns and clouds.

Greenhouse Effect and Global Warming

Carbon dioxide and methane are two of a number of so called "greenhouse gases". Greenhouses gases are responsible for the relatively warm temperature of the atmosphere. Without the blanket of greenhouse gases, the Earth would be a frozen ball of ice. The gases of our atmosphere are known as "selective absorbers" of radiant energy. That is, a particular gas absorbs and emits energy well at some wavelengths but not at others. Solar radiation (shortwave) passes through most of the atmospheric gases without being absorbed to a significant extent. However, longwave radiation emitted from the Earth's surface and directed toward the sky is readily absorbed by greenhouse gases. When absorbed, the temperature of the atmosphere increases. Some of this absorbed energy is emitted to space while some is emitted back towards the Earth. This is the basis for the greenhouse effect.

Global Warming

The fact that atmospheric gases contribute to the heating of the Earth is not new. A hundred years ago, Swedish scientist Svante Arrhenius became the first person to investigate the effect that doubling atmospheric carbon dioxide would have on global climate. Though all atmospheric scientists agree that there is a greenhouse effect, not all agree on the impact that human beings are having on it. In particular, many cannot agree that the present global warming that we are experiencing is a product of human activities. Analysis of ice cores has shown a significant variation in the carbon dioxide content of our atmosphere which has affected global air temperatures since the great ice sheets marched across the continents. Measurements of greenhouse gas concentrations over the last 150 years have shown a steady increase in carbon dioxide with an apparent increase in global temperatures as a result. Research has shown that there has been a 30% increase in the carbon dioxide content since the dawn of the industrial age. This increase is due to a number of activities such as fossil fuel burning, deforestation, and loss of other carbon dioxide "sinks" like wetlands and forests. The burning of fossil fuels releases stored carbon into the atmosphere raising the carbon dioxide content of the air. Forest removal leaves carbon dioxide in the air to enhance the natural greenhouse effect.

Rising levels of greenhouse gases is thought to cause a rise in global air temperatures. Global mean surface temperatures have increased by .5 - 1.0 F since the latter part of the 19th century. Rising temperatures have caused a decrease in snow cover and sea ice in the Northern Hemisphere. Global sea level has risen by 4-8 inches over the past hundred years. Additional sea level rise and inundation of coastal regions is feared as Antarctic ice sheets and shelves, and smaller alpine glaciers melt. The frequency of extreme precipitation events has increased throughout much of the United States.

Atmospheric Structure

If we examine the vertical structure the atmosphere in different places we will find it varies in height, being lowest at the poles and highest at the equator. The varying height is due to the spatial variation in heating of the Earth's surface and thus the atmosphere above. This fact makes it difficult to define exact heights for the layers of the atmosphere. The solution is to subdivide the atmosphere not on the basis of fixed heights, but on temperature change.

Troposphere and Tropopause

The troposphere is the layer closest to the Earth's surface. The graph of temperature change indicates that air temperature decreases with an increase in altitude through this layer. Air temperature normally decreases with height above the surface because the primary source of heating for the air is the Earth. The rate of change in temperature with altitude is called the environmental lapse rate of temperature (ELR) The ELR varies from day-to-day at a place, and from place to place on any given day. The normal lapse rate of temperature is the average value of the ELR, .65°C /100 meters. That is, at any particular place and on any given day the actual ELR may be larger or smaller, but on average has a value of .65°C /100

m. So if I went outside today it could be .62°C /100 m and then tomorrow it might be .68°C /100 m. The ELR also varies from place- to - place on a given day. That is, at Chicago, Illinois it might be .65°C /100 m and on the same day it could be .62°C /100 m over London, England .

Under the right conditions, the air temperature may actually increase with an increase in altitude above the Earth. When this occurs we are experiencing an inverted lapse rate of temperature, or simply an inversion. Shallow surface inversions are typical over the snow covered surfaces of subarctic and polar regions, and sometimes occur when high pressure cells inhabit a region.

The tropopause lies above the troposphere. Here the temperature tends to stay the same with increasing height. The tropopause acts as a "lid" on the troposphere preventing air from rising upwards into the stratosphere.

Stratosphere

Above the tropopause lies the stratosphere. If a layer of air exhibits no change in temperature with an increase in elevation we typically refer to it as an isothermal layer i.e. layer of equal temperature. Through most of the stratosphere the air temperature increases with an increase in elevation creating a temperature inversion. The inverted lapse rate of temperature is due to the presence of stratospheric ozone which is a good absorber of ultra-violet radiation emitted by the Sun. As energy penetrates downward, less and less is available for lower layers and hence the temperature decreases toward the bottom of the stratosphere. The downward reduction of heat transfer due to solar energy absorption from above is offset by the heat given off by the Earth creating the isothermal layer at the bottom of the stratosphere. At the top of the stratosphere lies the stratopause. Like the tropopause, the stratopause is an isothermal layer that separates the stratosphere from the mesosphere.

Mesosphere and beyond

It is the properties of the previously discussed layers that affects most of what we study in physical geography. Processes acting in layers above the stratopause have relatively little impact on our elemental study of Earth near-surface processes. In the mesosphere air temperatures begin to decrease with increasing altitude. 99.9 percent of the gases that comprise the atmosphere lie below this level. The air of the mesosphere is thus extremely thin and air pressure very small. With very few molecules like ozone capable of absorbing solar radiation, especially near the top of the layer, the air temperature decreases with height. The mesopause separates the mesosphere from the thermosphere above.

Here, energetic oxygen molecules absorb incoming solar radiation raising the layer's temperature. Because solar activity determines the temperature of the layer, temperature at the top of the layer is warmer than that near the bottom of the thermosphere. Even though the temperatures are quite high in the thermosphere, the heat content of the layer is very low due the low density of air at this level.

Functional Layers

Two layers, the ionosphere and ozonosphere are identified when using function as the criterion for subdivision. The ionosphere is not really a layer of the atmosphere, but an electrified field of ions and free electrons. The ionosphere absorbs cosmic rays, gamma rays, X-rays, and shorter wavelengths of ultraviolet radiation. The spectacular display auroral lights are generally found in this region.

The ozonosphere is the concentrated layer of ozone found in the stratosphere. Ozone (O_3) absorbs ultraviolet light between 0.1 - 0.3μm. Though relatively constant through millions of years, seasonal fluctuations of ozone especially over the Arctic and Antarctic are common.

The Earth System

The Earth system is a complex interaction between its subsystems the atmosphere, hydrosphere, biosphere, and lithosphere. The Earth system around us today is the result of millions of years of evolutionary processes tending toward a stable equilibrium. At times, assaults from within and outside have stressed the system and forced changes. Here you will explore the types of systems found on Earth and the sources of energy that drive them.

The Earth in Spacc

Earth Origin

Earth is the third planet from the Sun, one of eight "classical" planets recognized by the International Astronomical Union. Pluto, defined as a planet until recently was downgraded. It is thought that our Earth originated from the accretion of bits of solid matter left from the massive explosion of a star or supernova. Bits of material were scattered into space forming a slowly rotating cosmic gas cloud. Gravity slowly gathered the thinly spread atoms of the cosmic cloud. As the atoms moved closer together the gas became hotter and more dense. A new sun was born as hydrogen eventually became so tightly compressed and temperatures so high that nuclear burning began. A flattened rotating disc of gas and dust surrounded the young sun. Outer cooler parts of the disc or star nebulae began to condense to form the building blocks of future planets.

It is believed that the Earth was created by the accretion of cold particles and originally had a homogeneous composition throughout. During the later part of the accretion phase, the Earth was likely heated by kinetic energy of objects colliding with the surface. Combined with the heat generated from radioactive decay of isotopes in the developing earth, the high temperature environment caused the entire planet to melt. Iron was pulled inward toward the core by gravity as lighter minerals - silicon, magnesium and aluminum - migrated upward, cooling to form the Earth's crust about 4.6 billion years ago.

As the planet cooled, solar radiation stripped away its original gasses to be replaced by those trapped beneath the surface and later released by volcanic venting also known as outgassing. The volcanic vapors, like water vapor, vented into the evolving atmosphere and condensed to form clouds, and ice comets appear to have contributed water vapor to the atmosphere. However, the surface was still too hot for water to collect. That which fell to the surface as precipitation quickly vaporized and re-entered the atmosphere to condense once again. As the surface cooled, precipitation finally filled basins and depressions forming the first oceans. The Earth was now on its evolutionary way towards the planet we live on today. The tectonic forces creating the surface configuration of oceans and continents today will be taken up in other modules.

Describing the Earth

Size and Shape

Those involved in the study of measuring the Earth, called geodesists, don't know exactly what the true shape of the Earth is. We often describe it as a sphere, it is more technically called an oblate ellipsoid. That is, the Earth is wider in the middle and flatter at the poles. The equatorial bulge is due to the centrifugal force exerted on the Earth by its rotation. The equatorial diameter Earth is about 7926 miles (12,756 km) while the polar diameter is 7900 miles (12,714 km). The equatorial circumference is approximately 24,900 miles (40,075 km). On December 26th, 2004 subduction occurred between the India and Burma plates off the coast of Indonesia making for a slightly more compact Earth. The shift in the Earth's crust resulted in a magnitude 9 earthquake and large tsunami that devastated South Asia. Interestingly, the Earth became slightly more round and the North Pole shifted by about 2.5 cm (an inch) in the direction of 145 degrees East longitude (Science Daily, 2005).

From the height of Mt. Everest at 29,029 feet (8848 m) in the Himalayas, to the Mariana Trench in the Pacific at 6781 feet below sea level the Earth has a total relief of about 12 miles. Though this seems to be a great distance, it's a mere blimp when compared to the diameter of the Earth.

Great and Small Circles

If you pass a plane through the center of a sphere, the intersection of the plane and the surface of the sphere creates a great circle. Planes passing through any other part of a sphere without going through the center create small circles. An arc of a great circle is the smallest distance between two points on a sphere and therefore is the preferred route for planes traveling great distances, like crossing an ocean. The concept of great and small circles relates to meridians (longitude) and parallels (latitude). Meridians are half of a great circle (180o) whose ends are at the North and South poles. Parallels of latitude are small circles, except for the equator which is a great circle.

Natural Systems

A system is defined as a collection of interacting objects. The Earth and its atmosphere defines the Earth system. A system consists of three basic elements:

(1) a functioning set of components,

(2) a flow of energy which powers them, and

(3) a process for the internal regulation of their functioning called feedback (Trewartha, et. al., 1977).

System regulation

Most systems tend toward a state of equilibrium where system inputs are balanced by system outputs. Though natural systems change over long periods of time, on the scale of a human lifetime they appear to be static. In reality, the state of natural systems oscillates around a mean condition - a state known as dynamic equilibrium. For instance, the abundance and type of animal species in an ecosystem may fluctuate over a time, but the overall diversity remains constant. The Earth's atmospheric temperature has remained fairly constant through long periods of Earth history, even though at shorter time intervals, geologically speaking, the temperature has risen or fallen. If one or more controlling variables (climate, vegetation, soil, man) imposes a long-term stress to the system it will seek to establish a new state. A steady-state equilibrium is reached when the rates of system inputs and outputs are equal, and the amount of material stored in the system is constant over time.

The state of the system is a result of feedback mechanisms between system components.

Feedbacks

Outputs generated by the functioning of a system component either encourages change in the system (positive feedbacks) or discourage changes (negative feedbacks). Negative feedbacks act to regulate the system to keep it in a state of equilibrium. Though many theories have been proposed as to what caused the long periods of glaciation over the course of earth history, a change in the amount of solar radiation absorbed by the surface is common to many of them. One idea is that the orbit of the earth around the sun changed causing a decrease in the amount of solar radiation reaching the earth. This was accomplished by a change in the earth - sun distance or a change in the tilt of the earth's axis. Whatever the reason, a decrease in solar radiation reaching and being absorbed by the surface would have caused the air temperature to decrease. With colder temperatures increased snowfall likely occurred and less snow melted over the course of a year. The build of snow and subsequent change to ice enabled glaciers to form and grow. As the earth is covered with a light colored surface its reflectivity increases. With increased reflectivity, less solar radiation is absorbed. As less radiation is absorbed, cooler temperatures develop, snow duration increases, glaciers grow, and more of the earth is covered by the highly reflective surface of glaciers.

A negative feedback discourages system change. An example of a negative feedback is used to support the notion of biospheric regulation of the atmosphere called the "Gaia Hypothesis" Some feel that the relatively stable conditions on Earth (atmospheric gas composition, temperature, etc) is due to the regulatory influence of the biosphere over the atmosphere. If some perturbation causes environmental conditions to shift, activities of the biosphere bring them back into balance. To illustrate this process they developed a simple model called "Daisy World". What we know is that the output of the sun has increased since the time our galaxy was formed. As a result, more solar radiation has been reaching the earth through time. However, over long periods of geologic time the air temperature has not changed all that much. Scientists argue that this has been accomplished through various biospheric regulatory mechanisms that alter the gaseous composition of the atmosphere and the nature of the earth surface. Their Daisy World model shows how the distribution of plants can modify the radiation balance of the Earth to regulate temperatures. Their model begins with a world that is covered with 50% dark and 50% light colored daisies. As the output of energy from the Sun increases, more energy is absorbed by the earth which in turn increases air temperature. The darker daisies absorb more sunshine than the light colored daisies because of their color. If the output of solar energy continues to increase, it becomes too much for the dark daisies to endure causing them to begin to die off. The with the lack of competition and their ability to reflect more light and endure higher temperatures, the light colored daisies flourish. As Daisy World becomes covered in a higher percentage of light colored daisies, the reflectivity of the surface increases. This results in a decrease in the absorption of sunshine and a reduction of temperature. Thus the change in the composition of plants in Daisy World dampens the effect of increased solar output. If it gets too cold, the dark daisies begin to flourish, increasing absorption of solar radiation and raising temperatures, causing the cycle to begin again. The negative feedback that is set up ultimately causes the system to reach an equilibrium. All systems have leverage points, points of vulnerability where an imposed stress yields maximum change. For instance, human intervention in the hydrologic cycle is best achieved at the river-flow stage (dam and reservoir building) as opposed to the precipitation stage (cloud seeding). A trigger (fire, species invasion, fertilizer runoff) sets off an environmental change. Once a change is initiated, the system responds by adjusting the energy and mass exchanges. If the stress is released, a period of recovery to its previous state occurs. Should the system be stressed beyond its threshold, it will seek a new state of equilibrium.

Types of Systems

Systems can be classified as open, closed, or isolated. Open systems allow energy and mass to pass across the system boundary. A closed system allows energy but not mass across its system boundary. An isolated system allows neither mass or energy to pass across the system boundary.

Open Systems

The ocean is an example of an open system. The ocean is a component of the hydrosphere and the ocean surface represents the interface between the hydrosphere and the atmosphere that lies above. Solar radiation passes through the atmosphere and is absorbed by the ocean. The absorbed energy evaporates water from the ocean. As the water vapor (mass) enters the atmosphere it carries with it the heat used to evaporate the water (called latent heat). When the water vapor enters the air it raises the air's humidity. If the humidity is high enough, condensation occurs, latent heat is released, and clouds are created. Continued condensation creates precipitation (mass) that falls back into the ocean. Hence, energy and heat (solar radiation, latent heat) as well as mass (water vapor and precipitation) passes across the boundary between the atmosphere and hydrosphere.

Closed Systems

The Earth system as a whole is a closed system. The boundary of the Earth system is the outer edge of the atmosphere. Virtually no mass is exchanged between the Earth system and the rest of the universe (except for an occasional meteorite). However, energy in the form of solar radiation passes from the Sun, through the atmosphere to the surface. The Earth in turn emits radiation back out to space across the system boundary. Hence, energy passes across the Earth's system boundary, but not mass, making it a closed system.

The interface between systems is not always easy to identify. Others are easier to recognize. The interface between the hydrosphere and lithosphere at a shoreline is easy to recognize as a definite planar boundary between a solid and fluid. The interface between the atmosphere and hydrosphere is less easy to discern as the hydrosphere comprises both liquid water of the surface and water held in the air.

Earth as a System

The Earth system (left) is a complex functioning system that includes all the components of the various "spheres" like the solid Earth or geosphere, the gaseous envelope surrounding the Earth that is the atmosphere, biosphere comprised of all living organisms and the hydrosphere or "water sphere". The Earth system diagram shows arrows representing flows of energy and mass that connect and intertwine the four spheres. At the top, solar energy drives many of the environmental processes operating in the four spheres. Additional sources of energy to drive Earth systems come from the Earth's internal heat engine and the gravitational attraction of the moon. Though the Earth system is a closed system, the "spheres" that comprise it are open. That is, there is a constant cycling of energy and mass between the hydrosphere, lithosphere, atmosphere, and biosphere.

Biogeochemical Cycles

We have adopted a model of the Earth System as a set of interacting "spheres", the atmosphere, hydrosphere, biosphere, and lithosphere. Being open systems, energy and mass is constantly cycled between them. The transport and transformation of substances through the Earth system are known collectively as biogeochemical cycles. These include the hydrologic (water), nitrogen, carbon, and oxygen cycles.

Nitrogen Cycle

Nitrogen comprises 78.08 % of the atmosphere making it the largest constituent of the gaseous envelope that surrounds the Earth. Nitrogen is important in the make up of organic molecules like proteins. Unfortunately, nitrogen is inaccessible to most living organisms. Nitrogen must be "fixed" by soil bacteria living in association with the roots of particular plant like legumes, clover, alfalfa, soybeans, peas, peanuts, and beans. Living on nodules around the roots of legumes, the bacteria chemically combine nitrogen in the air to form nitrates (NO_3) and ammonia (NH_3) making it available to plants. Organisms that feed on the plants ingest the nitrogen and release it in organic wastes. Denitrifying bacteria frees the nitrogen from the wastes returning it to the atmosphere.

Oxygen Cycle

Oxygen is the second most abundant gas in Earth's atmosphere and an essential element of most organic molecules. Though oxygen is passed between the lithosphere, biosphere and atmosphere in a variety of ways, photosynthesizing vegetation is largely responsible for oxygen found in the atmosphere. The cycling of oxygen through the Earth system is also accomplished by weathering of carbonate rock. Some atmospheric oxygen is bound to water molecules from plant transpiration and evaporation. Oxygen is also bound to carbon dioxide and released into the atmosphere during animal respiration.

Carbon Cycle

Carbon is the fourth most abundant element in the Universe and is the building block for all living things. The conversion of carbon dioxide into living matter and then back is the main pathway of the carbon cycle. Plants draw about one quarter of the carbon dioxide out of the atmosphere and photosynthesize it into carbohydrates. Some of the carbohydrate is consumed by plant respiration and the rest is used to build plant tissue and growth. Animals consume the carbohydrates and return carbon dioxide to the atmosphere during respiration. Carbohydrates are oxidized and returned to the atmosphere by soil microorganisms decomposing dead animal and plant remains (soil respiration). Another quarter of atmospheric carbon dioxide is absorbed by the world's oceans through direct air-water exchange. Surface water near the poles is cool and more soluble for carbon dioxide. The cool water sinks and couples to the ocean's thermohaline circulation which transports dense surface water toward the ocean's interior. Marine organisms form tissue containing reduced carbon, and some also form carbonate shells from carbon extracted from the air. There is actually very little of the total carbon cycling through the Earth system at any one point in time. Most of the carbon is stored in geologic deposits - carbonate rocks, petroleum, and coal - formed from the burial and compaction of dead organic matter on sea bottoms. The carbon in these deposits is normally released by rock weathering.

Sources of Energy

Forces that shape the Earth derive their energy from a number of different sources. Exogenic processes are those driven by exogenic forces that primarily derive their energy from solar radiation. For instance, soil erosion is caused by the force of wind acting on bare ground. We can trace the energy that causes wind erosion to the receipt of solar radiation. How? Though we are jumping ahead ourselves, wind is a product of horizontal differences in pressure over distance caused by the unequal heating of the Earth's surface. Low pressure is created when heated air rises from the surface and then flows outward at a higher elevation. As air moves upward, the surface pressure decreases relative to the air around it. The variation in surface pressure causes air to move into the region of low pressure to replace that which is rising, thus creating a wind. Soil is detached when wind blows over an erodible surface. Water and glacial erosion are other examples of exogenic processes.

Endogenic processes are those that get their energy from endogenic forces originating deep within the Earth. Many of the great mountain systems like the Himalayas are a product of the collision of lithospheric plates. The movement of lithospheric plates is thought to result from convection currents in the mantle. Deep within the core of the Earth, heat is generated by the radioactive decay of elements like uranium, thorium, and potassium. The heat is transferred upward to warm the mantle causing it to slowly circulate and tug on the plates above. The movement of plates fractures and folds rock, and their collision creates vast mountain chains and volcanic cones. So in the final analysis, endogenic forces tend to build things up while exogenic forces wear things down.

Future Geographies: Feedbacks Driving Global Warming

In this chapter we have learned that there are two types of feedbacks, positive feedbacks that drive system change and negative feedbacks that seek to keep systems in a state of equilibrium. Geoscientists like physical geographers are recognizing that positive feedback mechanisms may drive the Earth system past thresholds and towards a new state of equilibrium. In so doing, a new physical geography of the Earth system will appear. The distribution of Earth's regional climate's and ecosystems may be irreversibly altered.

Examples of Feedbacks Driving Global Warming

Rising temperatures are expected to cause increased evaporation of water into the atmosphere, most of which will originate from oceans. The additional water vapor boosts the absorption of infrared radiation emitted by the earth resulting in more warming (a positive feedback). The increased warmth promotes more evaporation yielding an enhanced greenhouse effect. However, the addition of water may cause an increase in cloud cover resulting in a higher atmospheric albedo and reflection of incoming solar radiation. If this were to occur, the reduction in insolation would lead to cooling. Such contradictory consequences makes it difficult to determine what actually will occur in the future.

Throughout history, humans have cut forests to build structures, warm their homes, and cook their meals, and clear the land for agriculture. Removing forests removes a powerful sink for carbon dioxide. Leaving more CO_2 in the atmosphere enhances global warming and thus an increase in temperatures. As a result, temperature conditions that may be too warm to support healthy forest ecosystems. With less vegetation present, more carbon dioxide is left in the atmosphere causing more warming, another positive feedback driving the earth system toward ever warmer conditions. As temperatures increase, evaporation increases causing drier conditions and the threat of wildfires and forest destruction.

Geoscientists agree that the Arctic has been and will continue to be significantly impacted by global warming. Much of the land surface in the Arctic is underlain by permanently frozen ground called "permafrost". They uppermost "active layer" experiences seasonal thawing. Recent studies indicate that climatic warming my result in a 12 to 15% reduction in the area covered by permafrost and a 15 to 30% increases in the thickness of the active layer. As temperature rises permafrost melts, releasing stored carbon, but just as importantly, methane. Increased warming results in more permafrost melting pushing the earth system ever forward into a future enhanced greenhouse environment.

Changes in Arctic ecosystems has already occurred as a result of global warming. When permafrost melts, water collects in small ponds on the surface increasing the heat gain nearly ten-fold. The additional heat continues to melt the underlying permafrost causing it to collapse and increasing the size of the pond. This negative feedback further degrades the permafrost.

As noted earlier in this chapter, carbon dioxide makes up a greater proportion of the atmosphere by volume, but methane absorbs energy much more efficiently. Increased warming at high latitudes may cause an increase in the release of methane from bogs or peatlands. Methane release from organic decomposition in wetlands coupled with carbon dioxide from melting permafrost will drive greenhouse gas levels higher, creating warmer temperatures.

Changes to the reflectivity of the surface (called the albedo) affects the amount of solar radiation absorb by the Earth. As Arctic sea ice melts it exposes open water which is less reflective (albedo decreases). The reduction in albedo allows more light to be absorbed by the ocean. As the ocean water warms, more heat is added to the air creating a positive feedback and driving Arctic temperatures ever higher. The reduction in sea ice is having a significant impact on arctic ecosystems.

Tipping Points

Positive feedbacks drive the physical environment towards new physical states. In June of 2008, twenty years after his landmark testimony about global warming, Dr. James Hansen reiterated his warnings before the U.S. Congress. He cited several examples of earth systems reaching or nearing a tipping point. A tipping level (point) is a level at which "no additional forcing is required for large climate change and impacts." (Hansen, 2008). According to Hansen, a "point of no return" is reached when unstoppable and irreversible (on a practical time scale) occurs. The disintegration of the Greenland ice cap is an example. Time is also an important factor in assessing whether a tipping point has been reached or a point of no return. Some, like Josefino Comiso of the NASA Goddard Space Flight Center, feel that the tipping point for perennial Arctic sea ice has already passed. David Barber, of the University of Manitoba is projecting that the North Pole will be ice free for the first time in history. For example, sea ice may completely disappear from the Arctic Ocean during the summer in a few years. This would represent a new state for the Arctic ocean. But temperature conditions could change in the relatively near future to permit sea ice to reform during the summer.

Energy and Radiation

Solar radiation is the source of energy that drives most environmental processes acting at the surface of the Earth. The spatial variation of energy affects the spatial variation of temperature, wind, and moisture which determine the geography of soils, vegetation, climate and landforms. The awesome power of hurricanes is driven by the heating of water and subsequent heat release during condensation. Unequal heating of the Earth's surface creates wind that heaps sand into great dunes.

Energy and Heat

Energy is the ability to do work on matter. The work done is manifested in a variety of ways. Matter can be pushed, pulled, or lifted over distance when energy is applied. In other words, work done on matter implies a change of position or movement. Potential energy is the energy of position. A block of rock attached to a high cliff face has substantial potential energy due to its position above the ground. When it breaks away from the cliff and falls to the surface potential energy is converted into kinetic energy of motion. When the rock hits the ground, kinetic energy is converted into work when it dislodges surface material. Heat is the total energy associated with random atomic and molecular motions of a substance. Heat is transferred in three ways. Radiation is the transfer of energy via electromagnetic waves. Radiation does not need an intervening medium to pass heat energy from the emitter to the absorber. When radiation from the Sun is absorbed by the Earth it does work by setting molecules in motion and raising their kinetic energy level. In a solid, the molecules may vibrate more rapidly and collide with one another and transfer heat from warmer to colder portion of the mass by conduction. In fluids like air and water, heat is transferred by the circulation of molecules via the process of convection.

The calorie is used as a unit of measurement for heat. A calorie is the amount of heat required to raise the temperature of one gram of water through 1°C. Energy is also expressed in terms of joules. One joule is the equivalent of one watt of power radiated or dissipated for one second. Temperature is a measure of the average kinetic energy level of a substance, in other words, the degree of hotness or coldness. Don't think temperature and heat are the same thing. A boiling pan of water has a higher temperature than a tepid bathtub of water, but the tub contains more heat because there is more mass.

The Nature of Electromagnetic Radiation

Electromagnetic radiation travels through space in the form of waves. Unlike heat transfer by convection or conduction, heat transfer by electromagnetic radiation can travel through empty space, requiring no intervening medium to transmit it. The quantity of energy carried in a wave is associated with the height or amplitude of the wave. Everything else being equal, the amount of energy carried in a wave is directly proportional to the amplitude of the wave. The type or "quality" of radiation depends on the wavelength, the distance between successive crests. The greater the distance between wave crests, the longer the wavelength. Any body that has a temperature is emitting electromagnetic radiation. There are an infinite number of wavelengths that make up the electromagnetic spectrum though we group them into a number of bands. The shortest wavelengths fall into the gamma rays, the electromagnetic radiation we can see with our eyes and processed by our brains falls into the visible band, and radio waves are comprised of the longest wavelengths.

The maximum wavelength at which a body emits radiation depends on its temperature. Wein's (pronounced "weens") Law states that the peak wavelength of radiation emission is inversely related to the temperature of the emitting body. That is, the hotter the body, the shorter the wavelength of peak emission. The Sun being a much hotter body emits most of its radiation in the shortwave end and the Earth in the longwave end of the spectrum. The division between shortwave and longwave radiation occurs at about 3 micrometers.

Radiation as Particles

It's hard to imagine radiation moving as waves through empty space without a medium to transfer the wave form. For instance, the waves created when you drop a rock into a pool of water require molecules of H_2O to propagate them. Though we describe electromagnetic radiation as invisible waves of energy, at the smallest scale it behaves as a particle, like when light is emitted by a single atom or molecule. When energy is given off there is a change in the orbital pattern of the electrons that surround the nucleus of an atom. As the orbit changes, a bundle of energy called a "photon" is released. However, particles of light differ from particles of matter: they have no mass, occupy no space, and travel at the speed of light, 2.9998 X 108 m s^{-1}. The amount of energy carried by a photon varies inversely with wavelength, the shorter the wavelength, the more energetic the photon.

Selective Absorption of the Atmosphere

The gasses that comprise our atmosphere are referred to as selective absorbers. That is, each gas absorbs only particular wavelengths of light. Why? Electrons orbit the nucleus of an atom at fixed orbital distances called orbital shells. The orbital shell for each atom is different and discrete. That is, for a given atom like hydrogen, its electrons can only orbit at particular distances and are different than those for atoms of neon.

Each orbital shell is associated with a given energy level; the greater the distance from the nucleus the greater the energy level. Electrons jump to a higher shell when excited by the absorption of energy. The photon must have the exact amount of energy to move the electron from, say, shell one to shell two. If the photon doesn't have enough energy to move the electron to shell two, it cannot move the electron half way between shell one and two. The atom does not stay in this excited, unstable state for very long. Energy is given off and the electron returns to a stable state or its "ground state" (lowest energy level or orbital distance). Recall that the amount of energy carried by a photon depends on the wavelength. Thus the atoms that comprise a gas can only absorb, or emit, particular wavelengths of energy (i.e. photons of energy).

The graph shows very little absorption for the atmosphere as a whole in the shortwave end of the spectrum, especially in the visible light band (the band of maximum emission for the Sun). The atmosphere absorbs far better in the longwave end of the electromagnetic spectrum which is the region of maximum emission (10μm) for the Earth.

The Sun

The Sun is a giant thermonuclear furnace with an internal temperature estimated to be 15 million degrees Celsius. Hydrogen nuclei collide at such an extremely high speed they fuse to form helium nuclei generating enormous amounts of heat in the core. The heat works its way to the luminous outer surface called the photosphere. Here temperatures fall to about 6000oC generating a maximum wavelength of emission in the visible end of the electromagnetic spectrum. Sun spots are dark, cooler regions of strong magnetic fields on the photosphere. The number of sun spots vary through an eleven year cycle. Solar flares occur in the region of sun spots, sending energized, charged particles at great speeds toward Earth. Above the photosphere lies the chromosphere and the corona. The chromosphere acts as a boundary between the cooler photosphere and hotter outermost layer the corona.

The Solar Wind and Auroras

A continuous flow of charged particles (ions and electrons) is discharged as a solar wind. At the extremely high temperatures, violent collisions of gases strip them of electrons acquiring enough speed to escape the gravitational pull of the sun. When this solar wind comes close to the Earth they interact with Earth's magnetic field. When the solar wind strikes the Earth's magnetic field it deforms it into a tear-drop shaped cavity called the magnetosphere. Inside the magnetosphere are ionized gases from the solar wind and the upper most part of the Earth's atmosphere.

During periods of high solar activity, the solar wind is more dense, travels faster, and possesses more energy. Reaching the Earth' magnetic field they set off auroral displays by exciting atmospheric gases resulting in the emission of visible light. In the Northern Hemisphere the spectacular light show is the aurora borealis or northern lights. In the Southern Hemisphere they are called the aurora australis, or southern lights.

Earth-Sun Relations

Solar radiation is one of many sources of energy, and probably one of the most important sources, that drive environmental processes acting at the surface of the Earth. The amount and intensity of solar radiation reaching the Earth is affected by the geometric relationship of the Earth with respect to the Sun.

The Solar Constant

Though the temperature of the air near the ground is primarily determined by the heat released by Earth's surface, the principal source for heating the Earth is solar radiation. The Earth is "constantly" bathed in solar radiation propagated through space ultimately reaching the surface of the earth. On average, the Earth receives 1368 W/m2 (1.96 ly/min) of solar radiation at the outer edge of the atmosphere, called the "solar constant". However, the actual amount received at the edge of the atmosphere or the Earth's surface varies from place to place and day to day on account of the orientation of the Earth to the Sun.

Earth Revolution and Rotation

Earth, the third planet of our solar system revolves around the Sun once every 365 1/4 days. The elliptical orbit of the earth varies from 91.5 million miles on January 3 called "perihelion", to 94.5 million miles on July 4 called "aphelion" for an average earth-sun distance of 93 million miles. The elliptical path causes only small variations in the amount of solar radiation reaching the earth.

The Earth rotates at a uniform rate on its axis once every 24 hours. Turning in an eastward direction the Sun "rises" in the east and seemingly "travels" toward the west during the day. The Sun isn't actually moving, it's the eastward rotation towards the morning Sun that makes it appear that way. The Earth then rotates in the opposite direction to the apparent path of the Sun. Looking down from the North Pole yields a counterclockwise direction. From over the South Pole a clockwise direction of rotation occurs. You can demonstrate this by looking down at the North Pole of a counterclockwise rotating globe.

Axial Tilt

The plane of the ecliptic is a plane that cuts through the center of the Earth and the Sun in which the Earth revolves around the Sun. The Earth's axis is tilted 23 1/2 degrees from being perpendicular to the plane of the ecliptic. The axis of rotation remains pointing in the same direction as it revolves around the Sun, pointing toward the star Polaris. As a result, the Earth's axis of rotation remains parallel to its previous position as it orbits the sun, a property called "parallelism". The constant tilt and parallelism causes changes in the angle that a beam of light makes with respect to a point on Earth during the year, called the "sun angle". The most intense incoming solar radiation occurs where the sun's rays strike the Earth at the highest angle. As the sun angle decreases, the beam of light is spread over a larger area and decreases in intensity. During the summer months the Earth is inclined toward the Sun yielding high sun angles. During the winter, the Earth is oriented away from the Sun creating low sun angles. The tilt of the Earth and its impact on sun angle is the reason the Northern and Southern Hemisphere have opposite seasons. Summer occurs when a hemisphere is tipped toward the Sun and winter when it is tipped away from the Sun.

Path length and Insolation

The distance that a beam of light travels greatly affects the amount of solar energy that ultimately reaches the Earth. The Earth-Sun distance only varies by about 3 million miles compared to an average distance of about 93 million miles over the year. A more significant impact on insolation is the thickness of the atmosphere on depletion of a beam of light. As the amount of atmosphere through which the beam passes increases, the greater the chance for reflection and scattering of light, thus reducing insolation at the surface. Due to the curvature of the Earth, a beam of light striking the Equator passes through less atmosphere than one at a higher latitude.

Seasons and Earth-Sun Relations

The Earth's axis always remains pointing in the same direction as it revolves around the sun. As a result, the solar angle varies at a given place throughout the year. The variation in sun angle is the prime cause of our seasons. The orientation of the Earth with respect to the Sun also determines the length of day. Together, the sun angle and day length determine the total amount of solar radiation incident at the Earth. To illuminate this point (pardon the pun), let's follow the Earth as it progresses through its orbit around the Sun.

On about June 21st or June 22nd the Northern hemisphere is tipped toward the sun. At noon, the subsolar point, or place where the sun lies directly overhead at noon, is located at 23 1/2o north latitude. This date is known as the summer solstice, the longest day of the year for places located north of Tropic of Cancer. The 23 1/2o parallel was so named because it is during the astrological sign Cancer when the Sun's rays strike at their highest angle of the year north of this line. The North pole tips into the Sun and tangent rays strike at the Arctic and Antarctic Circles. (A tangent ray is one that meets a curve or surface in a single point). This creates a 24 hour period of daylight ("polar day") for places located poleward of 66 1/2o north. We find the South Pole tipped away from the Sun, sending places poleward of 66 1/2o south into 24 hours of darkness ("polar night").

On Sept 22nd or 23rd, the Earth has moved around the Sun such that the poles are neither pointing toward or away from the sun. On this day, the Sun is directly overhead 0 degrees, the equator, at noon. Tangent rays strike at the poles. It is the autumnal equinox and all places experience 12 hours of day light and 12 hours of darkness. The winter solstice occurs on December 21st or 22nd when the Earth has oriented itself so the North Pole is facing away from, and the South Pole into the Sun. Again, tangent rays strike at the Arctic and Antarctic circles. Places poleward of 66 1/2o north are in the grips of the cold, polar night. Places poleward of 66 1/2o south experience the 24 hour polar day. The Sun lies directly over 23 1/2o south. Occurring during the astrological sign of Capricorn, 23 1/2o south latitude is called the Tropic of Capricorn.

Continuing to March 20th or 21st (i.e. Spring Equinox) the Earth has positioned itself similar to that which occurs in September, only on the other side of the Sun. Once again tangent rays strike at the North and South poles, and the perpendicular rays of the Sun strike the Equator at noon. All places have equal day length (12 hours day;12 hours of night) as the circle of illumination cuts all latitudes in half. So over the course of a year, the Sun's rays are only perpendicular to the surface (directly over head) at places between 23 1/2o north and south. Places between the Tropic of Cancer and Capricorn experience two times when the Sun is directly over head over the course of a year. The sun angle does not vary much for places between 23 1/2o north and south, a larger range in sun angle occurs poleward of these latitudes. The greater the variation in sun angle, the greater the variation in surface heating.

Day Length and Seasons

Day length is determined by the length of time the Sun is above the horizon. Day length changes through the year as the orientation of the Earth to the Sun changes. The circle of illumination is the imaginary circle that separate day from night.

Note during December that more of a given latitude in the Southern hemisphere is exposed to the Sun. This is the longest day of the year for those living poleward of the Equator. In June the opposite occurs with longer day length in the Northern hemisphere. Note that in both cases, the circle of illumination bisects the Equator (cuts it in half). The Equator is the only place on Earth that experiences equal day length every day of the year.

Radiation and Energy Balance of the Earth System

Most of the environmental processes acting near the surface of the Earth derive their energy from exchanges of heat between the Earth and the atmosphere above. Much of this heat comes from radiant energy initially provided by the absorption of solar radiation. The absorbed energy is used to warm the atmosphere, evaporate water, warm the subsurface along with a host of other processes.

The Radiation Balance

The radiation balance of the Earth system is an accounting of the incoming and outgoing components of radiation. These components are balanced over long time periods and over the Earth as whole. If they weren't the Earth would be continually cooling or warming. However, over a short period of time, radiant energy is unequally distributed over the Earth.

Shortwave Radiation

Shortwave radiation from the Sun penetrates through space to the outer edge of the atmosphere unimpeded by the vacuum of outer space. If one places a surface oriented perpendicular to an incoming beam of light, 1.94 cal cm-2 min-1 of solar radiation will be received. This value is known as the solar constant but actually varies by a small amount as the Earth-Sun distance changes through the year. Once solar radiation begins to penetrate through the atmosphere this amount begins to decrease due to absorption and reflection.

About 30% of the available solar radiation at the top of the atmosphere is reflected or scattered back to space by particulates and clouds before it reaches the ground. The gases of the atmosphere are relatively poor absorbers of solar radiation, absorbing only about 20% of what is available at the outer edge of the atmosphere. The remaining solar radiation makes its way to surface as direct and diffuse solar radiation. Direct solar radiation (S) is shortwave radiation able to penetrate through the atmosphere without having been affected by constituents of the atmosphere in any way. Diffuse radiation (D) is shortwave radiation that has been scattered by gases in the atmosphere. Scattering is a process whereby a beam of radiation is broken down into many weaker rays redirected in other directions. Together, direct and diffuse shortwave radiation accounts for the total incoming solar radiation or insolation (KI). In equation form:

KI = S+D

A portion of the incoming solar radiation is absorbed by the surface and a portion is also reflected away. The proportion of light reflected from a surface is the albedo (a). Albedo values range from 0 for no reflection to 1 for complete reflection of light striking the surface. Albedo can be expressed as a percentage (albedo multiplied by 100) that for some is easier to understand. For instance, grass has an albedo of about .23.

This means that of the incoming solar radiation that strikes the grass, 23% of it is reflected away. On the other hand, highly reflective surfaces like snow have an albedo upwards of .87, or 87% of sunlight is reflected away.

The amount of reflection (K?) is given by the following equation:

KI = (S+D)a

The amount of reflection basically depends on the color of the surface, darker surfaces reflect less than lighter colored ones. For some surfaces, like water, the sun angle affects albedo. If you have been out on a lake during the day you might have noticed that the sun reflects off the surface more when the sun is lower in the sky than it does when it is more directly overhead.

Net shortwave radiation is the difference between incoming and outgoing shortwave radiation expressed as:

K*= (S+D) - (S+D)a

During the day, K* is a positive value as incoming always exceeds outgoing shortwave radiation. At night, K* is equal to zero as the Sun is below the horizon. (No, moonlight doesn't count!)

Longwave Radiation

The energy absorbed at the surface is radiated by the Earth as terrestrial longwave radiation (L?). The amount of energy emitted is primarily dependent on the temperature of the surface. The hotter the surface the more radiant energy it will emit.

The gases of the atmosphere are relatively good absorbers of longwave radiation and thus absorb the energy emitted by the Earth's surface. The absorbed radiation is emitted downward toward the surface as longwave atmospheric counter-radiation (L?) keeping near surface temperatures warmer than they would be without this blanket of gases. This is known as the "greenhouse effect".

The difference between incoming and outgoing longwave radiation is net longwave radiation expressed as:

L* = LI - LI

Net Radiation

Gathering all the radiation terms together we have net allwave radiation:

Q*= [(S+D) - (S+D)a] + LI - LI

Net radiation can be positive, negative, or even zero. Net radiation is a positive value when there is more incoming radiation than outgoing radiation. This typically occurs during the day time when the sun is out and the air temperature is the warmest. At night, net radiation is usually a negative value as there is no incoming solar radiation and net longwave is dominated by the outgoing terrestrial longwave flux. Net radiation is zero when the incoming and outgoing components are in perfect balance, which doesn't occur too often.

Energy Balance

Available net radiation is used to do work in the Earth system. The principal use of this energy is in the phase change of water (latent heat, LE), changing the temperature of the air (sensible heat, H), and subsurface (ground heat, G) or,

Q* = H + LE + G

Though there are other uses for net radiation like photosynthesis and the weathering of rocks, it is the three previously stated uses that are most important. LE, H, and G involve non-radiative transfers of heat. That is, conduction or convection/advection are responsible for the transfer of heat, not electromagnetic radiation.

When work is done, like heating the air above the surface, there is a transfer of energy (heat) from one place to the next. To illustrate the transfer of energy we'll use arrows either pointing away from or toward the surface of the Earth to indicate the direction of heat transfer.

We will also use positive and negative signs to indicate that heat is being added to, or taken away from a body. Following the conventions of Sellers (1965) and Oke (1987), non-radiative fluxes directed away from a surface are positive. Thus positive values indicates a loss of heat from the surface while negative values indicate a gain.

Sensible Heat Transfer (H)

Sensible heat is heat energy transferred between the surface and air when there is a difference in temperature between them. A change in temperature over distance is called a "temperature gradient". In this case, it is a vertical temperature gradient, i.e., between the surface and the air above. We feel the transfer of sensible heat as a rise or fall in the temperature of the air. Heat is initially transferred into the air by conduction as air molecules collide with those of the surface. As the air warms it circulates upwards via convection. Thus the transfer of sensible heat is accomplished in a two-step process. Because air is such a poor conductor of heat, it is convection that is the most efficient way of transferring sensible heat into the air.

When the surface is warmer than the air above, heat will be transferred upwards into the air as a positive sensible heat transfer. The transfer of heat raises the air's temperature but cools the surface. If the air is warmer than the surface, heat is transferred from the air to the surface creating a negative sensible heat transfer. If heat is transferred out of the air, the air cools and the surface warms. This situation may take place at night when the sun goes down and there is no input of solar radiation. At this time, the ground cools due to longwave emission and the air directly above the surface is warmer.

Latent Heat Transfer (LE)

When energy is added to water it will change states or phase. The phase change of a liquid to a gas is called evaporation. If we could see down to the molecular level we would find water being comprised of cluster of water molecules (H2O). The clusters are bound together by bonding between the hydrogen atoms of water molecules. The heat added during evaporation breaks the bonds between the clusters creating individual molecules that escape the surface as a gas. The heat used in the phase change from a liquid to a gas is called the latent heat of vaporization. We say it is "latent" because it is being stored in the water molecules to later be released during the condensation process. We can't sense or feel latent heat as it does not raise the temperature of the water molecules.

When evaporation is taking place we say there is a positive latent heat flux (transfer). A positive latent heat flux is illustrated with an arrow pointing up away from the surface of the earth. This indicates that the surface is losing energy to the air above. Evaporation is a cooling process for a surface because energy is removed from the water as molecules escape the surface. This causes the surface temperature to decrease. You've probably experienced this cooling when water or sweat evaporates from your skin.

Condensation is the phase change from a gas to a liquid. During the phase change, the latent heat that was taken up during evaporation is released from the water molecule and passed into the surrounding air. During this process latent heat is converted to sensible heat causing an increase in the temperature of the air.

When radiation is absorbed by the Earth it will raise the temperature of the surface. But if the surface is water, some of that energy is used in evaporation rather than heating the water. As a result, with equal inputs of energy to land and water surfaces, land will heat up more than water. This is one of the reasons why it is cooler near large bodies of water.

Ground Heat Transfer (G)

The third major use of radiant energy is to warm the subsurface of the Earth. Heat is transferred from the surface downwards via conduction. Like in the case of sensible heat transfer, a temperature gradient must exist between the surface and the subsurface for heat transfer to occur. Heat is transferred downwards when the surface is warmer than the subsurface (positive ground heat flux). If the subsurface is warmer than the surface then heat is transferred upwards (negative ground heat flux).

The transfer of energy to and from the surface varies over the course of a day. During the day net radiation is a positive value as incoming radiation exceeds outgoing radiation allowing the surface to gain energy. The energy is distributed over the three major categories of energy use, LE, H, and G. During the day, the available radiant energy is used to evaporate water into the air, raising the air's humidity. Sensible heat is transferred upwards to warm the air above the surface. Heat is also conducted down into the subsurface. At night the processes reverse. At night with no incoming solar radiation there is more outgoing radiation than incoming creating a negative value for net radiation. Under these circumstances the surface cools due to a loss of energy and heat is transferred from the air toward the surface. As air cools through the evening the loss of energy allow condensation to occur, so long as the air's humidity is at or near saturation. Notice that the arrow for the ground heat flux G is pointing upward toward the surface. This indicates that the energy that had been stored in the subsurface during the day is now conducted toward the surface. This occurs as the surface is cooler than the subsurface.

Water is available at the surface for evaporation and latent heat transfer into the air at moist locations. Without available water, no transfer of latent energy occurs, hence the absence of an LE flux for the dry surface. Most of the available energy, Q*, is allocated to sensible heat transfer creating warm air temperatures.

Global Patterns of Insolation, Net Radiation, and Heat

Patterns of insolation and net radiation which determine the location of plants, animals, climate, soils and other elements of our physical environment can be discerned from Figures ER.22 through ER.24. Figure ER.20 illustrates the latitudinal distribution of incoming solar radiation and outgoing terrestrial radiation. From approximately 35o N to 35o S latitude (the red area of the graph) there is a surplus of energy as incoming radiation exceeds outgoing.

The blue regions indicate that there is more outgoing energy than incoming, yielding a net loss of energy from the Earth's surface. One might ask then why the middle to higher latitudes aren't getting colder through time as a result of the net loss, and the subtropical to equatorial regions getting constantly hotter due to the net gain. The reason is that the energy is redistributed by circulation of the atmosphere and oceans. Heat gained in the tropics is transported poleward by the global circulation of air and warm ocean currents to heat higher latitude regions. Cooler air from the higher latitudes and cold ocean currents push equatorward to cool the lower latitudes. This process of redistributing energy in the Earth system helps maintain a long-term energy balance.

Insolation

For the Earth as a whole, particular patterns can be accounted for by variation in surface features that impact insolation. Insolation maxima are found in the tropical and subtropical deserts of the earth. Here, high sun angles and a lack of cloud cover in desert regions allow much solar radiation to the surface. Insolation decreases to a minimum at the poles where low sun angles and the fact that the Sun doesn't rise above the horizon nearly half the year reduces annual insolation.

Net radiation

Net radiation exhibits a different pattern from that of insolation. Maximum net radiation is found over the tropical and subtropical oceans. The sun angle is always high over the tropical oceans so the surface receives intense radiation throughout the year. With a high sun angle the albedo of the surface is low and absorption is high. However, the energy received is partitioned into warming the surface as well as evaporating water. The result is a lower surface temperature than one might expect with such high sun angles. Additionally, the high specific heat of water means that it takes much more energy to heat a unit mass of water than that of land, resulting in lower ocean surface temperatures. With lower surface temperatures the water surface does not radiate as much longwave radiation out to the atmosphere as nearby land at the same latitude. With much radiation coming in and little going out, the net value is large compared to land at the same latitude. Net radiation is at a minimum over the poles as the sunlight that comes in at a low angle is reflected from the ice-covered surface. Combined with the long polar night, very little net radiation is found at these latitudes.

Patterns of Energy Utilization

Global Patterns of Sensible and Latent Heat Transfer

Sensible heat transfer (H) into the air is dependent on the temperature gradient between the surface and the air above. An examination of the global distribution of sensible heat transfer reveals that it is at a maximum in the tropical and subtropical deserts. Here the high surface temperature conducts much heat into the air above. Sensible heat is lowest near the poles where the surface temperatures are quite cold. The maximum amount of latent heat transfer (LE) occurs over the subtropical oceans where there is a maximum of net radiation and, of course, water to evaporate. The lowest rates occur in desert locations. Even though there is ample available energy for LE, there is little water present. Off the east coast of midlatitude continents like North America, we'll find very high rates of latent energy transfer into the air. Here, dry air blows off the continent and over the warm ocean current that flows along the coast. This produces a large moisture gradient between the surface and the air above that induces evaporation and LE transfer.

Regional Patterns of Sensible and Latent Heat Transfer

West Palm Beach, Florida is located in a warm and moist climate. The annual variation of net radiation shows a typical pattern of Q* being at a maximum during the summer and minimum during the winter. Latent heat transfer (LE) is high at West Palm Beach because of the water availability near the ocean. Latent energy transfer into the air is greatest during the summer time which is the wettest period of the year, and when net radiation is the highest. Warmer summer time air can hold more moisture and hence there is a larger moisture gradient to drive latent heat transfer. The annual variation of sensible heat transfer is determined by the available net radiation and the temperature gradient between the air and surface, as well as use of energy for latent heat transfer. During the spring a larger temperature gradient between the surface and the air above exists. More important is the availability of water for evaporation. During the summer, appreciable rainfall occurs that provides water for evaporation. During this time period, sensible heat transfer decreases as net radiation is allocated to evaporation and latent heat transfer.

At the other extreme is Yuma, Arizona, a warm and dry climate. The most noticeable characteristic of this place is the lack of latent heat transfer. Though ample radiation is available here, there is no water to evaporate. Nearly all net radiation is used for sensible heat transfer which explains the hot dry conditions at Yuma.

Future Geographies: Radiative Forcing and the Earth's Heat Balance

The future physical geography of Earth as affected by global warming comes down to changes in the heat balance of the Earth system. Radiative forcing is a measure of the strength of agents, both natural and human, that cause climate change. Radiative forcing agents are factors that change the balance between incoming solar radiation and outgoing infrared radiation within the Earth's atmosphere. The radiative forcing of greenhouse gases is what will propel much of this change. Documented changes with relatively high level of scientific understanding from 1750 to 2005 has been presented by the Intergovernmental Panel on Climate Change.

The Present Picture

Two long-lived greenhouse gases produced from human activities, carbon dioxide and methane, are the most potent, contributing 1.66 and 0.48 (W/m2) respectively at the global scale. Shorter-lived tropospheric ozone contributes an average of 0.35 (W/m2), though we have only a medium level of scientific understanding of its contribution. Though human activities affect agents that increase radiative forcing, they also negatively impact radiative forcing. A notable impact, is that of the aerosol content of the atmosphere. Aerosols themselves can negatively impact radiative forcing by reflecting solar radiation. But a much larger impact, and one with less scientific certainty, is their role in creating clouds which also reflect solar radiation.

In addition to changes in the gaseous composition of the atmosphere, surface albedo changes from human activities also effects radiative forcing. This is particularly true when forests are cleared for agriculture. Forests generally have a lower albedo than open land thus absorbing more incident solar radiation. These changes induce a radiative forcing by effecting the shortwave radiation balance. This is particularly true when snow is present. Open land has a more complete cover of highly reflective snow, while the lower albedo trees stand above the snow.

Natural radiative forcing largely results from changes in solar output and volcanic eruptions. As noted earlier in this chapter [link here], sunspot activity varies on an 11-year cycle. But since the dawn of the industrial age, solar output has been slowly increasing and thus the the Sun has had a positive radiative forcing effect. Volcanic eruptions produce a variety gases, though their presence in the atmosphere is relatively short lived (2 to 3 years). The most notable is sulphate aerosols injected into the stratosphere causing a negative radiative forcing. The stratosphere is presently free of appreciable amounts of volcanic aerosols. The last major eruption to affect stratospheric aerosol content was Mt. Pinatubo in 1991. Adding the effects of other radiative forcing components like surface albedo changes, the combined net anthropogenic radiative forcing is estimated to be +1.6 (W/m2). This, according to the IPCC, indicates that since 1750, it is extremely likely that human activities have caused a substantial effect on warming Earth's climate. Additionally, is it likely that this estimate is five times greater than that which can be attributed to natural changes in the output of the Sun.

The radiative forcing is positive for most of the earth and principally associated with long-lived greenhouse gases like carbon dioxide. This is especially true for the southern hemisphere due to the higher levels of aerosols in the source-rich continental regions of the northern hemisphere midlatitudes. Wherever high concentrations of aerosols are found, especially in the northern hemisphere, surface forcing is negative. This is due to the influence of aerosols in reducing the shortwave radiation that reaches the ground. As aerosol concentrations are lower over much of the southern hemisphere oceans and at high latitudes. With less aerosols more shortwave radiation reaches the earth thus surface forcing becomes positive.

Future Forcings

Future heat balance conditions from the forcings is tricky and predictions from various AOGCMs do not precisely agree with one another, largely due to the radiatively active gases used, solar variability, land use change, and how radiation transfer is formulated. The range of forcing using "box and whisker" diagrams estimated by these models using a scenario where economic growth is rapid, world population peaks at 9 billion in 2050 and then declines, there is a quick and efficient spread of technologies, extensive social and cultural interaction occurs worldwide, and world-income and way of life converges between regions. Longwave forcing continues to increase fueling continued warming of the earth system.

Global warming will continue unabated without changes in how human activities impact radiative forcing agents. In future chapters, we'll investigate how changes in these agents will impact patterns of temperature, pressure and wind, weather, biotic systems, the hydrosphere and earth surface processes.

Air Temperature

The temperature of our atmosphere is controlled by a complex set of interactions between the biosphere, lithosphere, hydrosphere, and atmosphere. Energy is constantly exchanged between the surface and the air above, as well as circulating around the globe. Here we'll look at what controls the air temperature at a particular place by examining radiation and energy exchanges between the earth and air above. Then we'll examine how the global circulation of air and water affects air temperature.

Controls over air temperature

Temperature is a measure of the heat content of a body. It is a measure of the average speed of the random motion of molecules that comprise a substance. The air temperature at any place is determined by (1) radiation and heat transfers between the surface and the air above, (2) the location relative to a large body of water, and (3) the movement of vast pools of air called air masses.

Radiation, sensible heat and temperature

The air temperature at a place is determined by the exchange of radiant energy between the Sun, Earth, and its atmosphere. Solar radiation is the principle source of energy to heat the surface.

Shortwave solar radiation easily penetrates to the surface without much absorption by the gases that comprise the atmosphere. As the sun heats the surface during the day, the earth warms and increases its output of infra red, or longwave radiation. The gases of the atmosphere, being relatively good absorbers of longwave radiation, are warmed and experience a rise in temperature. Thus, the immediate source of energy to heat the air is the surface of the earth.

Solar radiation increases after sunrise to a maximum at noon and then decreases to a minimum at sunset. Outgoing radiation increases after sunrise but lags somewhat behind the insolation curve. The graph for air temperature follows the same pattern as that of outgoing radiation. This should seem reasonable as it is the absorption of outgoing energy from the surface that determines air temperature. The amount of time between maximum incoming energy and maximum temperature over the day is known as the daily temperature lag.

A similar type of lag occurs on an annual basis. The seasonal lag of temperature is the amount of time between the highest incoming insolation and highest temperature on an annual basis. For instance, in the midlatitudes the highest angle that the sun makes with the surface, and thus the most intense heating, occurs around June 22nd. It isn't until about a month later that the highest temperatures occur. The lag is often longer near a large body of water like the Great Lakes or the ocean. A temperature lag of two months is not uncommon for places located near large bodies of water.

Clouds have an impact on the radiation balance and air temperature of a place. Clouds can block incoming solar radiation by reflection of their tops. Clouds also act to diffuse light as it penetrates towards the surface. Both of these would act to cool the atmosphere. Clouds and water vapor are good absorbers of longwave radiation emitted by the earth's surface too. You've probably noticed that the warmest evenings tend to be when we have a heavy cover of clouds. These clouds absorb the radiation emitted by the earth and radiate it back down toward the earth's surface, warming the air. The coldest evenings occur during cloudless conditions. The lack of clouds in the desert creates large daily temperature ranges. During the day, sunlight streams to the earth's surface heating it to very high temperatures. Near surface air temperatures are very high as a result. At night, the absence of clouds allows emitted longwave radiation to escape to space causing the surface to cool and the air above to do so as well.

The atmosphere is also heated by the exchange of sensible heat between the surface and the air above. Sensible heat is transferred into the air by conduction and convection. Heat is most efficiently moved by turbulent eddies, or swirls of vertically moving air. The initial transfer is due to the presence of a temperature gradient between the surface and the air. If the surface of the earth is warmer than the air above, heat will be transferred upwards raising the temperature of the air. If the air is warmer than the surface, heat will be transferred towards the surface, thus cooling the air. The lag of temperature behind incoming radiation is also a result of the time it takes for sensible heat to transferred upwards.

Air Temperature, Water Bodies and Continentality

Air temperature is greatly affected by the location of a place relative to a large body of water. The impact of continental location on weather and climate characteristics of a place is called "continentality". Air temperature near or over bodies of water is much different from that over land due to differences in the way water and land heat and cool. Properties that affect water temperature are:

- Transparency
- Allocation of Q*
- Ability to circulate
- Specific heat

Water is a transparent medium and land is opaque. Water allows light to penetrate to depth, leaving the surface layers cooler than they would be if the surface was opaque. A cooler water surface results in cooler air temperatures above. When solar radiation strikes land, the energy is absorbed in a thin layer that heats relatively rapidly. Likewise, it readily gives up its heat to the atmosphere.

When radiant energy is absorbed by land, most of the net radiation is used for sensible heat transfer or ground heat transfer, only small amounts are used for latent heat transfer. As sensible heat transfer into the air is the dominant heat transfer, air temperatures increase over the land. Over water, much of the net radiation is used for evaporation. With little energy used for sensible heat transfer, air over water remains cooler than that over land. Being a fluid, water is able to freely circulate. Surface water that has been warmed by the sun can mix with cooler water at depth, thus keeping the body of water cool. Land can not circulate warmer surface layers with cooler ones below, resulting in high surface temperatures and higher air temperatures than these over water. Finally, the specific heat of water is higher than that of land. Specific heat is the amount of energy required to raise the temperature of one gram of substance through one degree Celsius. Water has a specific heat that is five times greater than land. This means that it takes five times more energy to heat one gram of water than one gram of land. So if adjacent land and water receive the same amount of insolation, the water will warm much slower than land, and give up its heat much more slowly than land.

Combining the above differences between the heating of land and water, a few observations can be made. First, air temperatures are usually lower over a water surface than over adjacent land. As this cooler maritime air comes ashore, air temperatures over land will be reduced. Because the water's temperature doesn't fluctuate as much as that of land, temperature ranges are smaller over water and coastal locations than those in the interior. Finally, seasonal temperature lags are longer, by about a month, for coastal locations than their interior counterparts. San Francisco, being located on the west coast of the United States, is influenced by the moderating effect of the Pacific Ocean. Wichita is in the center of the country is controlled by the thermal characteristics of land. Norfolk on the east coast is influenced by both the westerly winds from the continent and the moderating influence of the Atlantic Ocean. Thus the west coast location has the smallest temperature range (and longest seasonal lag), the interior location has the largest temperature range and the east coast location a moderate range.

Global Patterns of Air Temperature

Global patterns of air temperature are a reflection of the relative importance of the factors discussed in the preceding sections. Isotherms, or lines connecting points of equal air temperature are used to map the spatial pattern of temperature.

Latitudinal Patterns (north to south patterns)

The first thing to note on January and July temperature maps is the spacing and linearity (or lack thereof) of the isotherms. Overall, isotherms in the southern hemisphere tend to be more linear or run straight across the map. In the Northern Hemisphere the isotherms tend to be more wavy, dipping far to the south or north depending on season and location. This pattern reflects the impact of land-sea contrasts on the heating of the air. The southern hemisphere is a more uniform surface, mostly water. Where there is land, isotherms take sudden swings over the surface. The northern hemisphere has much more land surface and the configuration of the isotherms reflect it. Isotherms dip far to the south in January as cold temperatures occupy the continental interiors and coastal locations stay more mild being influenced by the ocean.

The values of the isotherms validate our general conception of the distribution of world temperatures. Low latitudes that experience the highest sun angles throughout the year have the highest air temperatures. The highest temperatures occur in the tropical and subtropical deserts of North Africa, Australia, and the southwestern portion of the United States. Because the angle of the sun doesn't vary much during the year and day length is about the same, annual temperature ranges tend to be small, on the order of only a few degrees. However, daily temperature ranges can be quite large as pointed out earlier in the chapter.

High latitude locations have much lower annual temperatures as the sun never gets directly overhead and sun angles are quite a bit lower than those in low latitudes. However, the seasonal temperature range is large. Cold air masses penetrate south dropping air temperatures during the winter months. During the summer, warm tropical air masses stream toward higher latitudes raising temperatures. The movement of air masses and more varied sun angles results in larger temperature ranges than one experiences in the low latitudes.

Longitudinal Patterns (west to east patterns)

Longitudinal patterns of temperature reflect the influence of continentality and ocean circulation. Let's examine the longitudinal temperature patterns one sees in the midlatitudes of North America. In the mid-latitudes the prevailing wind direction is from west to east. Places located along the coast receive a constant influx of oceanic air throughout the year. Because oceans don't change their temperature much during the year, the air above them doesn't change much either. When the oceanic air streams on to land, temperatures tend to be rather mild. The changes in air temperature one experiences as you travel from west to east across a midlatitude continent largely reflect the influence of continentality. The temperature range along the west coast of North America tends to be small due to the constant influx on oceanic air. Temperature extremes increase as distance from the coast increases. In the interior of the North American continent, warm air masses from the Gulf of Mexico work their way northward, especially during the summer. During the winter, cold continental polar air masses dominate. The great difference in the temperature of these two air masses results in a large temperature range. Air masses moving to the east from the interior tend to be warm, but the proximity to water keeps air temperatures mild giving east coast locations moderate ranges of temperatures.

Table: West - East comparison of Annual Temperature Range

City	January Temperature	July Temperature	Temperature Range
San Francisco, CA	9.6°C (49.3°F)	16.2°C (61.1°F)	6.6°C (11.8°F)
Dodge City, KS	-.4°C (31.3°F)	26.1°C (79°F)	26.5°C (47.7°F)
Atlantic City, NJ	0°C (32°F)	23.8°C (74.84°F)	23.8°C (42.8°F)

City

Future Geographies: Global Warming and Regional Temperature Patterns

An enhanced greenhouse effect caused by human activities will upset the radiation balance of the earth system creating a variety of changes in the geography of planet Earth, the most notable being air temperature. Temperature trends over the past 100-plus years clearly indicate rising temperatures on all continents and over the oceans.

Predicting changes to the global patterns of temperature is a challenging undertaking for scientists as they must rely on models for their forecasts. The models are numerical representations based on how our earth system functions. They are limited by our understanding of earth system processes and long-term data sets. Using a variety of models, geoscientists have forecast a range of possible scenarios. One thing is clear from their predictions, that the amount of temperature change varies geographically.

Arctic Regions

The arctic regions appear to be impacted the most. Observations of mean annual surface air temperature over the past 50 years has increased 2°C to 3°C in Alaska and Siberia and decreased by 1°C over southern Greenland. Mean annual surface air temperature over the Arctic region (north of 60° latitude) is projected to increase 1.1°F by 2050 and 4.4°C by 2100.

The Midlatitudes

Climate change is expected to increase the frequency of extreme events in midlatitude regions like the midwest United States. A severe drought in 1988, heat waves in 1995 and 1996, flooding on the Mississippi in 1993 (100-year flood) and 2002, and numerous tornadoes and severe thunderstorms can be expected in the future. Illinois will be become warmer, especially in the summer having temperatures more like present-day Oklahoma or Arkansas Wisconsin temperatures could rise 2.7°-5.5°C in the winter and by 4.4° - 9.4°C during the summer by 2100. Extreme heat will be more common than today. Southern Ontario's winter temperatures are expected to increase by 3°- 7°C and summer's to be 4°-8°C warmer. More southerly states like Illinois will experience less warmer. Winter temperatures are expected to increase by 2.7°-3.8°C during the winter in Indiana while summer temperatures are expected to increase by 4.4o - 5.5°C. Growing seasons could be 4 to 7 weeks longer in Wisconsin and 3 to 6 weeks longer to the south in Illinois. Under a medium -high emissions scenario, the IPCC predicts a 3°-4.9°C change in statewide in California.

Subtropical Regions

Though most geoscientists have felt that the Arctic will show the first true signs of a future climate, dramatic changes have been recorded in subtropical regions. Recent analysis of satellite data has found that each hemisphere's jet stream has moved poleward by about 1 degrees of latitude or 70 miles. Jet streams are found on the poleward limit of the tropics which means they are getting wider. Continued movement would mean the spread of subtropical deserts like the Sahara. Regional climate predictions for southern Africa during summer suggest a warm season increase of 2°C to 4°C over the subcontinent, with the doubling of carbon dioxide. Current climate models project regional temperature increases approximately 2 to 5.5°C by 2100, with an 4.5° to 8.3°C increase in the average summer heat index for the southeastern United States.

Tropical Regions

Most model predictions indicate the smallest change to temperature will occur in tropical latitudes. Depending on model assumptions and location, annual changes on the order of .1°C to 3°C are predicted. Analysis indicates that there may be significant differences within the tropics, especially in Asia, depending on proximity to the sea. Warming is projected to be least in the islands and coastal areas throughout Indonesia, the Philippines, and coastal south Asia and Indo-China and greatest inland. Even with relatively small temperatures, they can be devastating. A 3° Celsius rise in temperature would result in a 60 percent reduction in the arabica coffee area in Brazil, the world's largest producer.

Atmospheric and Ocean Circulation

The atmosphere around us is in constant motion, even if we don't feel the wind across our face. Molecules of air dart about transferring heat from one place to the next at a variety of geographic scales. Here you will learn how winds at a variety of spatial scales form and what controls their behavior. You'll look at how atmospheric pressure and wind patterns influence weather and climate. Finally you will delve into what causes oceanic circulation and how it relates to atmospheric motion.

2

AIR PRESSURE

PRESSURE VARIATIONS ACROSS THE EARTH

Air pressure is the force exerted by the weight of a column of air above a particular location. When the molecules of air collide with the inside surfaces of the container they exert a pressure. The amount of pressure they exert depends on the number of collisions that occur between the molecules and the inside surface of the container. We can change the pressure in two ways. First, we can increase the density of the air by either putting more air molecules into the container or reducing the volume of the container. Secondly, we can increase the temperature of the air to make the molecules move faster and thus collide with the sides more often. Therefore, changes in air pressure can come about by changes in air density or temperature.

In nature, pressure variations across the surface of the Earth are created by mechanical or thermal means. Mechanical changes in pressure occur when air flow is impeded causing a mass of air to build up over a particular location thus increasing air pressure. Heating and cooling the air (thermal mechanisms) also create variations in air pressure. When air is heated it rises, and if pushed away aloft, surface air pressure decreases. Conversely if air is cooled, it subsides toward the surface causing air pressure to increase.

Air pressure is measured using a barometer. Several different barometers exist, two of the most common are the mercury barometer and the aneroid barometer. The mercury barometer is a tube with a reservoir of mercury at one end. Under average sea level conditions, the atmosphere exerts enough pressure to push a column of mercury up to the height of 29.92 inches. The aneroid barometer uses an aneroid or sylphon cell to measure pressure. The aneroid cell is a metal chamber that expands and contracts with changing air pressure. Though inches of mercury are often reported on your daily weather forecast (especially in the United States), meteorologists use millibars as the units of measurement for air pressure. Under average sea level conditions the atmospheric pressure is 1013.2 millibars (29.92 inches of mercury). Average sea level pressure serves as the division between what we call "high pressure" and "low pressure" at the surface. High pressure is defined as values greater than 1013.2 mb and low pressure is below 1013.2 mb.

Air pressure decreases as one moves upward through the atmosphere because the length of the column of air shortens and hence there is less mass above a given location. However, the rate of decrease is not the same between two elevations. Because air is highly compressible, the air is closely packed together near the surface (high density) and less densely packed aloft. In fact, over 90% of the atmosphere is found below 10 miles. As a result, the air pressure decreases more rapidly between two elevations close to the surface than between two points separated by the same distance aloft.

As explained previously, we use an average value of sea level pressure to differentiate between high pressure and low pressure. Because air pressure decreases aloft, the average pressure at any point above the surface is less. At 5600 meters the average pressure is 500 mb. If on any given day the pressure is larger than 500 mb we consider it high pressure at this elevation. If we measure a smaller amount then it is low pressure at this elevation. Do not confuse high pressure with higher pressure and low pressure with lower pressure. Adding the "er" to the end of the word indicates a change relative to a previous state. For instance, lets say you measure the air pressure to be 1015 mb at the surface and 516 mb at 5600 meters. Both cases are under the influence of high pressure at their respective locations. However, the pressure is higher at the surface than at 5600 meters.

Analyzing Air Pressure Patterns

Meteorologists have a variety of ways to visualize weather data, a map being the most common. To analyze pressure patterns, a constant height map is often used. A constant height map (also known as a "constant height chart") shows the distribution of pressure at sea level. Isobars, lines connecting points of equal air pressure are used to show pressure patterns on constant height maps. Most of the maps of air pressure in this book are constant height maps.

Another map that is used to analyze pressure patterns is called a constant pressure map (also known as a "constant pressure chart"). A constant pressure map shows the change in elevation of an isobaric surface which is a surface upon which the pressure is the same at all locations. By examining the height of an isobaric surface relative to it's normal elevation, one can discern where areas of high and low pressure are. The 500 mb surface is commonly used to by meteorologists in weather forecasting. The normal height of 500 mb surface is 5600 meters. Recall, that at the surface we consider high pressure to be greater than normal sea level pressure and low pressure to be less than normal sea level pressure. In a similar way we can use the normal height of the 500 mb surface to identify where high and low pressure areas are located.

Controls over Wind Direction and Speed

Air is constantly moving to seek an equilibrium between areas of more air molecules (higher pressure) and those with less (lower pressure). You have probably experienced this by opening a container that has been vacuum packed. Because the container is vacuum packed, there is less air inside the can (lower pressure) than outside the can (higher pressure). When you open the container you here a "whoosh" as air rushes into it. The air rushing from outside the container into it is a wind, albeit at the microscale. Wind is nothing more than the movement of air molecules from one place to the next. The direction and speed of the wind represents the balance between three basic forces acting on it: the pressure gradient, the Coriolis force, and surface friction.

Pressure Gradient

Meteorologists use isobars to depict the distribution of surface pressure on maps. An isobar is a line that connects places of equal air pressure. The spacing of isobars indicates the change in pressure over distance otherwise known as a pressure gradient. We can induce a change in pressure over distance by the unequal heating of the Earth's surface. This can be done when one location receives more incoming energy than another, possibly because one place has a higher sun angle than another. Heating the air in one place causes it to rise off the surface promoting low pressure with the pressure increasing away from that location. The creation of a pressure gradient initially causes the air to flow from higher toward lower pressure creating a wind. So in terms of a cause-and-effect relationship:

Energy gradient -> temperature gradient ->
pressure gradient -> wind

The orientation or direction of a pressure gradient is always described as being from higher toward lower pressure. The speed of the wind is controlled by the strength of the pressure gradient, the stronger the pressure gradient the higher the wind speed. The strength of the pressure gradient can be discerned from the spacing of isobars on a weather map.

Let's consider a simple situation to understand how the height of an isobaric surface relates to air pressure. Recall that air pressure is related to force exerted by the weight of a column of air above a given point. If air temperature varies through any part of an air column, the density and pressure will also vary. The 500 mb surface is shown as the white surface dipping from left to right. Let's assume that the surface pressure remains constant. When air is heated it becomes bouyant causing it to rise and when cooled it sinks. As the warm air rises more air molecules will be found above 5600 meters than normal and thus the 500 mb surface is found at a higher elevation. To the right where cold air has sunk to the surface fewer air molecules than normal are found above 5600 meter and thus the 500 mb surface is found at a lower elevation. If there are more molecules above 5600 meter in the warm region, then high pressure is located at 5600 meters. If fewer air molecules are above 5600 meters in the cold region, then low pressure is located at 5600 meters.

Coriolis Force

The Coriolis force is the effect of earth rotation on the direction of the wind. The Coriolis force arises for two reasons, first our directional system of latitude and longitude has been fixed to a rotating earth. Thus, our frame of reference for monitoring the direction of a free-moving object above the Earth is constantly changing. The second reason is the amount of turning about a vertical axis varies from a maximum at the poles and minimum at the equator. Demonstrate this by standing a pencil on end at the north pole and turn the globe.

The pencil completes one full rotation. But standing the pencil on end at the equator and rotating the earth yields no rotation about a vertical axis. Because the Earth, and the target, has rotated underneath the free-moving missile, it appears that the missile has veered off course (changed direction). Such is the case for winds blowing above the surface. The deflection works the same way for an east-west wind, the path will curve to the right as it moves across the surface.

Though the air is deflected to the right of its path in the Northern hemisphere, in the Southern Hemisphere wind is deflected to the left of its path. Why the difference? It all has to do with perspective. Pick up a globe and spin it in a west to east direction. Now look down on it from above the North Pole. It appears to by spinning in counterclockwise direction. Now keep it spinning from west to east, lift the globe over your head and look at it from above the South Pole. It appears to be going in a clockwise direction.

Friction

Generally speaking wind speed increases with height above the surface as the frictional force of surface diminishes with height. The friction imposed on air mechanically slows the wind and diverts its direction. The friction layer is the layer of air that is influenced by friction caused by the surface. The friction layer varies in height across the Earth, but for the most part lies within about a kilometer of the surface.

Surface Circulation around Highs and Lows

Recall that air always flows from higher towards lower pressure. Around high pressure systems (H), air is directed outward from the center. Around low pressure systems (L) air is directed inward toward the center. If pressure gradient was the only force acting on the air, wind would move directly across isobars at a perpedicular angle. Wind instead moves across the isobars at an angle of anywhere from 10o to 45o. Because the Coriolis Effect bends the air to the right of it's path (i.e. the direction of the pressure gradient) in the Northern hemisphere, air takes on a clockwise flow around highs and counterclockwise around lows. In the Southern hemisphere, air circulates in a counterclockwise fashion around highs and clockwise around lows. Above the "friction layer", only the pressure gradient and Coriolis effect operate on wind. At particular latitudes, the opposing pressure gradient and Coriolis forces can balance one another high in the troposphere above the friction layer. When this occurs, winds tend to blow parallel to isobars. Winds that blow roughly parallel to isobars are called "geostrophic winds". The fast-moving jet streams are type of geostrophic wind.

Atmospheric Moisture

Water in its various forms sustains life, transports energy and erodes the surface beneath our feet. Water is needed for cell growth, photosynthesis, the formation of soil, and to absorb and transport nutrients in plants and animals. Without water, living things could not survive. Energy is transported between the various spheres of the Earth system via phase changes of water. Nearly every portion of the Earth has been sculpted by the movement of water across the surface at some point in geologic history. Here we'll look at water in its various forms, as a gas, liquid, and solid. We'll investigate how it moves through and the vital role it plays in the Earth system. You will become familiar with the geographic distribution of precipitation and its impact on the environment.

The Hydrologic Cycle

The hydrosphere is the sphere that contains all the water of the Earth system. This includes water in a gaseous state, liquid water found in rivers, lakes, and streams, and water in its solid state like that of glaciers and ice sheets. Water found in living plants and animals can be considered part of the hydrosphere. The water of the hydrosphere interacts with the other subsystems of the earth.

The hydrologic cycle refers to the movement of water through its various stores within the Earth system. The amount of water that cycles between the surface and the atmosphere is phenomenal. At any minute, nearly a billion tons of water is delivered to the atmosphere by evaporation and the same amount precipitated from it. The hydrologic cycle not only traces the movement of water through the Earth system, it is a path way for the movement of energy. Water is evaporated from tropical oceans where energy is abundant and is transported on the wind to high latitudes where energy is in short supply. There it condenses and gives off heat to the atmosphere. The exchange of energy from low latitudes to high latitudes helps maintain the energy balance of the Earth system.

Phases of Water

A water molecule is composed of two atoms of hydrogen and one atom of oxygen. The molecule looks kind of like Mickey Mouse, with the oxygen forming the head and the two hydrogen forming the ears. Water molecules cluster together by bonding to the hydrogen atoms of neighboring water molecules. The molecules that comprise a solid, like ice, are arranged in a particular order. The molecules do not circulate but they do move. That is, the molecules vibrate in place around an average location. Solids represent the lowest level of kinetic energy. The molecules of a liquid, like water, have a higher kinetic energy level than solids and thus are free to circulate as "clumps" of molecules but constrained by a surface. Molecules of a gas are free to circulate as well, but are unconfined and move about with the highest kinetic energy level.

In order for water to change from a solid to liquid and finally to a gas, the water molecule must gain energy. The energy absorbed by water is used to break the hydrogen bonds between groups of molecules. When the bonds are broken between the molecules of ice, it melts and they can circulate as a fluid. The energy required to convert ice into water is called the latent heat of fusion. It takes about 80 calories of heat to convert one gram of ice into water.

TRANSFER OF WATER INTO AND OUT OF THE ATMOSPHERE

Evaporation

Evaporation is the phase change of a liquid to a gas. There are three very important requirements for evaporation to take place, (1) available energy, (2) available water, and (3) a vertical moisture gradient. Approximately 600 calories of heat must be added to a gram of water for it to evaporate into the air. This energy is called "the latent heat of vaporization". Latent heat is used to break the hydrogen bonds that bind water molecules together. In doing so, the energy is "locked up" in the water molecules. The energy remains "latent" in the molecules until they combine during the condensation process to form a liquid. When this happens latent energy is released into the surrounding environment as sensible heat. Sensible heat warms the surrounding air, and thus is an important source of energy to heat the atmosphere.

Even if you have all the energy required for evaporation it will not occur unless there is water present. Desert regions are noted for their lack of precipitation. One reason is that they have little available water to evaporate to later condense and form precipitation. Eighty-eight percent of the water that is evaporated into the air comes from oceans that lie between 60o north and south latitude. Most of the evaporation occurs in the tropical and subtropical oceans where the highest amounts of net radiation occur.

The third requirement for evaporation is the presence of a vertical moisture gradient. That is, there is a difference in moisture content with increasing height above the surface. All this means is that the humidity is high at the evaporating surface (liquid water), and the air above has a lower humidity. Evaporation will be the predominate phase change until the air is saturated with moisture.

Though not required, wind aids in the evaporation process. Wind transfers water molecules away from the evaporating surface and hence maintains a vertical moisture gradient.

Transpiration

The principal way in which water enters the air is through evaporation. Plants are another important source of atmospheric moisture. Plants contribute water to the atmosphere by transpiration. Transpiration is the transfer of water into the air via leaf pores or stomata. Interestingly, the same three requirements for evaporation apply to transpiration. Approximately 600 cal/gm of energy is required to transpire water from leaves. The transfer of water into the air removes heat from the plant and so transpiration, like evaporation, is a cooling process. Thus transpiration is an important means of transporting heat between the surface and air above.

Water for transpiration comes from that which is stored in the soil and then extracted by plant roots. The amount of water that is held in the soil moisture zone is dependent on the texture and structure of the soil. Coarse textured soil dominated by sand-size particles holds less moisture than a finer textured soil.

How important is plant transpiration? Consider this, one mature oak tree can transpire as much as 100 gallons of water in a day. An acre of corn can transpire as much as 4000 gallons of water per day (EPA). The problem that many countries face is an ever dwindling resource of groundwater to promote agriculture in regions too dry to do so. Far too often, groundwater resources are extracted faster than they can naturally replenish themselves. Over pumping depletes groundwater reserves in aquifers and ultimately leads to their collapse. This is happening in the semiarid and arid regions of the United States. One aquifer in particular, the Ogallala Aquifer, is at risk of being depleted. The recharge area where water enters the aquifer is in the Rocky Mountains. The aquifer extends underground for hundreds of miles into the Great Plains. The aquifer is used to support agriculture and municipal water supplies on the Great Plains. Unfortunately, water is being pumped out of the aquifer much faster than the rate of replenishment. The fear is that over pumping will lead to the aquifer running dry causing severe stress on the Great Plains agricultural economy.

Moisture in the Atmosphere

Humidity is a measure of the water vapor content of the air. The amount of water vapor in the air depends on the controls over evaporation discussed earlier. There are several ways in which a meteorologist can express the humidity of the air. Each humidity measure is controlled to some degree by air temperature.

Absolute humidity is the weight of water vapor per unit volume of air, usually measured in units of grams of water vapor per cubic meter of air. Absolute humidity is not often used to express the moisture content of air because it is sensitive to changes in both the temperature of the air and atmospheric pressure. For instance, let's say that a 1 cubic meter parcel of air at the surface has 2 grams of water in it. Now lift the parcel of air upwards into the atmosphere. As the air rises upward the decrease in atmospheric pressure on the parcel allows it to expand outward occupying more space. Let's say that the parcel doubles in size as a result of uplift. Before rising, the absolute humidity was 2 gm/m3. As the air doubles in volume the new absolute humidity is 1 gm/ m3. In actuality the parcel still has the same weight of water in it, 2 grams. But given the way absolute humidity is calculated it appears the amount of water in the air has decreased.

Instead of absolute humidity, we use a measure that is not sensitive to volume changes in the air. Specific humidity is measured as the weight of water vapor in the air per unit weight of air, which includes the weight of water vapor. The units of measurement are grams of water vapor per kilogram of air. Given that weight is not significantly influenced by temperature or atmospheric pressure, specific humidity is much more useful as a measure of humidity. Another measure very similar to specific humidity is th mixing ratio. The mixing ratio is the weight of water vapor per unit weight of dry air. Because the atmosphere is made up of so little moisture by volume, the mixing ratio is virtually the same as the specific humidity.

Humidity is not only measured as a weight, but also by the pressure it creates. Vapor pressure is the partial pressure created by water vapor. Vapor pressure, like atmospheric pressure, is measured in millibars and is relatively insensitive to volumetric expansion or temperature. The saturation vapor pressure is simply the pressure that water vapor creates when the air is fully saturated.

When we think of air as being saturated with moisture we often say that the air is "holding all the moisture it can". This implies that once the air has reached saturation it won't "accept" anymore water by evaporation. This is wrong. So long as there is water available evaporation will continue even when the air is fully saturated. Let's examine the concept of saturation in more detail.

Imagine a beaker filled halfway with water. Let's put a top on it to constrain the movement of water molecules and eliminate the influence of wind on evaporation. As the water absorbs heat it begins to change phase and enter the air as water vapor. Above the surface, water vapor molecules dart about suspended in the air. However, near the surface water molecules are attaching themselves back the surface, thus changing back into liquid water (condensation) (A). As evaporation occurs the water level in the beaker decreases (B). This occurs because evaporation exceeds condensation of water back onto the surface. After some time, the amount of water entering the air from evaporation is equal to that condensing (C). When this occurs the air is said to be saturated.

The saturation level of the air is directly related to the air's temperature. As air temperature increases, more water can remain in a gas phase. As temperature decreases, water molecules slow down and there is a greater chance for them to condense on to surfaces. The graph below shows the relationship between air temperature and vapor pressure, a measure of the humidity, at saturation.

Note that below zero degrees Celsius the curve splits, one for the saturation point above a liquid surface (liquid-vapor) and one for a surface of ice (ice - vapor). The first thing you might be wondering is how water can exist as a liquid below the freezing point. Water that is not frozen below 0o C is called "super-cooled water". For water to freeze, the molecules must become properly aligned to attach to one another. This is less likely to occur especially with small amounts of water, like cloud droplets. Thus in clouds where temperatures are below freezing it is common to find both super-cooled liquid water and ice crystals.

Notice that the saturation vapor pressure at -20o C is lower for ice than for a liquid surface. Why would this be so? You may recall that to convert water from a liquid to a gas requires about 600 calories per gram. To convert water from a solid to a gas requires about 680 calories, hence it is more difficult to "liberate" a molecule of water from ice than water. Therefore, when the air is saturated, there are more molecules above a water surface (i.e. more vapor pressure) than an ice surface (i.e. less vapor pressure).

Dew point temperature is the temperature at which condensation takes place and is used as a measure of moisture content. The dew point temperature depends on the amount of moisture in the air, the more moisture in the air, the higher the dew point temperature. It gets its name "dew point" because dew will form on surfaces when the air reaches saturation.

Have you ever noticed that even though it's 100% relative humidity out, it feels a lot drier during the winter than the summer? To see why, we have to examine relative humidity. Relative humidity is the ratio of the amount of water vapor in the air to its saturation point. Often relative humidity is defined as the amount of water vapor in the air to "how much it can hold" at a given temperature. The notion of a holding capacity is dispelled when one considers what saturation really means. Regardless, what we do know is that the saturation level of the air with respect to water vapor depends on the air's temperature. We know that as air temperature increases, the ability for the air to keep water in its vapor state is easier. That is, as the air temperature increases it can keep more water in the vapor state. So why does saturated cold air feel drier than warm air at saturation? Let's look at an example.

Continental polar air (cP) has an average temperature of 5°C (41°F). Its saturation mixing ratio is 6 gm/kg. So continental air at 100% relative humidity is

RH = 6 gm/kg (in the air) / 6 gm/kg (saturation)

The average temperature of maritime tropical air (mT) is 22°C (71.6°F) with a saturation mixing ratio of 16 gm/kg. So maritime tropical air at 100% relative humidity is

RH =16 gm/kg (in the air) / 16 gm/kg (saturation)

Therefore, polar air is drier at 100% relative humidity because it has much less moisture in it at saturation than the warmer maritime tropical air.

The Condensation Process

Condensation is the phase change of water vapor into a liquid. During the condensation process, water molecules lose the 600 cal/gm of latent heat that were added during the evaporation process. When latent heat is released (called the "latent heat of fusion"), it is converted into sensible heat which warms the surrounding air. Warming the air increases its buoyancy and fuels the development of storms. Condensation takes place in the presence of condensation nuclei and when the air is nearly saturated.

Water vapor is darting around so fast in the air that the molecules tend to bounce off one another without bonding. Even if a few pure water molecules were to collide and bind together, the surface tension created by such a tiny sphere is so great that it is extremely difficult for additional water molecules to become incorporated into the mass. Hence condensation nuclei act as a platform for condensation to take place, increasing the size of a droplet and decreasing surface tension. Water absorbent clay minerals and sea salt are good condensation nuclei. Sulfates and nitrates are water absorbent and are responsible for creating acid rain.

The air must be at or near its saturation point for condensation to take place. Air can become saturated in two ways, (1) add water to the air by evaporation thus bringing it to saturation given its present temperature, or (2) cool the air to its dew point temperature. Cooling the air is the most common way for condensation to occur and create clouds. Air can be cooled through contact with a cold surface or by uplift. Contact cooling occurs when air comes in contact with a cooler surface and conduction transfers heat out of the air. Cooling by contact is called diabatic cooling.

Uplift Mechanisms

Adiabatic cooling occurs when air is uplifted from the surface causing the air to lose heat through the work of expansion. A parcel of air is uplifted when it initially gains heat from the surface causing convective uplift. When the air is warmed by the surface it will expand and become less dense relative to air that surrounds it. Being less dense than the air that surrounds it, the air becomes buoyant and begins to rise. Because atmospheric pressure decreases with height, the parcel of air expands and cools. If the air cools to its dew point temperature saturation occurs and condensation begins. The elevation above the surface where condensation begins is called the condensation level. Convergent uplift occurs when air enters a center of low pressure. As air converges into the center of a cyclone it is forced to rise off the surface. As the air rises it expands, cools, and water vapor condenses. Convergent and convective uplift are the two most important uplift mechanisms for condensation in the tropics. Under the intense sun, surface heating causes the moist tropical air to rise. Convergence of the trade winds in the Intertropical convergence zone creates copious rainfall in the wet tropics as well.

Orographic uplift is the forced ascent of air when it collides with a mountain. As air strikes the windward side, it is uplifted and cooled. Windward slopes of mountains tend to be the rainy sides while the leeward side is dry. Dry climates like steppes and desert are often found in the "rain shadow" of tall mountain systems that are oriented perpendicular to the flow of air. Frontal uplift occurs when greatly contrasting air masses meet along a weather front. For instance, when warm air collides with cool air along a warm front, the warm air is forced to rise up and over the cool air. As the air gently rises over the cool air, horizontally developed stratus-type clouds form. If cold air collides with warm air along a cold front, the more dense cold air can force the warmer air ahead to rise rapidly creating vertically developed cumulus-type clouds.

Adiabatic Temperature Change and Stability

In "The Atmosphere" we discovered that air temperature usually decreases with an increase in elevation through the troposphere. The decrease in temperature with elevation is called the environmental lapse rate of temperature or normal lapse rate of temperature. Recall that the normal lapse rate of temperature is the average lapse rate of temperature of .65°C / 100 meters. The environmental lapse rate of temperature is the actual vertical change in temperature on any given day and can be greater or less than .65°C / 100 meters. Also recall that the decrease in temperature with height is caused by increasing distance from the source of energy that heats the air, the Earth's surface. Air is warmer near the surface because it's closer to its source of heat. The further away from the surface, the cooler the air will be. It's like standing next to a fire, the closer you are the warmer you'll feel. Temperature change caused by an exchange of heat between two bodies is called diabatic temperature change. There is another very important way to change the temperature of air called adiabatic temperature change.

Adiabatic temperature change of air occurs without the addition or removal of energy. That is, there is no exchange of heat with the surrounding environment to cause the cooling or heating of the air. The temperature change is due to work done on a parcel of air by the external environment, or work done by a parcel of air on the air that surrounds it. What kind of work can be done? The work that is done is the expansion or compression of air.

Imagine an isolated parcel of air that is moving vertically through the troposphere. We know that air pressure decreases with increasing elevation. As the parcel of air moves upward the pressure exerted on the parcel decreases and the parcel expands in volume as a result. In order to expand (i.e.. do work), the parcel must use its internal energy to do so. As the air expands, the molecules spread out and ultimately collide less with one another. The work of expansion causes the air's temperature to decrease. You might have had personal experience with this kind of cooling if you've let the air out of an automobile or bicycle tire. Air inside the tire is under a great deal of pressure, and as it rushes outside it moves into a lower pressure environment. In so doing, the parcel quickly expands against the outside environment air. By placing your hand in front of the valve stem, you can feel the air cool as it expands. This is called adiabatic cooling. As air descends through the troposphere it experiences increasing atmospheric pressure. This causes the parcel volume to decrease in size, squeezing the air molecules closer together. In this case, work is being done on the parcel. As the volume shrinks, air molecules bounce off one another more often ricocheting with greater speed. The increase in molecular movement causes an increase in the temperature of the parcel. This process is referred to as adiabatic warming.

The rate at which air cools or warms depends on the moisture status of the air. If the air is dry, the rate of temperature change is 1°C/100 meters and is called the dry adiabatic rate (DAR). If the air is saturated, the rate of temperature change is .6°C/100 meters and is called the saturated adiabatic rate (SAR). The DAR is a constant value, that is, it's always 1°C/100 meters. The SAR varies somewhat with how much moisture is in the air, but we'll assume it to be a constant value here. The reason for the difference in the two rates is due to the liberation of latent heat as a result of condensation. As saturated air rises and cools, condensation takes place. Recall that as water vapor condenses, latent heat is released. This heat is transferred into the other molecules of air inside the parcel causing a reduction in the rate of cooling.

Stability of Air

Adiabatic temperature change is an important factor in determining the stability of the air. We can think of air stability as the tendency for air to rise or fall through the atmosphere under its own "power". Stable air has a tendency to resist movement. On the other hand, unstable air will easily rise. What gives air "power" to rise? The tendency for air to rise or fall depends on the adiabatic and environmental lapse rates.

Stable Air

Stable atmospheric conditions prevail when the environmental lapse rate is less than the saturated adiabatic rate. The surrounding air is changing its temperature at a rate of .65°C/100 meters. The parcel on this day is "dry" and will rise and cool at a temperature of 1°C/100 meters. After giving the parcel a slight upward push, it rises to a level of 1000 meters where it cools to a temperature of 20°C. A measurement of the air surrounding the parcel shows a temperature of 23.5°C. In other words, the parcel is colder (and more dense) than the surrounding air at 1000 meters. If the uplift mechanism ceased, the parcel of air would return to the surface.

Unstable Air

Air is unstable when the environmental lapse rate is greater than the dry adiabatic rate. Under these conditions, a rising parcel of air is warmer and less dense than the air surrounding it at any given elevation. Note that at any elevation above the surface the parcel temperature is higher than the air that surrounds it. Even as it reaches the dew point temperature at 2000 meters, the air remains warmer than the surrounding air. As a result it continues to rise and cool at the saturated adiabatic rate. Vertically developed clouds are likely to develop under unstable conditions such as this.

Weather Systems

Weather is the day - to - day state of the atmosphere. The weather of the humid tropics is very similar throughout the year as a constant flow of energy keeps temperatures uniformly high. However, the daily weather is quite variable in the midlatitudes. Here, huge air masses collide to create powerful storm systems that affect global heat distribution, the shaping of the earth surface, and our daily livelihood. In this chapter we'll examine weather systems at a variety of geographic scales that affect our daily lives.

AIR MASSES

Air Mass Source Regions

An air mass is a vast pool of air having similar temperature and moisture characteristics over its horizontal extent. An air mass occupies thousands of square miles of the Earth's surface. Air masses are born in a source region where they take on their characteristic temperature and moisture content. Source regions are often regions of low relief and calm wind that prevent turbulent mixing and allow the air to take on the conditions of the surface over which it forms. Radiation and vertical mixing of heat yield an equilibrium between the conditions at the source region and the properties of the overlying air mass after a period of 3 to 5 days. Areas dominated by high pressure serve as good source regions where subsidence pushes the air toward the surface. High pressure also enables the air to move outward from the source region.

Air Mass Classification

Atmospheric scientists have created definite temperature and humidity criteria to classify each air mass. We'll classify them based on their general conditions, e.g. warm and wet, cold and dry. The latitude of the source region fundamentally determines the temperature of an air mass. Arctic air masses form between 60o and 90o north latitude. Arctic air masses are characterized as being extremely cold air masses. Polar air masses form between 40o and 60o north or south latitude and are cold air masses but warmer than the higher latitude arctic air mass. Warm tropical air masses are found between 15o and 35o north and south latitude. The exceedingly warm equatorial air masses form near the equator. The type of surface over which air masses form also determines their humidity characteristics. Maritime (oceanic) air masses are typically moist, whereas those forming over the continents are usually dry. However, humidity is also determined by temperature so cooler maritime polar air masses are drier than warm maritime tropical air masses.

Air Mass Types

Continental arctic air (cA) is typically described as extremely cold and dry. Record setting temperatures in the middle and high latitudes are due to the invasion of this very cold mass of air. At about the same latitude in the Southern Hemisphere is found the continental Antarctic (cAA) air mass. This too is an exceedingly cold air mass and is drier than its arctic counterpart as the source region is the continent of Antarctica. Continental polar (cP) air is considered a cold and dry air mass that is warmer than the arctic air mass located to the north. Continental polar air is typically a stable or conditionally stable mass of air. Maritime polar (mP) air is cool and moist air that brings mild weather to coastal locations. Maritime polar air is warmer than continental polar air in the winter as the surface temperature of the ocean is higher. Similarly, mP air masses are typically cooler than cP air masses during the summer as the continents warm more than the ocean at these latitudes. Maritime polar air masses that enter the west coast are forced to rise up coastal mountain chains causing significant orographic uplift and precipitation. In Europe, mP air masses penetrate further inland due to the east - west orientation of the mountains. Thus smaller temperature ranges and higher humidity typical of maritime climate are found further inland in Europe than in the North America.

Maritime tropical (mT) air masses are warm and moist air masses that are responsible for much of the precipitation east of the Rocky mountains in the United States. Precipitation occurs when mT air collides with cP air causing the warmer and less dense mT air to rise, cool, and condense into clouds. In the southeast portion of the United States convective uplift of air also occurs to create precipitation. Over subtropical and tropical continents the source region for the hot and dry continental tropical (cT) air mass is found. Major source regions are the great deserts of the Earth such as the Sahara, Arabian, and Australian. The extremely low humidity is due to the lack of available water for evaporation as well as the subsidence of the subtropical high. The southwest desert of the United States serves as a source region for cT air too, but only during the summer. Surface temperatures in the winter are too cold to create a continental tropical air mass there. Near the equator the exceedingly warm and humid maritime equatorial air masses form. Convection and convergence of this air mass in the Intertropical Convergence Zone is one for the reason for the heavy rainfall experienced in the rain forests of this region.

Air Mass Modification

The trajectory that air masses affecting North America take as they move out of their source regions. As they traverse the surface, the temperature and moisture content of air masses are modified. Continental air masses traveling south out of central Canada move over warmer surfaces. To indicate that the air mass is colder than the surface over which it is traveling a "k" is added (cPk). Heat transfer into the air mass from the underlying surface creates unstable conditions. In the late fall and early winter cP air masses moving over the open water of the Great Lakes gain heat and moisture. As the air mass strikes the land, the air can be uplifted by topographic barriers causing the lake-effect snows.

Off the southwest coast of North America lies a source region for maritime tropical air. This air mass is typically unstable at its source. As it moves toward land the air passes over the cold California Current. As the air mass traverses the cold ocean current, heat is transferred out of the air mass near the surface. In addition, the subsidence of the air aloft due to the presence of the subtropical high in this region causes adiabatic warming of the air at higher elevations. As a result, the environmental lapse rate of temperature decreases or sometimes inverts, making the air stable. To show that the air mass has become stable an "s" is added to its abbreviation, e.g. mTs. Stable conditions inhibit uplift and reduce the possibility for precipitation. Conversely, off the east coast of the United States the warm Gulf Stream enhances the instability of the maritime air mass, and precipitation becomes more likely. In this case, a "u" is added to indicate that the air mass is unstable, e.g. mTu.

Fronts

Fronts are boundaries between contrasting masses of air. Atmospheric scientists recognize fronts of different spatial scales. These range from the quasi-stationary fronts along which cyclones form to "weather" fronts embedded in cyclones. Fronts are three-dimensional features. They are not only a boundary between contrasting air masses running along the surface, but extend upwards into the troposphere as we will later learn.

Quasi-stationary Fronts

At the global scale are quasi-stationary fronts found migrating within a particular latitudinal zone throughout most of the year. The polar front is the boundary between polar-type air and tropical-type air. The polar front migrates between about 35o and 65o, following the annual cycle of earth surface heating. Above the polar front is found the polar front jet stream, a high velocity corridor of wind that controls the development and movement of mid-latitude cyclones.

During the winter, the polar front slides equatorward along with invading cold air. During the summer, the polar front retreats northward. This seasonal migratory pattern moves cyclones into and out of the middle latitudes giving them quite variable weather conditions over the seasons.

Synoptic Scale Fronts

At a smaller or synoptic scale are the "weather" fronts e.g., cold, warm, occluded, and stationary. Cold fronts are those where cold air replaces warm air. A warm front is where warm air replaces cold air. A noticeable difference between warm and cold fronts is the slope of the front above the surface. The frontal surface, the portion extending upward above the surface, is much steeper for the cold front than warm front. The steepness of the frontal surface directly impacts the type of weather one experiences along these fronts.

An occluded front forms when a cold front catches up with a warm front. Air is often converging at a front producing a trough of low pressure along it. A decrease in pressure is often experienced with their passage. A stationary front is where no change in air masses or movement of the front occurs. The weather associated with these fronts is discussed later.

Weather Map Depiction

Meteorologists use both symbols and color to distinguish between synoptic scale fronts on weather maps. If printed in color, warm fronts are shown as a line of red semi-circles pointing in the direction of movement. Cold fronts are depicted as a line of blue triangles. Occluded fronts appear in purple with both warm and cold front symbols on the same side. The symbols point in the direction of the front is moving. Stationary fronts are alternating warm and cold front symbols on opposite sides, indicating no movement. The map depicts a wave cyclone as it is starting to occlude. We see an occluded front trailing southeast from the center branching into cold and warm fronts.

The location of air masses on weather maps are identified by their letter abbreviation, e.g., mT, cP, mP. Shading is used to show where areas of precipitation occur. Looking at the local environmental setting can give a clue as to what mechanism caused uplift for precipitation to form.

The distribution of air pressure is shown by isobars, lines connecting points of equal air pressure. Isobars are drawn in increments of 4 millibars on surface weather maps. Recall that it is the pressure gradient that controls wind speed. Strong pressure gradients and hence faster winds occur where the isobars are closely spaced. Weak pressure gradients and slow winds occur where the isobars are widely spaced.

Wave Cyclones

The variable nature of weather in the midlatitudes is in part due to the presence of midlatitude or extratropical cyclones. Appropriately called "wave cyclones", these systems take the form of an ocean wave when fully developed. Wave cyclones can grow to vast proportions, nearly 1000 miles (1600 km) wide. These vast areas of low pressure are born along the polar front where cold polar air from the north collides with warm tropical air to the south. In so doing, huge spiraling storms move across the surface guided by the polar front jet stream.

Initial Stage - Cyclogenesis

Wave cyclones form where surface convergence predominates. Cyclones often develop in the region of the Aleutian and Icelandic sub-polar low pressure cells. Wave cyclones also develop and intensify on the east slope of the Rocky Mountains, the Gulf Coast and east coasts of North America and Asia.

Especially during the spring and summer in the midlatitudes of North America, high pressure to the north pushes cold polar air southward from Canada. To the south, maritime tropical air streams northward toward the polar air.The polar front is depicted by the symbols for a stationary front (the alternating red semi-circle and blue triangles). At the location where the opposing streams of air meet, cyclonic shear is created from opposing air streams sliding by each other causing the air to spin. You can demonstrate what happens as a result of cyclonic shear by placing a pencil between your hands. Push your right hand away from you (warm southerly flow) and draw your left hand towards you (cold, northerly flow). (Go ahead and try this to see if I'm right.) Examine what happens to the pencil. If you followed directions the pencil should be rotating in a counterclockwise fashion.

Mature Stage

Once the air collides and cyclonic circulation commences, warm air from the south invades where cold air was once located north of the polar front. A warm front develops where warm air replaces the cold air. The position of a warm front on a weather map is depicted (in red) with a line showing the boundary between the air masses and semi-circles indicating the direction the front is moving. To the west of the center of the developing system, cold air is sliding south replacing warm air at the surface. A cold front (blue triangles) develops where cold air replaces the warm air. Soon the developing system takes on the characteristic wave form, hence their name "wave cyclone". The lowest pressure is found at the center or apex of the wave.

The less dense warmer air slides up and over the colder more dense air. Surface friction imposed by the ground slows the advance of the front compared to its position aloft yielding a gentle slope to the front.

Occluded Stage

Being more dense, the air behind the cold front can "bulldoze" the warmer and less dense air out of the way. The advancing warm air along the warm front cannot push the colder air in its path out of the way. Instead, the warm air rises off the surface and glides up and over the colder more dense air ahead of the warm front. As a result, there is less horizontal displacement and the warm front moves slower across the earth than does a cold front. Over time the cold front catches up with the warm front and the cyclone starts to occlude.

Dissolving Stage

The system enters the dissolving stage after it occludes and the lifting mechanism is cutoff. Without the convergence and uplift, the cyclone dissipates in the atmosphere.

Surface Cyclones and the Jet Stream

Above the polar front lies the polar front jet stream, a zone of faster moving air in the upper troposphere. The jet stream takes on a meandering pattern with regions of faster and slower air. Within the jet stream there are regions air convergence and divergence.

Recall that surface air converges and rises in low pressure systems. To maintain low pressure at the surface the rising air must diverge at the top. It is this upper air divergence in the jet stream that "pulls" air upward to help form surface cyclones. In so doing, surface cyclones tend to follow the path of the jet stream. We can see that where upper level convergence occurs air sinks to promote high pressure at the surface. Where upper-level divergence occurs air is pulled up from the surface to help create low pressure near the ground. Wave cyclones dissolve when they no longer have the upper level divergence to maintain them.

WEATHER AND WAVE CYCLONES

The weather associated with the passage of a wave cyclone is a product of the convergence and frontal uplift found in the system. The wave cyclone can be divided into three sectors: (1) the cool sector ahead of the warm front, (2) the warm sector between the cold and warm fronts, and (3) the cold sector located behind the cold front. During the spring, summer, and fall, cP air masses tend to occupy the cold and cool sectors while an mT air mass lies in the warm sector. The cold sector generally has the lowest temperatures as cold air is coming from a northerly direction. Air in the cool sector is coming from an easterly direction so it is warmer than the air in the cold sector. In the warm sector air is entering the system from the south so we should expect to find the warmest temperatures in this region. In the next few sections we'll examine the weather associated with the various sectors and fronts.

Weather Patterns

The bottom portion shows a simple profile (side) view along the line identified as the "Profile Transect" that connects points A, B, C, D on the weather map view.

Let's examine the weather map view first. Isobars have been constructed to show the distribution of pressure around the cyclone. Notice that the lowest pressure is at the center of the system and increases outward. Another thing to note about the isobars is the V-shape where they cross the fronts. This indicates that the front sits in a trough of lower pressure. As a front approaches you will experience a drop in atmospheric pressure. Once a front has passed the pressure will increase.

The flow of air around the system is indicated by the wind direction symbols (black dots with a line pointing in the direction of the wind). The symbols show the characteristic counterclockwise flow around a center of low pressure in the Northern Hemisphere. Ahead of the warm front, in the cool sector, the air is from an easterly direction. In the warm sector, mT air streams out of the south. Behind the cold front air comes from a westerly to northwesterly direction. The light blue area shows the distribution of precipitation. Notice there is a larger band of rain along the warm front than along the cold front.

Warm Front Weather

The warm front slopes gently up into the troposphere that has a direct bearing on the kinds of clouds that are produced. As the warm air behind the front collides with the cooler air ahead, the warmer less dense air is forced to glide upward.

A typical sequence of clouds develops as a result of this gentle uplift. The first clouds you see as a warm front approaches are the thin, wispy cirrus clouds. As the front approaches the clouds become thicker and the cloud base lowers. As the cirrus clouds pass by you, cirrostratus and then altostratus clouds approach. As the warm front is nearly at your location you will see the clouds completely cover the sky as stratus clouds. Nimbostratus clouds along the front create low intensity precipitation that might last for a long time. Ahead of the front the wind is generally cool and from a easterly direction. As the front passes by you the wind direction shifts toward the southeast and the south. As it does the temperatures start to rise as warm air replaces the cool air at your location.

Warm Sector Weather

Once the warm front passes your location you'll notice an increase in temperature and air pressure. Soon the stratus clouds of the warm front give way to broken and clearing skies. As the warm sector moves into your location you will notice an increase in the humidity of the air. The wind is out of the south so maritime tropical air begins to invade. During the afternoon you might see an occasional puffy cumulus cloud. These "fair weather" clouds are often created by convection and instability in the warm and humid afternoon air.

After a while the winds start to shift to the southwest and the humidity continues to rise. You notice the clouds begin to grow in height, merge into larger darker masses. This indicates the air is becoming much more unstable. Once again the air pressure starts to fall. Winds begin to gust and growing cumulus clouds can be seen on the horizon. It would appear that a cold front is approaching.

Cold Front Weather

Weather along an advancing cold front is much different than that along a warm front. Friction slows the advancing cold air causing a steep slope to the front. The steep slope pushes the air ahead of it rapidly upwards and vertically developed clouds (cumulus) are produced along the front. As with a warm front, you experience a drop in the atmospheric pressure as the front approaches. As the cold front passes you, the winds shift from south to southwest, and finally to a westerly direction.

With greatly contrasting air masses on either side of the front and potentially unstable conditions, violent weather can form. Towering cumulonimbus clouds are common along cold fronts producing intense downpours of rain lasting for a relatively short period of time. Tornadoes can form under the most extreme conditions ahead of an advancing cold front. Below is a table that briefly summarizes the weather conditions associated with wave cyclones and their associated fronts. Instead of reading from left to right, read the table from right to left.

Weather Element	Cold Sector	Warm Sector	Cool Sector
Air Mass	cP	mT	cP
Pressure Tendency	rising	falling -- rising	falling
Wind Direction	NW - W	SW - S - SE	SE -- E
Clouds	Clring - Cu	Cb - Cu - Clring	Ns - St - As - Cs - Ci
Precipitation		Intense but short duration at cold front	Light but long duration at warm front

Intense but short duration at cold front

Light but long duration at warm front

Cloud abbreviations:

- Ci - Cirrus
- Cs - Cirrostratus
- As - Altostratus
- St - Stratus
- Ns - Nimbostratus
- Clring - Clearing
- Cu - Cumulus
- Cb - Cumulonimbus

3

THE ATMOSPHERE

ATMOSPHERIC COMPOSITION

Table below lists the eleven most abundant gases found in the Earth's lower atmosphere by volume. Of the gases listed, nitrogen, oxygen, water vapor, carbon dioxide, methane, nitrous oxide, and ozone are extremely important to the health of the Earth's biosphere.

The table indicates that nitrogen and oxygen are the main components of the atmosphere by volume. Together these two gases make up approximately 99% of the dry atmosphere. Both of these gases have very important associations with life. Nitrogen is removed from the atmosphere and deposited at the Earth's surface mainly by specialized nitrogen fixing bacteria, and by way of lightning through precipitation. The addition of this nitrogen to the Earth's surface soils and various water bodies supplies much needed nutrition for plant growth. Nitrogen returns to the atmosphere primarily through biomass combustion and denitrification.

Oxygen is exchanged between the atmosphere and life through the processes of photosynthesis and respiration. Photosynthesis produces oxygen when carbon dioxide and water are chemically converted into glucose with the help of sunlight. Respiration is a the opposite process of photosynthesis. In respiration, oxygen is combined with glucose to chemically release energy for metabolism. The products of this reaction are water and carbon dioxide.

The next most abundant gas on the table is water vapor. Water vapor varies in concentration in the atmosphere both spatially and temporally. The highest concentrations of water vapor are found near the equator over the oceans and tropical rain forests. Cold polar areas and subtropical continental deserts are locations where the volume of water vapor can approach zero percent. Water vapor has several very important functional roles on our planet:

- It redistributes heat energy on the Earth through latent heat energy exchange.
- The condensation of water vapor creates precipitaion that falls to the Earth's surface providing needed fresh water for plants and animals.
- It helps warm the Earth's atmosphere through the greenhouse effect.

The fifth most abundant gas in the atmosphere is carbon dioxide. The volume of this gas has increased by over 35% in the last three hundred years. This increase is primarily due to human induced burning from fossil fuels, deforestation, and other forms of land-use change. Carbon dioxide is an important greenhouse gas. The human-caused increase in its concentration in the atmosphere has strengthened the greenhouse effect and has definitely contributed to global warming over the last 100 years. Carbon dioxide is also naturally exchanged between the atmosphere and life through the processes of photosynthesis and respiration.

Methane is a very strong greenhouse gas. Since 1750, methane concentrations in the atmosphere have increased by more than 150%. The primary sources for the additional methane added to the atmosphere (in order of importance) are: rice cultivation; domestic grazing animals; termites; landfills; coal mining; and, oil and gas extraction. Anaerobic conditions associated with rice paddy flooding results in the formation of methane gas. However, an accurate estimate of how much methane is being produced from rice paddies has been difficult to ascertain. More than 60% of all rice paddies are found in India and China where scientific data concerning emission rates are unavailable.

Nevertheless, scientists believe that the contribution of rice paddies is large because this form of crop production has more than doubled since 1950. Grazing animals release methane to the environment as a result of herbaceous digestion. Some researchers believe the addition of methane from this source has more than quadrupled over the last century. Termites also release methane through similar processes. Land-use change in the tropics, due to deforestation, ranching, and farming, may be causing termite numbers to expand. If this assumption is correct, the contribution from these insects may be important. Methane is also released from landfills, coal mines, and gas and oil drilling. Landfills produce methane as organic wastes decompose over time. Coal, oil, and natural gas deposits release methane to the atmosphere when these deposits are excavated or drilled.

The average concentration of the greenhouse gas nitrous oxide is now increasing at a rate of 0.2 to 0.3% per year. Its part in the enhancement of the greenhouse effect is minor relative to the other greenhouse gases already mentioned. However, it does have an important role in the artificial fertilization of ecosystems. In extreme cases, this fertilization can lead to the death of forests, eutrophication of aquatic habitats, and species exclusion. Sources for the increase of nitrous oxide in the atmosphere include: land-use conversion; fossil fuel combustion; biomass burning; and soil fertilization.

Most of the nitrous oxide added to the atmosphere each year comes from deforestation and the conversion of forest, savanna and grassland ecosystems into agricultural fields and rangeland. Both of these processes reduce the amount of nitrogen stored in living vegetation and soil through the decomposition of organic matter. Nitrous oxide is also released into the atmosphere when fossil fuels and biomass are burned. However, the combined contribution to the increase of this gas in the atmosphere is thought to be minor. The use of nitrate and ammonium fertilizers to enhance plant growth is another source of nitrous oxide. How much is released from this process has been difficult to quantify. Estimates suggest that the contribution from this source represents from 50% to 0.2% of nitrous oxide added to the atmosphere annually.

Ozone's role in the enhancement of the greenhouse effect has been difficult to determine. Accurate measurements of past long-term (more than 25 years in the past) levels of this gas in the atmosphere are currently unavailable. Moreover, concentrations of ozone gas are found in two different regions of the Earth's atmosphere. The majority of the ozone (about 97%) found in the atmosphere is concentrated in the stratosphere at an altitude of 15 to 55 kilometers above the Earth's surface. This stratospheric ozone provides an important service to life on the Earth as it absorbs harmful ultraviolet radiation. In recent years, levels of stratospheric ozone have been decreasing due to the buildup of human created chlorofluorocarbons in the atmosphere. Since the late 1970s, scientists have noticed the development of severe holes in the ozone layer over Antarctica. Satellite measurements have indicated that the zone from 65° North to 65° South latitude has had a 3% decrease in stratospheric ozone since 1978.

Ozone is also highly concentrated at the Earth's surface in and around cities. Most of this ozone is created as a by product of human created photochemical smog. This buildup of ozone is toxic to organisms living at the Earth's surface.

Table: Average composition of the atmosphere up to an altitude of 25 km.

Gas Name	Chemical Formula	Percent Volume
Nitrogen	N_2	78.08%
Oxygen	O_2	20.95%
*Water	H_2O	0 to 4%
Argon	Ar	0.93%
*Carbon Dioxide	CO_2	0.0360%
Neon	Ne	0.0018%
Helium	He	0.0005%
*Methane	CH_4	0.00017%
Hydrogen	H2	0.00005%
*Nitrous Oxide	N_2O	0.00003%
*Ozone	O_3	0.000004%

** variable gases*

THE LAYERED ATMOSPHERE

The Earth's atmosphere contains several different layers that can be defined according to air temperature. According to temperature, the atmosphere contains four different layers. The first layer is called the troposphere. The depth of this layer varies from about 8 to 16 kilometers. Greatest depths occur at the tropics where warm temperatures causes vertical expansion of the lower atmosphere. From the tropics to the Earth's polar regions the troposphere becomes gradually thinner. The depth of this layer at the poles is roughly half as thick when compared to the tropics. Average depth of the troposphere is approximately 11 kilometers.

About 80% of the total mass of the atmosphere is contained in troposphere. It is also the layer where the majority of our weather occurs. Maximum air temperature also occurs near the Earth's surface in this layer. With increasing height, air temperature drops uniformly with altitude at a rate of approximately 6.5° Celsius per 1000 meters. This phenomenon is commonly called the Environmental Lapse Rate. At an average temperature of -56.5° Celsius, the top of the troposphere is reached. At the upper edge of the troposphere is a narrow transition zone known as the tropopause.

Above the tropopause is the stratosphere. This layer extends from an average altitude of 11 to 50 kilometers above the Earth's surface. This stratosphere contains about 19.9% of the total mass found in the atmosphere. Very little weather occurs in the stratosphere. Occasionally, the top portions of thunderstorms breach this layer. The lower portion of the stratosphere is also influenced by the polar jet stream and subtropical jet stream. In the first 9 kilometers of the stratosphere, temperature remains constant with height. A zone with constant temperature in the atmosphere is called an isothermal layer. From an altitude of 20 to 50 kilometers, temperature increases with an increase in altitude.

The higher temperatures found in this region of the stratosphere occurs because of a localized concentration of ozone gas molecules. These molecules absorb ultraviolet sunlight creating heat energy that warms the stratosphere. Ozone is primarily found in the atmosphere at varying concentrations between the altitudes of 10 to 50 kilometers. This layer of ozone is also called the ozone layer . The ozone layer is important to organisms at the Earth's surface as it protects them from the harmful effects of the Sun's ultraviolet radiation. Without the ozone layer life could not exist on the Earth's surface.

Separating the mesosphere from the stratosphere is transition zone called the stratopause. In the mesosphere, the atmosphere reaches its coldest temperatures (about -90° Celsius) at a height of approximately 80 kilometers. At the top of the mesosphere is another transition zone known as the mesopause. The last atmospheric layer has an altitude greater than 80 kilometers and is called the thermosphere. Temperatures in this layer can be greater than 1200° C. These high temperatures are generated from the absorption of intense solar radiation by oxygen molecules (O_2). While these temperatures seem extreme, the amount of heat energy involved is very small. The amount of heat stored in a substance is controlled in part by its mass. The air in the thermosphere is extremely thin with individual gas molecules being separated from each other by large distances. Consequently, measuring the temperature of thermosphere with a thermometer is a very difficult process. Thermometers measure the temperature of bodies via the movement of heat energy. Normally, this process takes a few minutes for the conductive transfer of kinetic energy from countless molecules in the body of a substance to the expanding liquid inside the thermometer. In the thermosphere, our thermometer would lose more heat energy from radiative emission then what it would gain from making occasional contact with extremely hot gas molecules.

PHYSICAL BEHAVIOR OF THE ATMOSPHERE AND THE GAS LAWS

In the previous topic, we learned the atmosphere is composed of a mixture of many different gases. This mixture behaves in many ways as if it were a single gas. As a result of this phenomenon, the following generalizations describe important relationships between temperature, pressure, density and volume, that relate to the Earth's atmosphere.

(1) When temperature is held constant, the density of a gas is proportional to pressure, and volume is inversely proportional to pressure. Accordingly, an increase in pressure will cause an increase in density of the gas and a decrease in its volume.

(2) If volume is kept constant, the pressure of a unit mass of gas is proportional to temperature. If temperature increase

so will pressure, assuming no change in the volume of the gas.

(3) Holding pressure constant, causes the temperature of a gas to be proportional to volume, and inversely proportional to density. Thus, increasing temperature of a unit mass of gas causes its volume to expand and its density to decrease as long as there is no change in pressure.

These relationships can also be described mathematically by the Ideal Gas Law. Two equations that are commonly used to describe this law are:

Pressure × Volume = Constant × Temperature

and

Pressure = Density × Constant × Temperature

Atmospheric Pressure

Air is a tangible material substance and as a result has mass. Any object with mass is influenced by the universal force known as gravity. Newton's Law of Universal Gravitation states: any two objects separated in space are attracted to each other by a force proportional to the product of their masses and inversely proportional to the square of the distance between them. On the Earth, gravity can also be expressed as a force of acceleration of about 9.8 meters per second per second. As a result of this force, the speed of any object falling towards the surface of the Earth accelerates (1st second - 9.8 meters per second, 2nd second - 19.6 meters per second, 3rd second - 29.4 meters per second, and so on.) until terminal velocity is attained.

Gravity shapes and influences all atmospheric processes. It causes the density and pressure of air to decrease exponentially as one moves away from the surface of the Earth.

Measuring Atmospheric Pressure

Any instrument that measures air pressure is called a barometer. The first measurement of atmospheric pressure began with a simple experiment performed by Evangelista Torricelli in 1643. In his experiment, Torricelli immersed a tube, sealed at one end, into a container of mercury. Atmospheric pressure then forced the mercury up into the tube to a level that was considerably higher than the mercury in the container. Torricelli determined from this experiment that the pressure of the atmosphere is approximately 30 inches or 76 centimeters (one centimeter of mercury is equal to 13.3 millibars). He also noticed that height of the mercury varied with changes in outside weather conditions.

Torricelli's Barometer

The most common type barometer used in homes is the aneroid barometer. Inside this instrument is a small, flexible metal capsule called an aneroid cell. In the construction of the device, a vacuum is created inside the capsule so that small changes in outside air pressure cause the capsule to expand or contract. The size of the aneroid cell is then calibrated and any change in its volume is transmitted by springs and levers to an indicating arm that points to the corresponding atmospheric pressure.

For climatological and meteorological purposes, standard sea-level pressure is said to be 76.0 cm or 29.92 inches or 1013.2 millibars. Scientists often use the kilopascal (kPa) as their preferred unit for measuring pressure. 1 kilopascal is equal to 10 millibars. Another unit of force sometimes used by scientists to measure atmospheric pressure is the newton. One millibar equals 100 newtons per square meter (N/m^2).

ATMOSPHERIC PRESSURE AT THE EARTH'S SURFACE

During the winter months (December to February), areas of high pressure develop over central Asia (Siberian High), off the coast California (Hawaiian High), central North America (Canadian High), over Spain and northwest Africa extending into the subtropical North Atlantic (Azores High), and over the oceans in the Southern Hemisphere at the subtropics. Areas of low pressure occur just south of the Aleutian Islands (Aleutian Low), at the southern tip of Greenland (Iceland Low), and latitudes 50 to 80° South.

During the summer months (June to August), a number of dominant winter pressure systems disappear. Gone are the Siberian High over central Asia and the dominant low pressure systems near the Aleutian Islands and at the southern tip of Greenland. The Hawaiian and Azores High intensify and expand northward into their relative ocean basins. High pressure systems over the subtropical oceans in Southern Hemisphere also intensity and expand to the north. New areas of dominant high pressure develop over Australia and Antarctica (South Polar High). Regions of low pressure form over central Asia and southwest Asia (Asiatic Low). These pressure systems are responsible for the summer monsoon rains of Asia.

The Ozone Layer

The ozone layer is a region of concentration of the ozone molecule (O_3) in the Earth's atmosphere. The layer sits at an altitude of about 10-50 kilometers, with a maximum concentration in the stratosphere at an altitude of approximately 25 kilometers. In recent years, scientists have measured a seasonal thinning of the ozone layer primarily at the South Pole. This phenomenon is being called the ozone hole.

The ozone layer naturally shields Earth's life from the harmful effects of the Sun's ultraviolet (UV) radiation. A severe decrease in the concentration of ozone in the ozone layer could lead to the following harmful effects:

- An increase in the incidence of skin cancer (ultraviolet radiation can destroy acids in DNA).
- A large increase in cataracts and Sun burning.
- Suppression of immune systems in organisms.
- Adverse impact on crops and animals.
- Reduction in the growth of phytoplankton found in the Earth's oceans.
- Cooling of the Earth's stratosphere and possibly some surface climatic effect.

Ozone is created naturally in the stratosphere by the combining of atomic oxygen (O) with molecular oxygen (O_2). This process is activated by sunlight. Ozone is destroyed naturally by the absorption of ultraviolet radiation,

O_3 + UV >>> O_2 + O

and by the collision of ozone with other atmospheric atoms and molecules.

O_3 + O >>> $2O_2$

O_3 + O_3 >>> $3O_2$

Since the late 1970s, scientists have discovered that stratospheric ozone amounts over Antarctica in springtime (September - November) have decreased by as much as 60%. Satellite measurements (NIMBUS 7 - Total Ozone Mapping Spectrometer) have indicated a 2% decrease in ozone between 65 degrees North - 65 degrees South per decade since 1978. A reduction of about 3% per year has been measured at Antarctica where most of the ozone loss is occurring globally. During the late 1990s, large losses of ozone were recorded above Antarctica year after year in the months of September and August. In some years, spring levels of stratospheric ozone were more than 60% lower than the levels recorded months prior to the seasonal development of the hole.

It appears that human activities are altering the amount of stratospheric O_3. The main agent responsible for this destruction was human-made chlorofluorocarbons or CFCs. First produced by General Motors Corporation in 1928, CFCs were created as a replacement to the toxic refrigerant ammonia. CFCs have also been used as a propellant in spray cans, cleaner for electronics, sterilant for hospital equipment, and to produce the bubbles in styrofoam. CFCs are cheap to produce and are very stable compounds, lasting up to 200 years in the atmosphere. By 1988, some 320,000 metric tons of CFCs were used worldwide.

In 1987, a number of nations around the world met to begin formulating a global plan, known as the Montreal Protocol, to reduce and eliminate the use of CFCs. Since 1987, the plan has been amended in 1990 and 1992 to quicken the schedule of production and consumption reductions. By 1996, 161 countries were participating in the Protocol. The Montreal Protocol called for a 100

% reduction in the creation and use of CFCs by January 1, 1996 in the world's more developed countries. Less developed countries have until January 1, 2010 to stop their production and consumption of these dangerous chemicals.

CFCs created at the Earth's surface drift slowly upward to the stratosphere where ultraviolet radiation from the Sun causes their decomposition and the release of chlorine (Cl). Chlorine in turn attacks the molecules of ozone chemically converting them into oxygen molecules.

$$Cl + O_3 >>> ClO + O_2$$

$$ClO + O = Cl + O_2$$

A single chlorine atom removes about 100,000 ozone molecules before it is taken out of operation by other substances. Chlorine is removed from the stratosphere by two chemical reactions:

$$ClO + NO_2 >>> ClONO_2$$

$$CH_4 + Cl >>> HCl + CH_3$$

Normally, these two reactions would quickly neutralize the chlorine released into the stratosphere. However, the presence of polar stratospheric clouds, rich in nitrogen, and sunlight facilitates a series of reactions which prolongs the reactive life of chlorine in the atmosphere. Interestingly, these polar stratospheric clouds require very cold air (approximately -85° Celsius) for their formation. Stratospheric air of this temperature occurs normally every year above Antarctica in the winter and early spring months. Destruction of the ozone begins in Antarctica in the spring as this region moves from 24 hours of night to 24 hours of day. These clouds are less frequent in the Arctic stratosphere because winter cooling of the air in the stratosphere is less severe. NASA's Earth Probe -Total Ozone Mapping Spectrometer home page has the latest images describing the current status of global stratosphere ozone levels in the atmosphere. The average areal coverage of the Antarctic ozone hole has now leveled off at about 24 million square kilometers. Scientists believe that the ozone hole over Antarctica will maintain this size till about 2018. After this date, the ozone hole should begin to recover and be completely gone by about 2070.

ATMOSPHERIC EFFECTS ON INCOMING SOLAR RADIATION

Three atmospheric processes modify the solar radiation passing through our atmosphere destined to the Earth's surface. These processes act on the radiation when it interacts with gases and suspended particles found in the atmosphere. The process of scattering occurs when small particles and gas molecules diffuse part of the incoming solar radiation in random directions without any alteration to the wavelength of the electromagnetic energy. Scattering does, however, reduce the amount of incoming radiation reaching the Earth's surface. A significant proportion of scattered shortwave solar radiation is redirected back to space. The amount of scattering that takes place is dependent on two factors: wavelength of the incoming radiation and the size of the scattering particle or gas molecule. In the Earth's atmosphere, the presence of a large number of particles with a size of about 0.5 microns results in shorter wavelengths being preferentially scattered. This factor also causes our sky to look blue because this color corresponds to those wavelengths that are best diffused. If scattering did not occur in our atmosphere the daylight sky would be black.

If intercepted, some gases and particles in the atmosphere have the ability to absorb incoming insolation. Absorption is defined as a process in which solar radiation is retained by a substance and converted into heat energy. The creation of heat energy also causes the substance to emit its own radiation. In general, the absorption of solar radiation by substances in the Earth's atmosphere results in temperatures that get no higher than 1800° Celsius. According to Wien's Law, bodies with temperatures at this level or lower would emit their radiation in the longwave band. Further, this emission of radiation is in all directions so a sizable proportion of this energy is lost to space.

The final process in the atmosphere that modifies incoming solar radiation is reflection. Reflection is a process where sunlight is redirect by 180° after it strikes an atmospheric particle. This redirection causes a 100% loss of the insolation. Most of the reflection in our atmosphere occurs in clouds when light is intercepted by particles of liquid and frozen water. The reflectivity of a cloud can range from 40 to 90%.

Sunlight reaching the Earth's surface unmodified by any of the above atmospheric processes is termed direct solar radiation. Solar radiation that reaches the Earth's surface after it was altered by the process of scattering is called diffused solar radiation. Not all of the direct and diffused radiation available at the Earth's surface is used to do work (photosynthesis, creation of sensible heat, evaporation, etc.). As in the atmosphere, some of the radiation received at the Earth's surface is redirected back to space by reflection. The following image describes the spatial pattern of surface reflectivity as measured for the year 1987. The reflectivity or albedo of the Earth's surface varies with the type of material that covers it. For example, fresh snow can reflect up to 95% of the insolation that reaches it surface. Some other surface type reflectivities are:

- Dry sand 35 to 45%
- Broadleaf deciduous forest 5 to 10%
- Needleleaf confierous forest 10 to 20%
- Grass type vegetation 15 to 25%

Reflectivity of the surface is often described by the term surface albedo. The Earth's average albedo, reflectance from both the atmosphere and the surface, is about 30%. Of all the sunlight that passes through the atmosphere annually, only 51% is available at the Earth's surface to do work. This energy is used to heat the Earth's surface and lower atmosphere, melt and evaporate water, and run photosynthesis in plants. Of the other 49%, 4% is reflected back to space by the Earth's surface, 26% is scattered or reflected to space by clouds and atmospheric particles, and 19% is absorbed by atmospheric gases, particles, and clouds.

Global Patterns of Insolation Receipts

The following image describes the annual pattern of solar radiation absorption at the Earth's surface for the year 1987. The combined effect of Earth-Sun relationships (angle of incidence and day length variations) and the modification of the solar beam as it passes through the atmosphere produces specific global patterns of annual insolation receipt as seen on Figure above. After examining these patterns, the following trends can be identified:

- Highest values of insolation received occur in tropical latitudes. Within this zone there are localized maximums over the tropical oceans and deserts where the atmosphere has virtually no cloud development for most of the year. Insolation quantities at the equator over land during the solstices are approximately the same as values found in the middle latitudes during their summer.
- Outside the tropics, annual receipts of solar radiation generally decrease with increasing latitude. Minimum values occur at the poles. This pattern is primarily the result of Earth-Sun geometric relationships and its effect on the duration and intensity of solar radiation received.
- In middle and high latitudes, insolation values over the ocean, as compared to those at the same latitude over the land, are generally higher (see NASA images). Greater cloudiness over land surfaces accounts for this variation.

NASA's Surface Radiation Budget Project has used satellite data, computer models, and meteorological data to determine shortwave surface radiation fluxes for the period July 1983 to June 1991.

The following links display these fluxes for January and July globally:

Average Available Solar Insolation at the Earth's Surface: January 1984-1991 (K + k)

Average Available Solar Insolation at the Earth's Surface: July 1983-1990 (K + k)

Average Absorbed Solar Insolation at the Earth's Surface: January 1984-1991 [(K + k)(1 - a)]

Average Absorbed Solar Insolation at the Earth's Surface: July 1983-1990 [(K + k)(1 - a)]

In the equations above, the mathematical terms have the following definitions (see topic 7(i) for more information on radiation balance equations):

K = Shortwave Direct Radiation

k = Shortwave Indirect Radiation

a = Reflectivity of the Surface or Surface Albedo

The Greenhouse Effect

The greenhouse effect is a naturally occurring process that aids in heating the Earth's surface and atmosphere. It results from the fact that certain atmospheric gases, such as carbon dioxide, water vapor, and methane, are able to change the energy balance of the planet by absorbing longwave radiation emitted from the Earth's surface. Without the greenhouse effect life on this planet would probably not exist as the average temperature of the Earth would be a chilly -18° Celsius, rather than the present 15° Celsius.

As energy from the Sun passes through the atmosphere a number of things take place. A portion of the energy (26% globally) is reflected or scattered back to space by clouds and other atmospheric particles. About 19% of the energy available is absorbed by clouds, gases (like ozone), and particles in the atmosphere. Of the remaining 55% of the solar energy passing through the Earth's atmosphere, 4% is reflected from the surface back to space. On average, about 51% of the Sun's radiation reaches the surface. This energy is then used in a number of processes, including the heating of the ground surface; the melting of ice and snow and the evaporation of water; and plant photosynthesis.

The heating of the ground by sunlight causes the Earth's surface to become a radiator of energy in the longwave band (sometimes called infrared radiation). This emission of energy is generally directed to space. However, only a small portion of this energy actually makes it back to space. The majority of the outgoing infrared radiation is absorbed by the greenhouse gases.

Absorption of longwave radiation by the atmosphere causes additional heat energy to be added to the Earth's atmospheric system. The now warmer atmospheric greenhouse gas molecules begin radiating longwave energy in all directions. Over 90% of this emission of longwave energy is directed back to the Earth's surface where it once again is absorbed by the surface. The heating of the ground by the longwave radiation causes the ground surface to once again radiate, repeating the cycle described above, again and again, until no more longwave is available for absorption.

The amount of heat energy added to the atmosphere by the greenhouse effect is controlled by the concentration of greenhouse gases in the Earth's atmosphere. All of the major greenhouse gases have increased in concentration since the beginning of the Industrial Revolution (about 1700 AD). As a result of these higher concentrations, scientists predict that the greenhouse effect will be enhanced and the Earth's climate will become warmer. Predicting the amount of warming is accomplished by computer modeling. Computer models suggest that a doubling of the concentration of the main greenhouse gas, carbon dioxide, may raise the average global temperature between 1 and 3° Celsius.

However, the numeric equations of computer models do not accurately simulate the effects of a number of possible negative feedbacks. For example, many of the models cannot properly simulate the negative effects that increased cloud cover would have on the radiation balance of a warmer Earth. Increasing the Earth's temperature would cause the oceans to evaporate greater amounts of water, causing the atmosphere to become cloudier. These extra clouds would then reflect a greater proportion of the Sun's energy back to space reducing the amount of solar radiation absorbed by the atmosphere and the Earth's surface. With less solar energy being absorbed at the surface, the effects of an enhanced greenhouse effect may be counteracted.

A number of gases are involved in the human caused enhancement of the greenhouse effect. These gases include: carbon dioxide (CO_2); methane (CH_4); nitrous oxide (N_2O); chlorofluorocarbons (CFxClx); and tropospheric ozone (O_3). Of these gases, the single most important gas is carbon dioxide which accounts for about 55% of the change in the intensity of the Earth's greenhouse effect. The contributions of the other gases are 25% for chlorofluorocarbons, 15% for methane, and 5% for nitrous oxide. Ozone's contribution to the enhancement of greenhouse effect is still yet to be quantified.

Average concentrations of atmospheric carbon dioxide in the year 2005 were about 380 parts per million. Prior to 1700, levels of carbon dioxide were about 280 parts per million. This increase in carbon dioxide in the atmosphere is primarily due to the activities of humans. Beginning in 1700, societal changes brought about by the Industrial Revolution increased the amount of carbon dioxide entering the atmosphere.

The major sources of this gas include fossil fuel combustion for industry, transportation, space heating, electricity generation and cooking; and vegetation changes in natural prairie, woodland, and forested ecosystems. Emissions from fossil fuel combustion account for about 65% of the extra carbon dioxide now found in our atmosphere. The remaining 35% is derived from deforestation and the conversion of prairie, woodland, and forested ecosystems primarily into agricultural systems. Natural ecosystems can hold 20 to 100 times more carbon dioxide per unit area than agricultural systems.

Artificially created chlorofluorocarbons are the strongest greenhouse gas per molecule. However, low concentrations in the atmosphere reduce their overall importance in the enhancement of the greenhouse effect.

Current measurements in the atmosphere indicate that the concentration of these chemicals may soon begin declining because of reduced emissions. Reports of the development of ozone holes over the North and South Poles and a general decline in global stratospheric ozone levels over the last two decades has caused many nations to cutback on their production and use of these chemicals. In 1987, the signing of the Montreal Protocol agreement by forty-six nations established an immediate timetable for the global reduction of chlorofluorocarbons production and use.

Since 1750, methane concentrations in the atmosphere have increased by more than 150%. The primary sources for the additional methane added to the atmosphere (in order of importance) are rice cultivation, domestic grazing animals, termites, landfills, coal mining, and oil and gas extraction. Anaerobic conditions associated with rice paddy flooding results in the formation of methane gas. However, an accurate estimate of how much methane is being produced from rice paddies has been difficult to obtain. More than 60% of all rice paddies are found in India and China where scientific data concerning emission rates are unavailable.

Nevertheless, scientists believe that the contribution of rice paddies is large because this form of crop production has more than doubled since 1950. Grazing animals release methane to the environment as a result of herbaceous digestion. Some researchers believe the addition of methane from this source has more than quadrupled over the last century. Termites also release methane through similar processes.

Land-use change in the tropics, due to deforestation, ranching, and farming, may be causing termite numbers to expand. If this assumption is correct, the contribution from these insects may be important. Methane is also released from landfills, coal mines, and gas and oil drilling. Landfills produce methane as organic wastes decompose over time. Coal, oil, and natural gas deposits release methane to the atmosphere when these deposits are excavated or drilled.

The average concentration of nitrous oxide in the atmosphere is now increasing at a rate of 0.2 to 0.3% per year. Sources for this increase include land-use conversion; fossil fuel combustion; biomass burning; and soil fertilization.

Most of the nitrous oxide added to the atmosphere each year comes from deforestation and the conversion of forest, savanna and grassland ecosystems into agricultural fields and rangeland. Both of these processes reduce the amount of nitrogen stored in living vegetation and soil through the decomposition of organic matter. Nitrous oxide is also released into the atmosphere when fossil fuels and biomass are burned. However, the combined contribution of these sources to the increase of this gas in the atmosphere is thought to be minor.

The use of nitrate and ammonium fertilizers to enhance plant growth is another source of nitrous oxide. Accurate measurements of how much nitrous oxide is being released from fertilization have been difficult to obtain. Estimates suggest that the contribution from this source may represent from 50% to 0.2% of nitrous oxide added to the atmosphere annually.

Ozone's role in the enhancement of the greenhouse effect has been difficult to determine scientifically. Accurate measurements of past long-term (more than 25 years in the past) levels of this gas in the atmosphere are currently unavailable. Concentrations of ozone gas are found in two different regions of the Earth's atmosphere. The majority of the ozone (about 97%) found in the atmosphere is localized in the stratosphere at an altitude of 15 to 55 kilometers above the Earth's surface.

In recent years, the concentration of the stratospheric ozone has been decreasing because of the buildup of chlorofluorocarbons in the atmosphere. Since the late 1970s, scientists have discovered that total column ozone amounts over Antarctica in the springtime have decreased by as much as 70%. Satellite measurements have indicated that the zone from 65° North to 65° South latitude has had a 3% decrease in stratospheric ozone since 1978. Ozone is also highly concentrated at the Earth's surface. Most of this ozone is created as an artificial by product of photochemical smog.

In summary, the greenhouse effect causes the atmosphere to trap more heat energy at the Earth's surface and within the atmosphere by absorbing and re-emitting longwave energy. Of the longwave energy emitted back to space, 90% is intercepted and absorbed by greenhouse gases.

Without the greenhouse effect the Earth's average global temperature would be -18° Celsius, rather than the present 15° Celsius. In the last few centuries, the activities of humans have directly or indirectly caused the concentration of the major greenhouse gases to increase.

Scientists predict that this increase may enhance the greenhouse effect making the planet warmer. Some experts estimate that the Earth's average global temperature has already increased by 0.3 to 0.6° Celsius, since the beginning of this century, because of this enhancement. Predictions of future climates indicate that by the middle of the next century the Earth's global temperature may be 1 to 3° Celsius higher than today.

Table: Gases involved in the Greenhouse Effect: past and present concentration and sources.

Green-house Gas	Concen-tration 1750	Concen-tration 2003	% age	Natural and Anthropogenic Sources
Carbon Dioxide	280 ppm	376 ppm	34%	Organic decay; Forest fires; Volcanoes; Burning fossil fuels; Deforestation; Land-use change
Methane	0.71 ppm	1.79 ppm	152%	Wetlands; Organic decay; Termites; Natural gas & oil extraction; Biomass burning; Rice cultivation; Cattle; Refuse landfills
Nitrous Oxide	270 ppb	319 ppb	18%	Forests; Grasslands; Oceans; Soils; Soil cultivation; Fertilizers; Biomass burning; Burning of fossil fuels
Chlorofluorocarbons (CFCs)	0	880 ppt	Not Applicable	Refrigerators; Aerosol spray propellants; Cleaning solvents
Ozone	Unknown	Varies with latitude and altitude in the atmosphere	Global levels have generally decreased in the stratosphere and increased near the Earth's surface	Created naturally by the action of sunlight on molecular oxygen and artificially through photochemical smog production

NET RADIATION AND THE PLANETARY ENERGY BALANCE

Shortwave radiation from the Sun enters the surface-atmosphere system of the Earth and is ultimately returned to space as longwave radiation (because the Earth is cooler than the Sun). A basic necessity of this energy interchange is that incoming solar insolation and outgoing radiation be equal in quantity. One way of modeling this balance in energy exchange is described graphically with the use of the following two cascade diagrams. The Global Shortwave Radiation Cascade describes the relative amounts (based on 100 units available at the top of the atmosphere) of shortwave radiation partitioned to various atmospheric processes as it passes through the atmosphere. The diagram indicates that 19 units of insolation are absorbed (and therefore transferred into heat energy and longwave radiation) in the atmosphere by the following two processes: Stratospheric Absorption of the Ultraviolet Radiation by Ozone 2 units; and Tropospheric Absorption of Insolation by Clouds and Aerosols 17 units.

23 units of solar radiation are scattered in the atmosphere subsequently absorbed at the surface as diffused insolation. 28 units of the incoming solar radiation are absorbed at the surface as direct insolation. Total amount of solar insolation absorbed at the surface equals 51 units. The total amount of shortwave radiation absorbed at the surface and in the atmosphere is 70 units. Three main losses of solar radiation back to space occur in the Earth's shortwave radiation cascade. 4 units of sunlight are returned to space from surface reflection. Cloud reflection returns another 20 units of solar radiation. Back scattering of sunlight returns 6 units to space. The total loss of shortwave radiation from these processes is 30 units. The term used to describe the combined effect of all of these shortwave losses is Earth albedo.

The Global Longwave Radiation Cascade indicates that energy leaves the Earth's surface through three different processes. 7 units leave the surface as sensible heat. This heat is transferred into the atmosphere by conduction and convection. The melting and evaporation of water at the Earth's surface incorporates 23 units energy into the atmosphere as latent heat. This latent heat is released into the atmosphere when the water condenses or becomes solid. Both of these processes become part of the emission of longwave radiation by the atmosphere and clouds. The surface of the Earth emits 117 units of longwave radiation. Of this emission only 6 units are directly lost to space. The other 111 units are absorbed by greenhouse gases in the atmosphere and converted into heat energy and then into atmospheric emissions of longwave radiation (the greenhouse effect). The atmosphere emits 160 units of longwave energy. Contributions to this 160 units are from surface emissions of longwave radiation (111 units), latent heat transfer (23 units), sensible heat transfer (7 units), and the absorption of shortwave radiation by atmospheric gases and clouds. Atmospheric emissions travel in two directions. 64 units of atmospheric emission is lost directly to space. 96 units travel to the Earth's surface where it is absorbed and transferred into heat energy.

The total amount of energy lost to space in the global longwave radiation cascade is 70 units (surface emission 6 units + atmospheric emission 64 units.) This is the same amount of energy that was added to the Earth's atmosphere and surface by the Global Shortwave Radiation Cascade. Finally, to balance the surface energy exchanges in this cascade we have to account for 51 units of missing energy [atmosphere and cloud longwave emission (96 units) minus surface longwave emission (117 units) minus latent heat transfer (23 units) minus sensible heat transfer (7 units) = -51 units]. This missing component to the radiation balance is the 51 units of energy absorbed at the Earth's surface as direct and diffused shortwave radiation. The following equations can be used to mathematically model net shortwave radiation balance, net longwave radiation balance, and net radiation balance for the Earth's surface at a single location or for the whole globe for any temporal period:

$$K^* = (K + k)(1 - a)$$

$$L^* = (LD - LU)$$

$$Q^* = (K + k)(1 - a) - LU + LD$$

where

Q^* is surface net radiation (global annual values of $Q^* = 0$, because input equals output, local values can be positive or negative),

K* is surface net shortwave radiation,

K is surface direct shortwave radiation,

k is diffused shortwave radiation (scattered insolation) at the surface,

a is the albedo of surface,

L* is net longwave radiation at the surface,

LD is atmospheric counter-radiation directed to the Earth's surface, and

LU is longwave radiation lost from the Earth's surface.

NASA's Surface Radiation Budget Project has used satellite data, computer models, and meteorological data to determine surface net shortwave radiation, net longwave radiation, and net radiation balances for the period July 1983 to June 1991. The following links display these balances for January and July globally:

Average Net Shortwave Radiation at the Earth's Surface: January 1984-1991 (K*)

Average Net Shortwave Radiation at the Earth's Surface: July 1983-1990 (K*)

Average Net Longwave Radiation at the Earth's Surface: January 1984-1991 (L*)

Average Net Longwave Radiation at the Earth's Surface: July 1983-1990 (L*)

Average Net Radiation at the Earth's Surface: January 1984-1991 (Q*)

Average Net Radiation at the Earth's Surface: July 1983-1990 (Q*)

GLOBAL HEAT BALANCE: INTRODUCTION TO HEAT FLUXES

Figure below illustrates the annual values of net shortwave and net longwave radiation from the South Pole to the North Pole. On closer examination of this graph one notes that the lines representing incoming and outgoing radiation do not have the same values. From 0 - 35 ° latitude North and South incoming solar radiation exceeds outgoing terrestrial radiation and a surplus of energy exists. The reverse holds true from 35 - 90° latitude North and South and these regions have a deficit of energy. Surplus energy at low latitudes and a deficit at high latitudes results in energy transfer from the equator to the poles. It is this meridional transport of energy that causes atmospheric and oceanic circulation. If there were no energy transfer the poles would be 25° Celsius cooler, and the equator 14° Celsius warmer!

The redistribution of energy across the Earth's surface is accomplished primarily through three processes: sensible heat flux, latent heat flux, and surface heat flux into oceans. Sensible heat flux is the process where heat energy is transferred from the Earth's surface to the atmosphere by conduction and convection. This energy is then moved from the tropics to the poles by advection, creating atmospheric circulation. As a result, atmospheric circulation moves warm tropical air to the polar regions and cold air from the poles to the equator. Latent heat flux moves energy globally when solid and liquid water is converted into vapor. This vapor is often moved by atmospheric circulation vertically and horizontally to cooler locations where it is condensed as rain or is deposited as snow releasing the heat energy stored within it. Finally, large quantities of radiation energy are transferred into the Earth's tropical oceans. The energy enters these water bodies at the surface when absorbed radiation is converted into heat energy. The warmed surface water is then transferred downward into the water column by conduction and convection. Horizontal transfer of this heat energy from the equator to the poles is accomplished by ocean currents.

The following equation describes the partitioning of heat energy at the Earth's surface:

$Q^* = H$ (Sensible heat) + L (Latent heat) + S (Surface heat flux into soil or water)

The actual amount of net radiation being partitioned into each one of these components is a function of the following factors:

- Presence or absence of water in liquid and solid forms at the surface.

- Specific heat of the surface receiving the net radiation.
- Convective and conductive characteristics of the receiving surface.
- Diffusion characteristics of the surface's overlying atmosphere.

THE CONCEPT OF TEMPERATURE

Temperature and Heat

- Temperature and heat are not the same phenomenon. Temperature is a measure of the intensity or degree of hotness in a body. Technically, it is determined by getting the average speed of a body's molecules. Heat is a measure of the quantity of heat energy present in a body. The spatial distribution of temperature in a body determines heat flow. Heat always flows from warmer to colder areas.
- The heat held in a object depends not only on its temperature but also its mass. For example, let us compare the heating of two different masses of water. In this example, one mass has a weight of 5 grams, while the other is 25 grams. If the temperature of both masses is raised from 20 to 25° Celsius, the larger mass of water will require five times more heat energy for this increase in temperature. This larger mass would also contain contain 5 times more stored heat energy.

Table: Heat energy required to raise two different quantities of water 5° Celsius.

Mass of the Water	Starting Temperature	Ending Temperature	Heat Required
5 grams	20° Celsius	25° Celsius	25 Calories of Heat
25 grams	20° Celsius	25° Celsius	125 Calories of Heat

Temperature Scales

A number of measurement scales have been invented to measure temperature. The most commonly used scale for measuring temperature is the Celsius system. The Celsius scale was developed in 1742 by the Swedish astronomer Anders Celsius. In this system, the melting point of ice was given a value of 0, the boiling point of water is 100, and absolute zero is -273. The Fahrenheit system is a temperature scale that is used exclusively in the United States. This system was created by German physicist Gabriel Fahrenheit in 1714. In this scale, the melting point of ice has a value of 32, water boils at 212, and absolute zero has a temperature of -460. The Kelvin scale was proposed by British physicist Lord Kelvin in 1848. This system is often used by scientists because its temperature readings begin at absolute zero and due to the fact that this scale is proportional to the amount of heat energy found in an object. The Kelvin scale assigns a value of 273 for the melting temperature of ice, while the boiling point of water occurs at 373.

MEASUREMENT OF AIR TEMPERATURE

A thermometer is a device that is used to measure temperature. Thermometers consist of a sealed hollow glass tube filled with some type of liquid. Thermometers measure temperature by the change in the volume of the liquid as it responds to the addition or loss of heat energy from the environment immediately outside its surface. When heat is added, the liquid inside the thermometer expands. Cooling cause the liquid to contract. Meteorological thermometers are often filled with either alcohol or mercury. Alcohol thermometers are favored in very cold environments because of this liquid's low freezing point (-112° Celsius).

By international agreement, the nations of the world have decided to measure temperature in a similar fashion. This standardization is important for the accurate generation of weather maps and forecasts, both of which depend on having data determined in a uniform way. Weather stations worldwide try to determine minimum and maximum temperatures for each and every day. By averaging these two values, daily mean temperatures are also calculated.

Many stations also take temperature readings on the hour. Temperature measurements are determined by thermometers designed and approved by the World Meteorological Organization. These instruments are housed in specially designed instrument shelters that allow for the standardization of measurements taken anywhere on the Earth.

DAILY AND ANNUAL CYCLES OF TEMPERATURE

Daily Cycles of Air Temperature

At the Earth's surface quantities of insolation and net radiation undergo daily cycles of change because the planet rotates on its polar axis once every 24 hours. Insolation is usually the main positive component making up net radiation. Variations in net radiation are primarily responsible for the particular patterns of rising and falling air temperature over a 24 hour period. The following three graphs show hypothetical average curves of insolation, net radiation, and air temperature for a typical land based location at 45° of latitude on the equinoxes and solstices.

Insolation

In the above graph, shortwave radiation received from the Sun is measured in Watts. For all dates, peak reception occurs at solar noon when the Sun attains its greatest height above the horizon.

Net Radiation

The net radiation graph indicates that there is a surplus of radiation during most of the day and a deficit throughout the night. The deficit begins just before sunset when emitted longwave radiation from the Earth's surface exceeds solar insolation and longwave radiation from the atmosphere.

Temperature

The relative placement of the temperature profiles for the various dates correlates to the amount of net radiation available for daily surface absorption and heat generation. The more energy available, the higher up the Y-axis the profile is on the graph.

September equinox is warmer than the March equinox because of the heating that occurred in the previous summer months. For all dates, minimum temperature occurs at sunrise. Temperature drops throughout the night because of two processes. First, the Earth's radiation balance at the surface becomes negative after sunset. Thus, the surface of the Earth stops heating up as solar radiation is not being absorbed. Secondly, conduction and convection transport heat energy up into the atmosphere and the warm air that was at the surface is replaced by cooler air from above because of atmospheric mixing. Temperature begins rising as soon as the net radiation budget of the surface becomes positive. Temperature continues to rise from sunrise until sometime after solar noon. After this time, mixing of the Earth's surface by convection causes the surface to cool despite the positive addition of radiation and heat energy.

Annual Cycle of Air Temperature

As the Earth revolves around the Sun, locations on the surface may under go seasonal changes in air temperature because of annual variations in the intensity of net radiation. Variations in net radiation are primarily controlled by changes in the intensity and duration of received solar insolation which are driven by variations in daylength and angle of incidence. The discussion below examines how changes in net radiation can effect mean monthly temperatures for the following five locations:

- o Manaus, Brazil, 3° South latitude.
- o Bulawayo, Zimbabwe, 20° South latitude.
- o Albuquerque, USA, 35° North latitude.
- o London, England, 52° North latitude.
- o Fairbanks, USA, 65° North latitude.

Manaus, Brazil - 3° South, 60° West

At Manaus, values of monthly net radiation average about 135 Watts per square meter. Monthly variation in net radiation is only about 35 Watts over the entire year. Two peaks in net radiation are visible on the graph. Both of these peaks occur during the equinoxes when the height of the Sun above the horizon is at its maximum

(90° above the horizon). Minimum values of net radiation correspond to the time of the year when the Sun reaches its minimum height of only 66.5° above the horizon at solar noon. Because of the consistent nature of net radiation, mean monthly air temperature only varies by 2° Celsius over the entire year.

Bulawayo, Zimbabwe - 20° South, 29° East

Net radiation at Bulawayo has a single peak and trough over the one year period graphed. This pattern is primarily controlled by variations in the intensity and duration of incoming solar insolation. During the December solstice, the Sun reaches its highest altitude above the horizon and daylength is at a maximum (13 hours and 12 minutes). The lowest values of net radiation occur around the June solstice when the Sun reaches its lowest altitude above the horizon and daylength is at a minimum (10 hours and 48 minutes) in the Southern Hemisphere. Monthly temperature variations follow the monthly change in net radiation. Net radiation represents energy available to do work. When received at the Earth's surface much of this energy is used to create sensible heat.

Albuquerque, USA - 35° North, 107° West

At Albuquerque, maximum net radiation occurs in May. The timing of this peak roughly coincides with the June solstice when daylengths are at their longest and solar heights are their greatest. However, monthly temperature variations do not mirror the changes in net radiation exactly. Peak monthly temperatures occur about two months after the net radiation maximum. This lag is probably caused by the delayed movement of stored heat energy in the ground into the atmosphere. Minimum monthly temperatures do coincide with the lowest values of net radiation which occur during the December solstice.

London, England - 52° North, 1° East

The annual patterns of net radiation and mean monthly temperature for ***London*** are quite similar to those already described for Albuquerque. London does, however, experience a greater annual variation in net radiation. This greater variation can be explained by the effect increasing latitude has on annual variations of insolation. During the winter months, outgoing **longwave radiation** actually exceeds incoming **insolation** producing negative net radiation values. This was not seen in Albuquerque. The variation in monthly mean temperature is also less extreme in London when compared to Albuquerque. Intuitively, one would expect London to have a greater annual change in temperature because of the greater variation in net radiation over the year. However, London's climate is moderated by the frequent addition of **latent heat** energy from seasonal precipitation.

Fairbanks, USA - 65° North, 148° West

Of the five locations examined, Fairbanks has the greatest variations in mean monthly temperature. Fairbanks is also the coldest of the climates examined. This is primarily due to the fact that during six months of the year net radiation is negative because outgoing longwave radiation exceeds incoming insolation. Fairbanks also receives the least cumulative amount of net radiation over the entire year. Mean month temperature is at its maximum in July which is one month ahead of the peak in net radiation.

Global Surface Temperature Distribution

If the Earth was a homogeneous body without the present land/ocean distribution, its temperature distribution would be strictly latitudinal. However, the Earth is more complex than this being composed of a mosaic of land and water. This mosaic causes latitudinal zonation of temperature to be disrupted spatially.

The following two factors are important in influencing the distribution of temperature on the Earth's surface:

- The latitude of the location determines how much solar radiation is received. Latitude influences the angle of incidence and duration of daylength.
- Surface properties - surfaces with high albedo absorb less incident radiation. In general, land absorbs less insolation that water because of its lighter color. Also, even if two surfaces have the same albedo, a surface's **specific heat**

determines the amount of heat energy required for a specific rise in temperature per unit mass. The specific heat of water is some five times greater than that of rock and the land surface. As a result, water requires the input of large amounts of energy to cause a rise in its temperature.

Table: Specific Heat of Various Substances.

Substance	Specific Heat
Water	1.00
Air	0.24
Granite	0.19
Sand	0.19
Iron	0.11

Mainly because of specific heat, land surfaces behave quite differently from water surfaces. In general, the surface of any extensive deep body of water heats more slowly and cools more slowly than the surface of a large land body. Other factors influencing the way land and water surfaces heat and cool include:

- Solar radiation warms an extensive layer in water, on land just the immediate surface is heated.
- Water is easily mixed by the process of convection.
- Evaporation of water removes energy from water's surface.

The following images illustrate the Earth's temperature distribution patterns for an average January and July based on 39 years of data. Note that the spatial variations of temperature on these figures is mostly latitudinal. However, the horizontal banding of isotherms is somewhat upset by the fact that water heats up more slowly in the summer and cools down more slowly in the winter when compared to land surfaces. During January, much of the terrestrial areas of the Northern Hemisphere are below freezing. Some notable Northern Hemisphere cold-spots include the area around Baffin Island Canada, Greenland, Siberia, and the Plateau of Tibet. Temperatures over oceans tend to be hotter because of the water's ability to hold heat energy.

In the Southern Hemisphere, temperatures over the major landmasses are generally greater than 20° Celsius with localized hot-spots in west-central Australia, the Kalahari Desert in Africa, and the plains of Bolivia, Paraguay, and Argentina. Subtropical oceans are often warmer than landmass areas near the equator. At this latitude, land areas receive less incoming solar radiation because of the daily convective development of cumulus and cumulonimbus clouds. In the mid-latitudes, oceans are often cooler than landmass areas at similar latitudes. Terrestrial areas are warmer because of the rapid heating of land surfaces under frequently clear skies. Antarctica remains cold and below zero degrees Celsius due to the presence of permanent glacial ice which reflects much of the solar radiation received back to space.

In July, the Northern Hemisphere is experiencing its summer season because the North Pole is now tilted towards the Sun. Some conspicuous hot-spots include the south-central United States, Arizona and northwest Mexico, northern Africa, the Middle East, India, Pakistan, and Afghanistan. Temperatures over oceans tend to be relatively cooler because of the land's ability to heat quickly. Two terrestrial areas of cooler temperatures include Greenland and the Plateau of Tibet. In these regions, most of the incoming solar radiation is sent back to space because of the presence of reflective ice and snow.

In the Southern Hemisphere, temperatures over the major landmasses are generally cooler than ocean surfaces at the same latitude. Antarctica is bitterly cold because it is experiencing total darkness. Note that Antarctica is much colder than the Arctic was during its winter season.

The Arctic consists mainly of ocean. During the summer, this surface is able to absorb considerable quantities of sunlight which is then converted into heat energy. The heat stored in the ocean is carried over into the winter season. Antarctica has a surface composed primarily of snow and ice. This surface absorbs only a small amount of the solar radiation during the summer. So it never really heats up. As a result, the amount of heat energy stored into the winter season is minimal.

Forces Acting to Create Wind

Wind can be defined simply as air in motion. This motion can be in any direction, but in most cases the horizontal component of wind flow greatly exceeds the flow that occurs vertically. The speed of wind varies from absolute calm to speeds as high as 380 kilometers per hour (Mt. Washington, New Hampshire, April 12, 1934). In 1894, strong winds in Nebraska pushed six fully loaded coal cars over 160 kilometers in just over three hours. Over short periods of time surface winds can be quite variable.

Wind develops as a result of spatial differences in atmospheric pressure. Generally, these differences occur because of uneven absorption of solar radiation at the Earth's surface. Wind speed tends to be at its greatest during the daytime when the greatest spatial extremes in atmospheric temperature and pressure exist.

Wind is often described by two characteristics: wind speed and wind direction. Wind speed is the velocity attained by a mass of air traveling horizontally through the atmosphere. Wind speed is often measured with an anemometer in kilometers per hour (kmph), miles per hour (mph), knots, or meters per second (mps). Wind direction is measured as the direction from where a wind comes from. For example, a southerly wind comes from the south and blows to the north. Direction is measured by an instrument called a wind vane. Both of these instruments are positioned in the atmospheric environment at a standard distance of 10 meters above the ground surface.

Wind speed can also be measured without the aid of instruments using the Beaufort wind scale. This descriptive scale was originally developed by Admiral Beaufort of the British Navy in the first decade of the 17th century. The purpose for this system was to allow mariners to determine wind speed from simple observations. The Beaufort system has undergone several modifications to standardize its measurement scale and to allow for its use on land. Users of this scale look for specific effects of the wind on the environment to determine speed.

Winds are named according to the compass direction of their source. Thus, a wind from the north blowing toward the south is called a northerly wind. Figure below describes the sixteen principal bearings of wind direction. Most meterological observations report wind direction using one of these sixteen bearings.

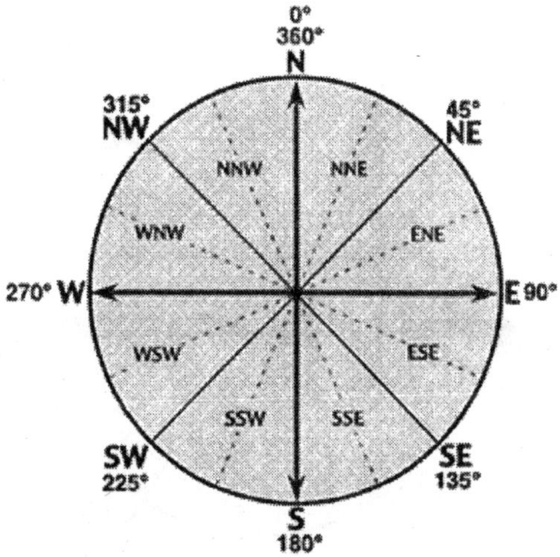

Figure: Wind compass describing the sixteen principal bearings used to measure wind direction. This compass is based on the 360 degrees found in a circle.

Horizontally, at the Earth's surface wind always blows from areas of high pressure to areas of low pressure (vertically, winds move from areas of low pressure to areas of high pressure), usually at speeds determined by the rate of air pressure change between pressure centers. This situation is comparable to someone skiing down a hill. The skier will of course move from the top of the hill to the bottom of the hill, with the speed of their descent controlled by the gradient or steepness of the slope. Likewise, wind speed is a function of the steepness or gradient of atmospheric air pressure found between high and low pressure systems. When expressed scientifically, pressure change over a unit distance is called pressure gradient force, and the greater this force the faster the winds will blow.

On weather maps, pressure is indicated by drawing isolines of pressure, called isobars, at regular 4 millibar intervals (e.g., 996 mb, 1000 mb, 1004 mb, etc.). If the isobars are closely spaced, we can expect the pressure gradient force to be great, and wind speed to be high. In areas where the isobars are spaced widely apart, the pressure gradient is low and light winds normally exist. High speed winds develop in areas where isobars are closer.

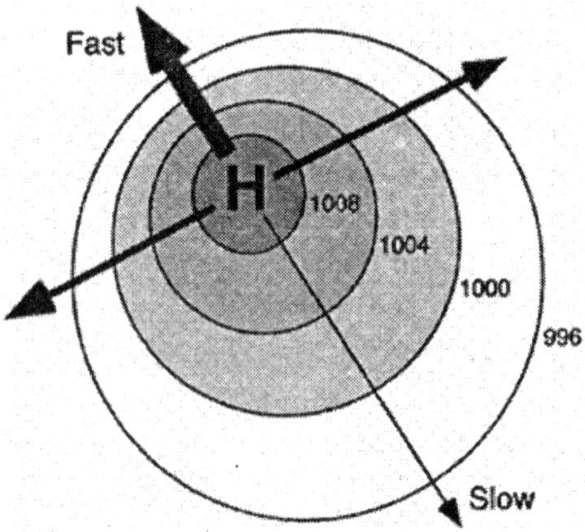

Figure: Association between wind speed and distance between isobars. In the illustration above thicker arrows represent relatively faster winds.

Driving Forces

To better understand wind we must recognize that it is the result of a limited number of accelerating and decelerating forces, and that the action of these forces is controlled by specific fundamental natural laws. Sir Isaac Newton formulated these laws as several laws of motion. The first law suggests that an object that is stationary will remain stationary, and an object in motion will stay in motion as long as no opposing force is put on the object. As a result of this law, a puck sent in flight from a blade of a hockey stick will remain in motion until friction slows it down or the goalie makes a save. This law also suggests that once in motion an object's path should be straight. Newton's second law of motion suggests that the force put on an object equals its mass multiplied by the acceleration produced. The term force in this law refers to the total or net effect of all the forces acting on an object. Mathematically, this law is written as:

Force = Mass × Acceleration

or

Acceleration = Force/Mass

From this natural law of motion we can see that the acceleration of an object is directly proportional to the net force pushing or pulling that body and inversely proportional to the mass of the body. Thus, the greater the force created by the movement of a hockey player's stick the faster the puck will travel. This law also suggests that if the player used a larger (more massive) puck more force would have to be applied to it to get it to travel as fast as a puck with less mass.

In the previous lecture we briefly examined one of the forces, pressure gradient force, acting on wind. Let us return to this force and examine it in greater detail and in relation to Newton's laws of motion. We will also examine the effects of three other forces that act on air in motion.

Pressure gradient force is the primary force influencing the formation of wind from local to global scales. This force is determined by the spatial pattern of atmospheric pressure at any given moment in time. Figure below illustrates two different pressure gradient scenarios and their relative effect on wind speed.

The two diagrams display the relative relationship between pressure gradient and wind speed. This relationship is linear and positive. As a result, quadrupling the pressure gradient increases wind speed by a factor of four. This is what we would expect according to Newton's second law of motion, assuming the mass of the wind is unchanged.

We can also describe pressure gradient acceleration mathematically with the following equation:

$$F(m/s^2) = \left| \frac{1}{D} \bullet \left(\frac{P_1 - P_2}{n} \right) \right|$$

where:

D = density of air (average density of surface air is 1.29 kilograms per cubic meter)

P_2 = pressure at point 2 in Newtons/m^2 ($N\ m^{-2}$)

P_1 = pressure at point 1 in Newtons/m^2 ($N\ m^{-2}$)

n = distance between the two points in meters

From this equation we can determine wind acceleration between two points in meters per second squared by knowing three variables: the density of the moving air; the change in pressure between the points of interest in newtons; and the distance between the two points in meters. For example, to determine the wind speed between two points for moving air with a density of 1.29 kilograms per cubic meter, a pressure difference of 400 Newtons/m^2, and a distance of 300,000 meters, the following calculations would be performed:

$$F(m/s^2) = \left| \frac{1}{1.29} \bullet \left(\frac{400}{300{,}000} \right) \right| = 0.00103 m/s^2$$

From the calculated value of acceleration we can determine wind speed, V, from the formula:

$V = V0 + Ft$

Where V0 is the initial velocity of the wind and t is the time during which F is applied.

The rotation of the Earth creates another force, termed Coriolis force, which acts upon wind and other objects in motion in very predictable ways. According to Newton's first law of motion, air will remain moving in a straight line unless it is influenced by an unbalancing force. The consequence of Coriolis force opposing pressure gradient acceleration is that the moving air changes direction. Instead of wind blowing directly from high to low pressure, the rotation of the Earth causes wind to be deflected off course. In the Northern Hemisphere, wind is deflected to the right of its path, while in the Southern Hemisphere it is deflected to the left. The magnitude of the Coriolis force varies with the velocity and the latitude of the object. Coriolis force is absent at the equator, and its strength increases as one approaches either pole. Furthermore, an increase in wind speed also results in a stronger Coriolis force, and thus in greater deflection of the wind. Coriolis force only acts on air when it has been sent into motion by pressure gradient force.

Finally, Coriolis force only influences wind direction and never wind speed.

Centripetal acceleration is the third force that can act on moving air. It acts only on air that is flowing around centers of circulation. Centripetal acceleration is also another force that can influence the direction of wind. Centripetal acceleration creates a force directed at right angles to the flow of the wind and inwards towards the centers of rotation (e.g., low and high pressure centers). This force produces a circular pattern of flow around centers of high and low pressure. Centripetal acceleration is much more important for circulations smaller than the mid-latitude cyclone.

The last force that can influence moving air is frictional deceleration. Friction can exert an influence on wind only after the air is in motion. Frictional drag acts in a direction opposite to the path of motion causing the moving air to decelerate (see Newton's first and second laws of motion). Frictional effects are limited to the lower one kilometer above the Earth's surface.

Geostrophic Wind

Air under the influence of both the pressure gradient force and Coriolis force tends to move parallel to isobars in conditions where friction is low (1000 meters above the surface of the Earth) and isobars are straight. Winds of this type are usually called geostrophic winds. Geostrophic winds come about because pressure gradient force and Coriolis force come into balance after the air begins to move.

Finally, Buy Ballot's Law states that when you stand with your back to a geostrophic wind in the Northern Hemisphere the center of low pressure will be to your left and the high pressure to your right. The opposite is true for the Southern Hemisphere.

Gradient Wind

Wind above the Earth's surface does not always travel in straight lines. In many cases winds flow around the curved isobars of a high (anticyclone) or low (cyclone) pressure center. A wind that blows around curved isobars above the level of friction is called a gradient wind. Gradient winds are slightly more complex than geostrophic winds because they include the action of yet another physical force. This force is known as centripetal force and it is always directed toward the center of rotation. The following figure describes the forces that produce gradient winds around high and low pressure centers. Around a low, the gradient wind consists of the pressure gradient force and centripetal force acting toward the center of rotation, while Coriolis force acts away from the center of the low. In a high pressure center, the Coriolis and centripetal forces are directed toward the center of the high, while the pressure gradient force is directed outward.

Friction Layer Wind

Surface winds on a weather map do not blow exactly parallel to the isobars as in geostrophic and gradient winds. Instead, surface winds tend to cross the isobars at an angle varying from 10 to 45°. Close to the Earth's surface, friction reduces the wind speed, which in turn reduces the Coriolis force. As a result, the reduced Coriolis force no longer balances the pressure gradient force, and the wind blows across the isobars toward or away from the pressure center. The pressure gradient force is now balanced by the sum of the frictional force and the Coriolis force. Thus, we find surface winds blowing counterclockwise and inward into a surface low, and clockwise and out of a surface high in the Northern Hemisphere. In the Southern Hemisphere, the Coriolis force acts to the left rather than the right. This causes the winds of the Southern Hemisphere to blow clockwise and inward around surface lows, and counterclockwise and outward around surface highs.

4

LOCAL AND REGIONAL WIND SYSTEMS

Thermal Circulations

As discussed earlier, winds blow because of differences in atmospheric pressure. Pressure gradients may develop on a local to a global scale because of differences in the heating and cooling of the Earth's surface. Heating and cooling cycles that develop daily or annually can create several common local or regional thermal wind systems. The basic circulation system that develops is described in the generic illustrations below.

In this first diagram, there is no horizontal temperature or pressure gradient and therefore no wind. Atmospheric pressure decreases with altitude as depicted by the drawn isobars (1000 to 980 millibars). In the second diagram, the potential for solar heating is added which creates contrasting surface areas of temperature and atmospheric pressure. The area to the right receives more solar radiation and the air begins to warm from heat energy transferred from the ground through conduction and convection. The vertical distance between the isobars becomes greater as the air rises. To the far left, less radiation is received because of the presence of cloud, and this area becomes relatively cooler than the area to the right. In the upper atmosphere, a pressure gradient begins to form because of the rising air and upward spreading of the isobars. The air then begins to flow in the upper atmosphere from high pressure to low pressure.

Below the upper atmosphere low is a thermal high created by the relatively cooler air temperatures and enhanced by the descending air from above. Surface air temperatures are cooler here because of the obstruction of shortwave radiation absorption at the Earth's surface by the cloud. At the surface, the wind blows from the high to the low pressure. Once at the low, the wind rises up to the upper air high pressure system because of thermal buoyancy and outflow in the upper atmosphere. From the upper high, the air then travels to the upper air low, and then back down to the surface high to complete the circulation cell. The circulation cell is a closed system that redistributes air in an equitable manner. It is driven by the greater heating of the surface air in the right of the diagram.

Sea and Land Breezes

Sea and land breezes are types of thermal circulation systems that develop at the interface of land and ocean. At this interface, the dissimilar heating and cooling characteristics of land and water initiate the development of an atmospheric pressure gradient which causes the air in these areas to flow.

During the daytime land heats up much faster than water as it receives solar radiation from the Sun. The warmer air over the land then begins to expand and rise forming a thermal low. At the same time, the air over the ocean becomes a cool high because of water's slower rate of heating. Air begins to flow as soon as there is a significant difference in air temperature and pressure across the land to sea gradient. The development of this pressure gradient causes the heavier cooler air over the ocean to move toward the land and to replace the air rising in the thermal low. This localized air flow system is called a sea breeze. Sea breeze usually begins in midmorning and reaches its maximum strength in the later afternoon when the greatest temperature and pressure contrasts exist. It dies down at sunset when air temperature and pressure once again become similar across the two surfaces.

At sunset, the land surface stops receiving radiation from the Sun. As night continues the land surface begins losing heat energy at a much faster rate than the water surface. After a few hours, air temperature and pressure contrasts begin to develop between the land and ocean surfaces. The land surface being cooler than the water becomes a thermal high pressure area. The ocean becomes a warm thermal low. Wind flow now moves from the land to the open ocean. This type of localized air flow is called a land breeze.

MOUNTAIN AND VALLEY BREEZES

Mountain and valley breezes are common in regions with great topographic relief. A valley breeze develops during the day as the Sun heats the land surface and air at the valley bottom and sides. As the air heats it becomes less dense and buoyant and begins to flow gently up the valley sides. Vertical ascent of the air rising along the sides of the mountain is usually limited by the presence of a temperature inversion layer. When the ascending air currents encounter the inversion they are forced to move horizontally and then back down to the valley floor. This creates a self-contained circulation system. If conditions are right, the rising air can condense and form into cumuliform clouds.

During the night, the air along the mountain slopes begins to cool quickly because of longwave radiation loss. As the air cools, it becomes more dense and begins to flow downslope causing a mountain breeze. Convergence of the draining air occurs at the valley floor and forces the air to move vertically upward. The upward movement is usually limited by the presence of a temperature inversion which forces the air to begin moving horizontally. This horizontal movement completes the circulation cell system. In narrowing terrain, mountain winds can accelerate in speed because of the venturi effect. Such winds can attain speeds as high has 150 kilometers per hour.

Monsoon Winds

Monsoons are regional scale wind systems that predictably change direction with the passing of the seasons. Like land/sea breezes, these wind systems are created by the temperature contrasts that exist between the surfaces of land and ocean. However, monsoons are different from land/sea breezes both spatially and temporally. Monsoons occur over distances of thousands of kilometers, and their two dominant patterns of wind flow act over an annual time scale.

During the summer, monsoon winds blow from the cooler ocean surfaces onto the warmer continents. In the summer, the continents become much warmer than the oceans because of a number of factors. These factors include:

- Specific heat differences between land and water.
- Greater evaporation over water surfaces.
- Subsurface mixing in ocean basins which redistributes heat energy through a deeper layer.

Precipitation is normally associated with the summer monsoons. Onshore winds blowing inland from the warm ocean are very high in humidity, and slight cooling of these air masses causes condensation and rain. In some cases, this precipitation can be greatly intensified by orographic uplift. Some highland areas in Asia receive more than 10 meters of rain during the summer months.

In the winter, the wind patterns reverse as the ocean surfaces are now warmer. With little solar energy available, the continents begin cooling rapidly as longwave radiation is emitted to space. The ocean surface retains its heat energy longer because of water's high specific heat and subsurface mixing. The winter monsoons bring clear dry weather and winds that flow from land to sea.

Figure below illustrates the general wind patterns associated with the winter and summer monsoons in Asia. The Asiatic monsoon is the result of a complex climatic interaction between the distribution of land and water, topography, and tropical and mid-latitudinal circulation. In the summer, a low pressure center forms over northern India and northern Southeast Asia because of higher levels of received solar insolation. Warm moist air is drawn into the thermal lows from air masses over the Indian Ocean. Summer heating also causes the development of a strong latitudinal pressure gradient and the development of an easterly jet stream at an altitude of about 15 kilometers and a latitude of 25° North. The jet stream enhances rainfall in Southeast Asia, in the Arabian Sea, and in South Africa.

When autumn returns to Asia the thermal extremes between land and ocean decrease and the westerlies of the mid-latitudes move in. The easterly jet stream is replaced with strong westerly winds in the upper atmosphere. Subsidence from an upper atmosphere cold low above the Himalayas produces outflow that creates a surface high pressure system that dominates the weather in India and Southeast Asia. Monsoon wind systems also exist in Australia, Africa, South America, and North America.

GLOBAL SCALE CIRCULATION OF THE ATMOSPHERE

Simple Model of Global Circulation

We can gain an understanding of how global circulation works by developing two simplified graphical models of processes that produce this system. The first model will be founded on the following simplifying assumptions:

- The Earth is not rotating in space.
- The Earth's surface is composed of similar materials.
- The global reception of solar insolation and loss of longwave radiation cause a temperature gradient of hotter air at the equator and colder air at the poles.

Based on these assumptions, air circulation on the Earth should approximate the patterns shown on Figure below. In this illustration, each hemisphere contains one three-dimensional circulation cell.

Surface air flow is from the poles to the equator. When the air reaches the equator, it is lifted vertically by the processes of convection and convergence. When it reaches the top of the troposphere, it begins to flow once again horizontally. However, the direction of flow is now from the equator to the poles. At the poles, the air in the upper atmosphere then descends to the Earth's surface to complete the cycle of flow.

Three Cell Model of Global Circulation

If we eliminate the first assumption, the pattern of flow described in the model above would be altered, and the mesoscale flow of the atmosphere would more closely approximate the actual global circulation on the Earth. Planetary rotation would cause the development of three circulation cells in each hemisphere rather than one. These three circulation cells are known as the: Hadley cell; Ferrel cell; and Polar cell.

In the new model, the equator still remains the warmest location on the Earth. This area of greater heat acts as zone of thermal lows known as the intertropical convergence zone (ITCZ). The Intertropical Convergence Zone draws in surface air from the subtropics. When this subtropical air reaches the equator, it rises into the upper atmosphere because of convergence and convection. It attains a maximum vertical altitude of about 14 kilometers (top of the troposphere), and then begins flowing horizontally to the North and South Poles. Coriolis force causes the deflection of this moving air in the upper atmosphere, and by about 30° of latitude the air begins to flow zonally from west to east. This zonal flow is known as the subtropical jet stream. The zonal flow also causes the accumulation of air in the upper atmosphere as it is no longer flowing meridionally. To compensate for this accumulation, some of the air in the upper atmosphere sinks back to the surface creating the subtropical high pressure zone. From this zone, the surface air travels in two directions.

A portion of the air moves back toward the equator completing the circulation system known as the Hadley cell. This moving air is also deflected by the Coriolis effect to create the Northeast Trades (right deflection) and Southeast Trades (left deflection). The surface air moving towards the poles from the subtropical high zone is also deflected by Coriolis acceleration producing the Westerlies. Between the latitudes of 30 to 60° North and South, upper air winds blow generally towards the poles. Once again, Coriolis force deflects this wind to cause it to flow west to east forming the polar jet stream at roughly 60° North and South. On the Earth's surface at 60° North and South latitude, the subtropical Westerlies collide with cold air traveling from the poles. This collision results in frontal uplift and the creation of the subpolar lows or mid-latitude cyclones. A small portion of this lifted air is sent back into the Ferrel cell after it reaches the top of the troposphere. Most of this lifted air is directed to the polar vortex where it moves downward to create the polar high.

ACTUAL GLOBAL SURFACE CIRCULATION

Upper Air Winds and the Jet Streams

Winds at the top of the troposphere are generally poleward and westerly in direction. Figure below describes these upper air westerlies along with some other associated weather features. Three zones of westerlies can be seen in each hemisphere on this illustration. Each zone is associated with either the Hadley, Ferrel, or Polar circulation cell. The polar jet stream is formed by the deflection of upper air winds by coriolis acceleration. It resembles a stream of water moving west to east and has an altitude of about 10 kilometers. Its air flow is intensified by the strong temperature and pressure gradient that develops when cold air from the poles meets warm air from the tropics. Wind velocity is highest in the core of the polar jet stream where speeds can be as high as 300 kilometers per hour. The jet stream core is surrounded by slower moving air that has an average velocity of 130 kilometers per hour in winter and 65 kilometers per hour in summer.

Associated with the polar jet stream is the polar front. The polar front represents the zone where warm air from the subtropics (pink) and cold air (blue) from the poles meet. At this zone, massive exchanges of energy occur in the form of storms known as the mid-latitude cyclones. The shape and position of waves in the polar jet stream determine the location and the intensity of the mid-latitude cyclones. In general, mid-latitude cyclones form beneath polar jet stream troughs. The following satellite image, taken from above the South Pole, shows a number of mid-latitude cyclones circling Antarctica. Each mid-latidude cyclone wave is defined by the cloud development associated with frontal uplift.

The subtropical jet stream is located approximately 13 kilometers above the subtropical high pressure zone. The reason for its formation is similar to the polar jet stream. However, the subtropical jet stream is weaker. Its slower wind speeds are the result of a weaker latitudinal temperature and pressure gradient.

Air Masses and Frontal Transitional Zones

An air mass is a large body of air of relatively similar temperature and humidity characteristics covering thousands of square kilometers. Typically, air masses are classified according to the characteristics of their source region or area of formation. A source region can have one of four temperature attributes: equatorial, tropical, polar or arctic. Air masses are also classified as being either continental or maritime in terms of moisture characteristics. Combining these two categories, several possibilities are commonly found associated with North America: maritime polar (mP), continental polar (cP), maritime tropical (mT), continental tropical (cT), and continental arctic (A). The following diagram describes the source regions and common patterns of movement for the various types of air masses associated with North America.

Frequently, two air masses, especially in the middle latitudes, develop a sharp boundary or interface, where the temperature difference between them becomes intensified. Such an area of intensification is called a frontal zone or a front. The boundary between the warm and cold air masses always slopes upwards over the cold air. This is due to the fact that cold air is much denser than warm air. The sloping of warm air over the cold air leads to a forced uplifting (frontal lifting) of the warm air if one air mass is moving toward the other. In turn, this uplifting causes condensation to occur and the possibility of precipitation along the frontal boundary.

Frontal zones where the air masses are not moving against each other are called stationary fronts. In transitional areas where there is some air mass movement, cold or warm fronts can develop. Figure below illustrates a vertical cross-section of a cold front. A cold front is the transition zone in the atmosphere where an advancing cold, dry stable air mass displaces a warm, moist unstable subtropical air mass. On a weather map, the cold front is drawn as a solid blue line with triangles. The position of the triangles shows the direction of frontal movement. Cold fronts move between 15 to 50 kilometers per hour in a southeast to east direction. The formation of clouds and precipitation at the frontal zone is caused by frontal lifting. High altitude cirrus clouds are found well in advance of the front. Above the surface location of the cold front, high altitude cirrostratus and middle altitude altocumulus are common. Precipitation is normally found just behind the front where frontal lifting has caused the development of towering cumulus and cumulonimbus clouds. Table below describes some of the weather conditions associated with a cold front. A warm front is the transition zone in the atmosphere where an advancing warm subtropical, moist air mass replaces a retreating cold, dry polar air mass. On a weather map, a warm front is drawn as a solid red line with half-circles. The position of the half-circles shows the direction of frontal movement. Warm fronts move about 10 kilometers per hour in a northeast direction. This is less than half the speed of a cold front. The formation of clouds and precipitation ahead of the frontal zone is caused by gradual frontal lifting. High altitude cirrus, cirrostratus and middle altitude altostratus clouds are found well in advance of the front. About 600 kilometers ahead of the front, nimbostratus clouds occur. These clouds produce precipitation in the form of snow or rain. Between the nimbostratus clouds and the surface location of the warm front, low altitude stratus clouds are found. Finally, a few hundred kilometers behind the front scattered stratocumulus are common in the lower troposphere. Table below describes some of the weather conditions associated with a warm front.

Occluded fronts are produced when a fast moving cold front catches and overtakes a slower moving warm front. Two types of occluded fronts are generally recognized. A cold type occluded front occurs when the air behind the front is colder than the air ahead of the front. When the air behind the front is warmer than the air ahead of the front a warm type occluded front is produced. Warm type occlusions are common on the west coast of continents and generally form when maritime polar air collides with continental polar or arctic air. Note that in the occlusion process the invading mild moist air that was found behind the warm front has been lifted into the upper troposphere.

Finally, the frontal systems described on this page are often associated with a storm system known as the mid-latitude cyclone. The next section will describe this weather phenomenon in detail.

The Mid-Latitude Cyclone

Mid-latitude or frontal cyclones are large traveling atmospheric cyclonic storms up to 2000 kilometers in diameter with centers of low atmospheric pressure. An intense mid-latitude cyclone may have a surface pressure as low as 970 millibars, compared to an average sea-level pressure of 1013 millibars. Normally, individual frontal cyclones exist for about 3 to 10 days moving in a generally west to east direction. Frontal cyclones are the dominant weather event of the Earth's mid-latitudes forming along the polar front.

Mid-latitude cyclones are the result of the dynamic interaction of warm tropical and cold polar air masses at the polar front. This interaction causes the warm air to be cyclonically lifted vertically into the atmosphere where it combines with colder upper atmosphere air. This process also helps to transport excess energy from the lower latitudes to the higher latitudes.

The mid-latitude cyclone is rarely motionless and commonly travels about 1200 kilometers in one day. Its direction of movement is generally eastward. Precise movement of this weather system is controlled by the orientation of the polar jet stream in the upper troposphere. An estimate of future movement of the mid-latitude cyclone can be determined by the winds directly behind the cold front. If the winds are 70 kilometers per hour, the cyclone can be projected to continue its movement along the ground surface at this velocity.

The patterns of wind flow, surface pressure, fronts, and zones of precipitation associated with a mid-latitude cyclone in the Northern Hemisphere. Around the low, winds blow counterclockwise and inwards (clockwise and inward in the Southern Hemisphere). West of the low, cold air traveling from the north and northwest creates a cold front extending from the cyclone's center to the southwest. Southeast of the low, northward moving warm air from the subtropics produces a warm front. Precipitation is located at the center of the low and along the fronts where air is being uplifted.

Mid-latitude cyclones can produce a wide variety of precipitation types. Precipitation types include: rain, freezing rain, hail, sleet, snow pellets, and snow. Frozen forms of precipitation (except hail) are common with storms that occur in the winter months. Hail is associated with severe thunderstorms that form along or in front of cold fronts during spring and summer months.

Figure below describes a vertical cross-section through a mature mid-latitude cyclone. In this cross-section, we can see how air temperature changes as we move from behind the cold front to a position ahead of the warm front. Behind the surface position of the cold front, forward moving cold dense air causes the uplift of the warm lighter air in advance of the front. Because this uplift is relatively rapid along a steep frontal gradient, the condensed water vapor quickly organizes itself into cumulus and then cumulonimbus clouds. Cumulonimbus clouds produce heavy precipitation and can develop into severe thunderstorms if conditions are right. Along the gently sloping warm front, the lifting of moist air produces first nimbostratus clouds followed by altostratus and cirrostratus. Precipitation is less intense along this front, varying from moderate to light showers some distance ahead of the surface location of the warm front.

Frontal cyclone development is related to polar jet stream processes. Within the jet stream, localized areas of air outflow can occur because of upper air divergence. Outflow results in the development of an upper air vacuum. To compensate for the vacuum in the upper atmosphere, surface air flows cyclonically upward into the outflow to replenish lost mass. The process stops and the mid-latitude cyclone dissipates when the upper air vacuum is filled with surface air.

Mid-latitude cyclones cause far less damage than tropical cyclones or hurricanes. Hurricanes involve much greater amounts of atmospheric energy exchange. As one goes away from the equator, the energy available to fuel a weather system decreases as the amount of solar radiation and heat declines. Mid-latitude cyclones can have winds as strong as what is associated with a weak hurricane. But, this is a rare occurrence. Frontal cyclones tend to be most disruptive to human activity during winter months. Winter storms can produce heavy snowfalls or freezing rain which slows down transportation, snaps powerlines, and kills vegetation. In January 1998, a winter storm in eastern North America resulted in more than 20 human deaths, billions of dollars of damage, the loss of electrical power in some areas for up to two weeks, and the destruction of many deciduous trees because of the weight of ice.

THUNDERSTORMS AND TORNADOES

Thunderstorms

Thunderstorms form when moist, unstable air is lifted vertically into the atmosphere. Lifting of this air results in condensation and the release of latent heat. The process to initiate vertical lifting can be caused by:

(1) Unequal warming of the surface of the Earth.

(2) Orographic lifting due to topographic obstruction of air flow.

(3) Dynamic lifting because of the presence of a frontal zone.

Immediately after lifting begins, the rising parcel of warm moist air begins to cool because of adiabatic expansion. At a certain elevation the dew point is reached resulting in condensation and the formation of a cumulus cloud. For the cumulus cloud to form into a thunderstorm, continued uplift must occur in an unstable atmosphere. With the vertical extension of the air parcel, the cumulus cloud grows into a cumulonimbus cloud. Cumulonimbus clouds can reach heights of 20 kilometers above the Earth's surface. Severe weather associated with some these clouds includes hail, strong winds, thunder, lightning, intense rain, and tornadoes.

Generally, two types of thunderstorms are common:

(1) Air mass thunderstorms which occur in the mid-latitudes in summer and at the equator all year long.

(2) Thunderstorms associated with mid-latitude cyclone cold fronts or dry lines. This type of thunderstorm often has severe weather associated with it.

The most common type of thunderstorm is the air mass storm. Air mass thunderstorms normally develop in late afternoon hours when surface heating produces the maximum number of convection currents in the atmosphere. The life cycle of these weather events has three distinct stages. The first stage of air mass thunderstorm development is called the cumulus stage. In this stage, parcels of warm humid air rise and cool to form clusters of puffy white cumulus clouds. The clouds are the result of condensation and deposition which releases large quantities of latent heat. The added heat energy keeps the air inside the cloud warmer than the air around it. The cloud continues to develop as long as more humid air is added to it from below. Updrafts dominate the circulation patterns within the cloud.

When the updrafts reach their maximum altitude in the developing cloud, usually 12 to 14 kilometers, they change their direction 180° and become downdrafts. This marks the mature stage. With the downdrafts, precipitation begins to form through collision and coalescence. The storm is also at its most intense stage of development and is now a cumulonimbus cloud The top of the cloud takes on the familiar anvil shape, as strong stratospheric upper-level winds spread ice crystals in the top of the cloud horizontally. At its base, the thunderstorm is several kilometers in diameter. The mature air mass thunderstorm contains heavy rain, thunder, lightning, and produces wind gusts at the surface.

The mature thunderstorm begins to decrease in intensity and enters the dissipating stage after about half an hour. Air currents within the convective storm are now mainly downdrafts as the supply of warm moist air from the lower atmosphere is depleted. Within about 1 hour, the storm is finished and precipitation has stopped.

Thunderstorms form from the equator to as far north as Alaska. They occur most commonly in the tropics were convectional heating of moist surface air occurs year round. Many tropical land based locations experience over 100 thunderstorm days per year. Thunderstorm formation over tropical oceans is less frequent because these surfaces do not warm rapidly. Outside the tropics, thunderstorm formation is more seasonal occurring in those months where heating is most intense.

According to this map, the greatest incidence of thunderstorms occurs in the southeast and in parts of Colorado, Arizona, and New

Mexico. This particular spatial distribution suggests that extreme solar heating is not the only requirement for thunderstorm formation. Another important prerequisite is the availability of warm moist air. In the United States, the Gulf of Mexico supplies adjacent continental areas with moist maritime tropical air masses. These air masses are relatively unstable quickly forming cumulonimbus clouds when surface heating is intense. The secondary maximums found in Colorado, Arizona, and New Mexico are due to another climatic factor. All of these areas are on the leeward side of the Rocky Mountains. Mountain slopes in these areas that face the Sun absorb more direct solar radiation and become relatively warmer creating strong updrafts that form into cumulus clouds. If the differential heating is also supplemented by winds from the east, the cumulus clouds are further enhanced to become thunderstorms. Few thunderstorms occur along the west coast of the United States. This region is dominated by cool maritime polar air masses which suppress convectional uplift over land.

Severe Thunderstorms

Most thunderstorms are of the variety described above. However, some can form into more severe storms if the conditions exist to enhance and prolong the mature stage of development. Severe thunderstorms are defined as convective storms with frequent lighting, accompanied by local wind gusts of 97 kilometers per hour, or hail that is 2 centimeters in diameter or larger. Severe thunderstorms can also have tornadoes!

In most severe thunderstorms, the movement of the storm, in roughly an easterly direction, can refresh the storm's supply of warm humid air. With a continual supply of latent heat energy, the updrafts and downdrafts within the storm become balanced and the storm maintains itself indefinitely. Movement of the severe storm is usually caused by the presence of a mid-latitude cyclone cold front or a dry line some 100 to 300 kilometers ahead of a cold front. In the spring and early summer, frontal cyclones are common weather events that move from west to east in the mid-latitudes. At the same time, the ground surface in the mid-latitudes is receiving elevated levels of insolation which creates ideal conditions for air mass thunderstorm formation.

When the cold front or dry line of a frontal cyclone comes in contact with this warm air it pushes it like a bulldozer both horizontally and vertically. If this air has a high humidity and extends some distance to the east, the movement of the mid-latitude cyclone enhances vertical uplift in storm and keeps the thunderstorms supplied with moisture and energy. Thus, the mid-latitude cyclone converts air mass thunderstorms into severe thunderstorms that last for many hours. Severe thunderstorms dissipate only when no more warm moist air is encountered. This condition occurs several hours after nightfall when the atmosphere begins to cool off.

This storm would be moving from left to right because of the motion associated with a mid-latitude cyclone. The upper-level dry air wind is generated from the mid-latitude cyclone. It causes the tilting of vertical air currents within the storm so that the updrafts move up and over the downdrafts. The green arrows represent the updrafts which are created as warm moist air is forced into the front of the storm. At the back end of the cloud, the updrafts swing around and become downdrafts (blue arrows). The leading edge of the downdrafts produces a gust front near the surface. As the gust front passes, the wind on the surface shifts and becomes strong with gusts exceeding 100 kilometers per hour, temperatures become cold, and the surface pressure rises. Warm moist air that rises over the gust front may form a roll cloud. These clouds are especially prevalent when an inversion exists near the base of the thunderstorm.

Some severe thunderstorms develop a strong vertical updraft, commonly known as a mesocyclone. Mesocyclones measure about 3 to 10 kilometers across and extend from the storm's base to its top. They are also found in the southwest quadrant of the storm. In some cases, mesocyclones can overshoot the top of the storm and form a cloud dome. About half of all mesocyclones spawn tornadoes. When a tornado occurs, the mesocyclone lengthens vertically, constricts, and spirals down to the ground surface. Scientists speculate that mesocyclones form when strong horizontal upper air winds interact with normally occurring updrafts. The shearing effect of this interaction forces the horizontal wind to flow upward intensifying the updraft.

Tornadoes

A tornado is a vortex of rapidly moving air associated with some severe thunderstorms. Tornadoes that travel across lakes or oceans are called waterspouts. Winds within the tornado funnel may exceed 500 kilometers per hour. High velocity winds cause most of the damage associated with these weather events. Tornadoes also cause damage through air pressure reductions. The air pressure at the tornado center is approximately 800 millibars (average sea-level pressure is 1013 millibars) and many human made structures collapse outward when subject to pressure drops of this magnitude. The destructive path of a tornado is usually about half a kilometer wide, and usually no more than 25 kilometers long. However, a spring tornado in 1917 traveled 570 kilometers across Illinois and Indiana lasting well over 7 hours.

About 74% of all tornadoes have wind speeds between 65 and 181 kilometers per hour. These events are classified according to the Fujita tornado intensity scale as being weak. Damage from these tornadoes varies from broken windows and tree branches to shingles blowing off roofs and moving cars pushed from roads. Weak tornadoes have a path that is about 1.5 kilometers long and 100 meters wide, and they generally last for only 1 to 3 minutes. According to the Fujita scale, strong tornadoes can have wind speeds between 182 and 332 kilometers per hour. These phenomena cause considerable damage and occur about 25% of the time. Strong tornadoes can have a course up to 100 kilometers long and half a kilometer wide, and they can last for more than 2 hours. The rarest tornadoes are those with either a F4 or F5 rating. These events have wind speeds between 333 to 513 kilometers per hour and are very destructive and violent. F4 tornadoes occur only about 1% of the time, while F5 are even more rare with a chance of about 1 in 1000 of happening.

Tornadoes occur in many parts of the world. Some notable hots spots include South Africa, Australia, Europe, New Zealand, northern India, Canada, Argentina, Uruguay, and the United States. Of these locations, the United States has some specific regions within its boundaries that have an extremely high number of events per year. Tornado occurrence has some interesting temporal characteristics. In the United States, most tornadoes occur in April, May, June, and July. It is during these months that we get the conditions necessary for the formation of severe thunderstorms. Tornadoes also have particular times of the day in which they form. Most tornadoes form in the afternoon and early evening. During this eriuod of time, the Earth's surface is reaching its maximum daily temperature because of the continued absorption of solar radiation. Large amounts of this heat energy are also being transfered by conduction and convection into the atmosphere creating strong rapidly rising updrafts. If these updrafts influence the vertical development of a thunderstorm, they can also result in the formation of a tornado.

In the United States, about 40,000 tornadoes have occurred in the last fifty years (1950-1999). Data for the period 1916 to 1996 indicates that the frequency of tornadoes in the United States has increased substantially. However, part of this trend may be due to increased population densities. More people per unit area means a greater chance of seeing this relatively rare weather event. Two other factors that could also be responsible for the perceived increase in tornado numbers may be satellite imaging and weather radar. Both of these technologies allow us to pinpoint the thunderstorms that may generate funnels.

Total damage from tornadoes over the last 50 years has been estimated to be about 25 billion dollars. Tornadoes also take a heavy toll on human lives. Table below describes the ten deadliest tornado events in the United States. However, weather forecasting technology has played an important role in reducing the number of lives lost. In the decade of the 1930s, before the advent of severe weather forecasting, 1945 people were killed by tornadoes. From 1986 to 1995, only 418 individuals perished suggesting a 90% decrease in fatalities. This reduction is even more astonishing when you consider that the population of the United States doubled from 1935 to 1990.

Table: Ten deadliest tornado events in the United States.

DATE	LOCATION(S)	DEATHS
March 18, 1925	Missouri, Illinois, Indiana	689
May 6, 1840	Natchez, Mississippi	317
May 27, 1896	St. Louis, Missouri	255
April 5, 1936	Tupelo, Mississippi	216
April 6, 1936	Gainesville, Georgia	203
April 9, 1947	Woodward, Oklahoma	181
April 24, 1908	Amite, Louisiana and Purvis, Mississippi	143
June 12, 1899	New Richmond, Wisconsin	117
June 8, 1953	Flint, Michigan	115
May 11, 1953	Waco, Texas	114

Tornadoes can cause considerable damage to natural and human made structures on the Earth's surface. Often, they also cause the injury and death of people. One particular event that set new monetary records in destruction occurred in Oklahoma on May 3, 1999. The destruction from this meteorological event began at 4:45 in the afternoon and ended about six hour later. During this time period, about 70 tornadoes were spawned along a 240-kilometer long swath that began in southwest Oklahoma.

Oklahoma receives more tornadoes per square kilometer than any other region found on our planet. It also receives most of these severe events in the month of May when warm moist air from the Gulf of Mexico interacts with cold fronts descending from the northwest. On the morning of May 3rd, forecasters at NOAA's Storm Prediction Center predicted only a slight risk for severe weather across parts of Oklahoma, Texas, and Kansas. However, by the afternoon conditions for tornado generation had improved greatly. Clearing skies provided the solar radiation required to increase surface temperatures and enhance convective development of severe thunderstorms.

A kink in the jet stream, known as a short wave, strengthened upper air winds traveling from the east. Strong upper air winds have a tendency to enhance the vertical mesocyclonic circulation occurring inside developing thunderstorms. This information was added to the high-resolution computer forecast model at the Storm Prediction Center. At 3:49, the Storm Prediction Center updated the forecast and issued a tornado watch. Less than an hour later the damage began.

The greatest damage on May 3 occurred when the funnels cut through Oklahoma City. The damage to the urban area stretched over 60 kilometers and was at times more than a kilometer wide. In some places, winds from the funnel were traveling about 420 to 510 kilometers per hour! More than 2500 buildings were destroyed and another 7500 were damaged. Total damage to structures and other property was estimated to be about 1.2 billion dollars. The toll on human life, for the entire state, was 40 individuals. This number would have certainly been much higher if radio and television warning systems did not exist.

TROPICAL WEATHER AND HURRICANES

Tropical Weather

The tropics can be defined as the area of the Earth found between the Tropic of Cancer (23.5° North) and the Tropic Capricorn (23.5° South). In this region, the Sun will be directly overhead during some part of the year. The temperature of the tropics does not vary much from season to season because high quantities of solar insolation are received here regardless of the time of the year. Weather in the tropics is dominated by convective storms that develop mainly along the intertropical convergence zone (ITCZ), the subtropical high pressure zone, and oceanic disturbances in the trade winds that sometimes develop into hurricanes.

One of the most important weather features found in the tropics is the intertropical convergence zone. The intertropical convergence zone is distinguished by a wide band of cumulus and cumulonimbus clouds that are created by dynamic atmospheric lifting due to convergence and convection. In general, the intertropical convergence zone delineates the location where the noonday Sun is directly overhead. Because of the high Sun, the intertropical convergence zone receives the greatest quantity of daily solar insolation in the tropics. At the intertropical convergence zone, this energy is used to evaporate large amounts of water and is converted into sensible heat at the ground surface and within the atmosphere. Often, these processes lead to an almost daily development of convective thunderstorms by providing moisture and heat for the development of cumulonimbus clouds. The intertropical convergence zone also represents the location of convergence of the northeast and southeast trade winds. The convergence of these wind systems enhances the development of convective rain clouds at the tropics.

The intertropical convergence zone moves seasonally with the tilt of the Earth's axis. The convective rains that accompany the passage of the intertropical convergence zone are the primary source of precipitation for locations roughly 10 to 23.5° North and South latitude. The other important weather feature in the tropics is the subtropical high-pressure zone. Airflow in the subtropical high-pressure zone is primarily descending. This creates clear skies, low humidity, and hot daytime temperatures. Like the intertropical convergence zone, the subtropical high-pressure zone migrates seasonally. It generally influences locations 10 to 23.5° North and South during some part of the year.

Easterly Waves

Weather disturbances in the trade winds, known as easterly waves, are another source of cloud development and precipitation in the tropics. Easterly waves develop first as a weak disturbance in the atmosphere, usually because of the presence of localized warmer ocean temperatures. On a weather map these weather systems appear as a wave in the isobars. On the eastern side of this wave, convergence occurs forming numerous thunderstorms (divergence occurs on the western side). If the convergence is strong enough, the storm system may intensify and organize into a hurricane. On average, about 10% of the weather disturbances associated with easterly waves develop into hurricanes.

HURRICANES

Hurricanes are intense cyclonic storms that develop over the warm oceans of the tropics. These tropical storms go by other names in the various parts of the world: India/Australia - cyclones;

western North Pacific - typhoons; and the Philippines - baguio. By international agreement, the term tropical cyclone is used by most nations to describe hurricane-like storms that originated over tropical oceans. Surface atmospheric pressure in the center of a hurricane tends to be extremely low. The lowest pressure reading ever recorded for a hurricane (typhoon Tip, 1979) is 870 millibars (mb). However, most storms have an average pressure of 950 millibars. To be classified as a hurricane, sustained wind speeds must be greater than 118 kilometers per hour at the storm's center. Wind speed in a hurricane is directly related to the surface pressure of the storm. The following graph shows the relationship between surface pressure and sustained wind speed for a number of tropical low pressure systems.

Hurricanes have no fronts associated with them like the mid-latitude cyclones of the polar front. They are also smaller than the mid-latitude cyclone, measuring on average 550 kilometers in diameter. One of the largest hurricanes ever measured was Typhoon Tip (October 12, 1979) which had a diameter of about 2100 kilometers. Mature hurricanes usually develop a cloud-free eye at their center. In the eye, air is descending creating clear skies. The eye of the hurricane may be 20 to 50 kilometers in diameter. Surrounding the eye are bands of organized thunderstorm clouds formed as warm air move in and up into the storm. The strongest winds and heaviest precipitation are found in the area next to the eye where a vertical wall of thunderstorm clouds develops from the Earth's surface to the top of the troposphere.

HURRICANE DEVELOPMENT, MOVEMENT, AND DISSIPATION

Hurricanes are powered by the latent heat energy released from condensation. To form and develop, they must be supplied with a constant supply of warm humid air for this process. Surface air with enough energy to generate a hurricane only exists over oceans with a temperature greater than 26.5° Celsius (80° F). Further, this warm surface water must exist in a layer that is at least 200 meters (600 feet) deep. Ocean temperatures this high only occur in selected regions of our planet and during particular seasons. Hurricane development can also be prevented by the presence of a temperature inversion in the atmosphere. Inversions develop in the tropics when subtropical high pressure systems produce sinking air.

Hurricanes go through a number of different stages of development. Initially, these powerful storms begin their lives as a group of unorganized thunderstorms that develop over the specific areas of the tropical oceans. However, not all of these types of tropical disturbances become hurricanes. To develop into a hurricane, significant cyclonic circulation must occur around the disturbances. This type of circulation enhances the development of the group of thunderstorms by providing additional moisture and latent heat energy. With more moisture and latent heat energy, the strength and number of the thunderstorms in the tropical disturbance increases causing the disturbance to intensify.

The thunderstorms also begin to organize themselves into spiral bands that swirl cyclonically toward the center of the storm. If the sustained wind speed around the disturbance increases to between 37 and 63 kilometers per hour (23 to 39 miles per hour), the storm becomes classified as a tropical depression. Tropical depressions appear on the weather map as a cyclonic low with several closed isobars circling the storm's center. A tropical depression can continue to intensify and become a tropical storm, the next stage in hurricane development. Tropical storms have a lower central pressure, several more closed isobars on a weather map, and winds that are between 64 and 118 kilometers per hour. Finally, tropical storms officially become hurricanes when their sustained wind speed exceeds 118 kilometers per hour.

Figure below shows the tropical and subtropical ocean areas where hurricanes typically form on our planet. These areas generally extend poleward to a maximum latitude of about 25 to 30° North or South. The exclusion of hurricanes from around the equator is related to the fact that Coriolis force is almost negligible here. A specific threshold quantity of Coriolis force is required to initiate cyclonic flow. Note that hurricanes do not form over the southeastern Pacific Ocean, South Atlantic Ocean, and off the coast of northern

Africa. In these regions, cool ocean temperatures or the presence of temperature inversions restrict formation.

Hurricanes are seldom motionless after their initial formation. On average, hurricanes that form in the North Atlantic and North Pacific move in a west or northwestward path. In reality, the track taken by any individual storm is often very chaotic. Hurricanes can suddenly change both their speed and direction of travel.

Of these three regions, the northwest Pacific Ocean basin produced the most hurricanes for this period, an average of 17.7 storms per year. The mainland of North America is often influenced by storms that form in the North Atlantic and northeast Pacific which produce a yearly average of 5.9 and 7.4 hurricanes, respectively. Most of the storms that form in the northeast Pacific travel away from North America out to open ocean.

Tropical storms and hurricanes also have very specific seasonal patterns. The peak season for these weather events in the Southern Hemisphere is January to March. In the Northern Hemisphere, most tropical storms and hurricanes develop in the months of June to November. Figure below describes the month frequency of storm formation in the three ocean basins found in the Northern Hemisphere for the period 1951 to 2002. Each basin has slightly different patterns. Tropical storms and hurricanes rarely form during the months December to April in the North Atlantic and North Pacific basins. The Northwest Pacific basin has a significant number of storms forming in all months.

Hurricanes dissipate when the availability of latent heat energy is substantially reduced. This occurs either with landfall or storm movement into cooler seas. Most hurricanes live for about a week. However, if a hurricane remains over warm water its life can be extended. In 1992, hurricane Tina was an active tropical storm for 24 days over the North Pacific.

Hurricane Classification

The most commonly used system to classify the strength of hurricanes is the Saffir-Simpson scale. This classification scheme was developed so the public could quickly estimate the potential damage a hurricane's winds and storm surge could have on a coastal area. The first two categories describe the two stages that occur before a storm becomes a hurricane: TD – tropical depression and TS – tropical storm. Hurricanes are categorized into 5 scales of intensity that ranges from 1 to 5. A major hurricane is considered to be category 3 and above.

Hurricane Damage and Destruction

Tropical cyclones are the most deadly and destructive type of severe weather event on our planet. One of the most destructive hurricanes in the last 100 years was the Bhola cyclone (category 3) that made landfall on the Bangladesh coastline on November 12 of 1970. This storm had a minimal pressure reading of 966 millibars and maximum sustained winds of about 185 km/hr. Estimates suggest that over 300,000 people died from this storm. Most of these deaths were caused by flooding due to the storm surge and heavy rains. The high death toll caused by this hurricane was due to lack of prepareness. It is believed that less than 1% of the population took shelter in fortified buildings. One of the deadliest Atlantic storms is hurricane Mitch (category 5). Hurricane Mitch encountered populated areas of Central America twice: in late October and early November 1998. Estimates suggest that over 11,000 people died from this storm. Most of these deaths were caused by flooding and mudslides due to heavy rains.

The damage that hurricanes inflict is caused by high wind speeds, heavy rainfall, storm surge, and tornadoes. Wind speed in a hurricane is usually directly related to atmospheric pressure. The lower the pressure the faster the winds blow. Wind speed also varies within the storm. As discussed earlier, winds are usually strongest at the edge of the hurricane's eye. High winds inflict damage by blowing down objects, creating choppy waves and high seas, and by inundating coastal areas with seawater. Rainfall withi a hurricane can often exceed 60 centimeters (24 inches) in a 24-hour period. If this rainfall occurs on land, flooding often occurs. Storm surge is an increase in the height of the ocean's surface in the region beneath and around the eye of the storm. It occurs when low atmospheric pressure causes the ocean surface to expand and because the hurricane's cyclonic winds blow seawater towards the eye. Hurricane Camille (1969 – category 5) had a storm surge of more than seven meters (23 feet) with a central pressure of 909 millibars. A considerable amount of damage can also occur because of tornadoes. About 25% of the hurricanes that make landfall have associated tornadoes. Some scientists also suspect that the thunderstorms that occur near the eye of a hurricane can produce very strong downbursts (vertical downward movements of air). The year 2005 was extremely bad for the development of tropical storms and hurricanes in the Atlantic Ocean. During the late summer and fall of that year, 28 tropical storms developed of which 15 became hurricanes. Table below describes some of the characteristics of each of the storms that developed into hurricanes. Seven of the tropical storms and hurricanes made landfall in the United States causing more than 100 billion US dollars worth of damage. Katrina was the most destructive storm of the 2005 season causing over 81 billion dollars of damage. This hurricane made landfall at the mouth of the Mississippi River on August 29th and flooded 80% of New Orleans. The strongest hurricane of the 2005 season was hurricane Wilma with a minimum storm pressure of 882 mb. This is the lowest pressure reading ever recorded for the Altantic Ocean in modern times.

CLIMATE CLASSIFICATION AND CLIMATIC REGIONS OF THE WORLD

Climate Classification

The Köppen Climate Classification System is the most widely used system for classifying the world's climates. Its categories are based on the annual and monthly averages of temperature and precipitation. The Köppen system recognizes five major climatic types; each type is designated by a capital letter.

A - Tropical Moist Climates: all months have average temperatures above 18° Celsius.

B - Dry Climates: with deficient precipitation during most of the year.

C - Moist Mid-latitude Climates with Mild Winters.

D - Moist Mid-Latitude Climates with Cold Winters.

E - Polar Climates: with extremely cold winters and summers.

Tropical Moist Climates (A)

Tropical moist climates extend northward and southward from the equator to about 15 to 25° of latitude. In these climates all months have average temperatures greater than 18° Celsius. Annual precipitation is greater than 1500 mm. Three minor Köppen climate types exist in the A group, and their designation is based on seasonal distribution of rainfall. Af or tropical wet is a tropical climate where precipitation occurs all year long. Monthly temperature variations in this climate are less than 3° Celsius. Because of intense surface heating and high humidity, cumulus and cumulonimbus clouds form early in the afternoons almost every day. Daily highs are about 32° Celsius, while night time temperatures average 22° Celsius. Am is a tropical monsoon climate. Annual rainfall is equal to or greater than Af, but most of the precipitation falls in the 7 to 9 hottest months. During the dry season very little rainfall occurs. The tropical wet and dry or savanna (Aw) has an extended dry season during winter. Precipitation during the wet season is usually less than 1000 millimeters, and only during the summer season.

Dry Climates (B)

The most obvious climatic feature of this climate is that potential evaporation and transpiration exceed precipitation. These climates extend from 20 - 35° North and South of the equator and in large continental regions of the mid-latitudes often surrounded by mountains. Minor types of this climate include:

- BW - dry arid (desert) is a true desert climate. It covers 12% of the Earth's land surface and is dominated by xerophytic vegetation. The additional letters h and k are used generally to distinguish whether the dry arid climate is found in the subtropics or in the mid-latitudes, respectively.
- BS - dry semiarid (steppe). Is a grassland climate that covers 14% of the Earth's land surface. It receives more precipitation than the BW either from the intertropical convergence zone or from mid-latitude cyclones. Once again, the additional letters h and k are used generally to distinguish whether the dry semiarid climate is found in the subtropics or in the mid-latitudes, respectively.

Moist Subtropical Mid-Latitude Climates (C)

This climate generally has warm and humid summers with mild winters. Its extent is from 30 to 50° of latitude mainly on the eastern and western borders of most continents. During the winter, the main weather feature is the mid-latitude cyclone. Convective thunderstorms dominate summer months. Three minor types exist: Cfa - humid subtropical; Cs - Mediterranean; and Cfb - marine. The humid subtropical climate (Cfa) has hot muggy summers and frequent thunderstorms. Winters are mild and precipitation during this season comes from mid-latitude cyclones. A good example of a Cfa climate is the southeastern USA. Cfb marine climates are found on the western coasts of continents.

They have a humid climate with short dry summer. Heavy precipitation occurs during the mild winters because of the continuous presence of mid-latitude cyclones. Mediterranean climates (Cs) receive rain primarily during winter season from the mid-latitude cyclone. Extreme summer aridity is caused by the sinking air of the subtropical highs and may exist for up to 5 months. Locations in North America are from Portland, Oregon to all of California.

Moist Continental Mid-latitude Climates (D)

Moist continental mid-latitude climates have warm to cool summers and cold winters. The location of these climates is pole ward of the C climates. The average temperature of the warmest month is greater than 10° Celsius, while the coldest month is less than -3° Celsius. Winters are severe with snowstorms, strong winds, and bitter cold from Continental Polar or Arctic air masses. Like the C climates there are three minor types: Dw - dry winters; Ds- dry summers; and Df - wet all seasons.

Polar Climates (E)

Polar climates have year-round cold temperatures with the warmest month less than 10° Celsius. Polar climates are found on the northern coastal areas of North America, Europe, Asia, and on the landmasses of Greenland and Antarctica. Two minor climate types exist. ET or polar tundra is a climate where the soil is permanently frozen to depths of hundreds of meters, a condition known as permafrost. Vegetation is dominated by mosses, lichens, dwarf trees and scattered woody shrubs. EF or polar ice caps has a surface that is permanently covered with snow and ice.

Factors Influencing the World Climatic Regions

So far in this online textbook we have discovered that the climate of a particular place is the function of a number of factors. These factors include:

(1) Latitude and its influence on solar radiation received.

(2) Air mass influences.

(3) Location of global high and low pressure zones.

(4) Heat exchange from ocean currents.

(5) Distribution of mountain barriers.

(6) Pattern of prevailing winds.

(7) Distribution of land and sea.

(8) Altitude.

At a macro-level, the first three factors are most important in influencing a region's climate. The animated graphic below provides us with a generalized model of the Earth's annual climatic variations. It also describes the latitudinal effects of these top three factors through the following climatic features:

- Relative annual latitudinal location of the overhead Sun at solar noon.
- Intertropical convergence zone and its area of uplift, cloud development and precipitation.
- Subtropical high pressure zone and its associated descending air currents and clear skies.
- Polar front and its area of uplift, cloud development and precipitation.
- Polar vortex and its associated descending air currents and clear skies.
- Relative location of tropical/subtropical (red) and polar (light blue) air masses.

In the animation we can see that the intertropical convergence zone, the subtropical high pressure zone, polar front and the position of tropical/subtropical and polar air masses all move in response to the seasonal movements of the Sun. It is important to understand this concept because of its climatic ramifications for locations on the globe. The type of climate that a location experiences is to a large extent a function of seasonal migration of these weather features. For example, a location at 15° North latitude is influenced by the subtropical high pressure zone during winter solstice and by the intertropical convergence zone during the summer solstice. Another location, at 60° North latitude, would be influenced by polar air masses during the winter solstice, the polar front during the equinoxes, and by subtropical air masses and the subtropical high pressure zone during the summer solstice.

When studying about the Earth's Climatic Regions as described below, use this animation as a guide to understanding the large scale climatic processes that produce each location's particular climate.

5

CLIMATOLOGY

Urban Climatology

Urban and rural environments differ substantially in their micro-climate. These climatic differences are primarily caused by the alteration of the Earth's surface by human construction and the release of artificially created energy into the environment.

Energy Characteristics of Urban Areas

In a city, concrete, asphalt, and glass replace natural vegetation, and vertical surfaces of buildings are added to the normally flat natural rural landscape. Urban surfaces generally have a lower albedo, greater heat conduction, and more heat storage than the surfaces they replaced. The geometry of city buildings causes the absorption of a greater quantity of available incoming solar radiation and outgoing terrestrial infrared radiation. Even in early morning and late afternoon the urban areas are intercepting and absorbing radiation on their vertical surfaces.

In urban areas, large amounts of heat energy are added to the local energy balance through transportation, industrial activity, and the heating of buildings. In winter, the amount of heat generated from the burning of fossil fuels in New York City is 2.5 times greater than the heat absorbed from the Sun. Finally, in rural areas, evaporation and transpiration from various natural surfaces act to cool the land surface and local atmosphere. In urban locations, drainage systems have been created to quickly remove surface water. Thus, little water is available for cooling.

Observed Climate of Cities

Urban areas tend to be warmer than the surrounding countryside. These differences in temperature are best observed at night under stable conditions when atmospheric mixing is at a minimum. Climatologists call this phenomenon the urban heat island. The urban heat island is strongest at the city center where population densities are highest and industrial activity is at a maximum. The heat island effect has been described in many cities around the world, and temperature differences between city and country can be as high as 6° Celsius.

Wind in urban areas is generally calmer than those in rural areas. This reduction in velocity is due the frictional effects of the city's vertical surfaces. However, some street and building configurations within a city can channel the wind and increase its velocity through a venturi effect. Certain parts of downtown Chicago and Winnipeg are noted for their unusually high wind speeds.

Climatologists have measured about up to 10% more rainfall in urban areas. This increase may be due to the combined effect of particulate air pollution and increased convectional uplift. Air pollution may enhance rainfall by increasing the number of condensation nuclei through the atmospheric addition of smoke and dust particles. The additional generation of heat within the city increases the number of convection currents over that surface. Convection is required to initiate the development of thunderstorms.

EARTH'S CLIMATIC HISTORY

Reconstructing Past Climates

A wide range of evidence exists to allow climatologists to reconstruct the Earth's past climate. This evidence can be grouped into three general categories.

The first category is meteorological instrument records. Common climatic elements measured by instruments include temperature, precipitation, wind speed, wind direction, and atmospheric pressure. However, many of these records are temporally quite short as many of the instruments used were only created and put into operation during the last few centuries or decades. Another problem with instrumental records is that large areas of the Earth are not monitored. Most of the instrumental records are for locations in populated areas of Europe and North America. Very few records exist for locations in less developed countries (LDCs), in areas with low human populations, and the Earth's oceans. Over the last half century many meteorological stations have been added in land areas previously not covered. Another important advancement in developing a global record of climate has been the recent use of remote satellites.

Written documentation and descriptive accounts of the weather make up the second general category of evidence for determining climate change. Weather phenomena commonly described in this type of data includes the prevailing character of the seasons of individual years, reports of floods, droughts, great frosts, periods of bitter cold, and heavy snowfalls. Large problems exist in the interpretation of this data because of its subjective nature.

Many types of physical and biological data can provide fossil evidence of the effects of fluctuations in the past weather of our planet. Scientists refer to this information as "proxy data" of past weather and climate. Examples of this type of data include tree ring width and density measurements, fossilized plant remains, insect and pollen frequencies in sediments, moraines and other glacial deposits, marine organism fossils, and the isotope ratios of various elements. Scientists using this type of data assume uniformity in the data record. Thus, the response measured from a physical or biological character existing today is equivalent to the response of the same character in the past. However, past responses of these characters may also be influenced by some other factor not accounted for. Some common examples of proxy data include:

Glacial Ice Deposits. Fluctuations in climate can be determined by the analysis of gas bubbles trapped in the ice which reflect the state of the atmosphere at the time they were deposited, the chemistry of the ice (concentration or ratio of major ions and isotopes of oxygen and hydrogen), and the physical properties of the ice. Biological Marine Sediments. Climate change can be evaluated by the analysis of temporal changes in fossilized marine fauna and flora abundance, morpological changes in preserved organisms, coral deposits, and the oxygen isotopic concentration of marine organisms.

Inorganic Marine Sediments. This type of proxy data includes clay mineralogy, aeolian terrestial dust, and ice rafted debris.

Terrestrial Geomorphology and Geology Proxy Data. There are a number of different types of proxy data types in this group including glacial deposits, glacial erosional features, shoreline features, aeolian deposits, lake sediments, relict soil deposits, and speleothems (depositional features like stalactites and stalagmites).

Terrestial Biology Proxy Data. Variations in climate can be determined by the analysis of biological data like annual tree rings, fossilized pollen and other plant macrofossils, the abundance and distribution of insects and other organisms, and the biota in lake sediments.

Earth's Climatic History

Climatologists have used various techniques and evidence to reconstruct a history of the Earth's past climate. From this data, they have found that during most of the Earth's history global temperatures were probably 8 to 15 degrees Celsius warmer than today. In the last billion years of climatic history, warmer conditions were broken by glacial periods starting at 925, 800, 680, 450, 330, and 2 million years before present.

The period from 2,000,000 - 14,000 B.P. (before present) is known as the Pleistocene or Ice Age. During this period, large glacial ice sheets covered much of North America, Europe, and Asia for extended periods of time. The extent of the glacier ice during the Pleistocene was not static. The Pleistocene had periods when the glacier retreated (interglacial) because of warmer temperatures and advanced because of colder temperatures (glacial). During the coldest periods of the Ice Age, average global temperatures were probably 4 - 5 degrees Celsius colder than they are today.

The most recent glacial retreat is still going on. We call the temporal period of this retreat the Holocene epoch. This warming of the Earth and subsequent glacial retreat began about 14,000 years ago (12,000 BC). The warming was shortly interrupted by a sudden cooling, known as the Younger-Dryas, at about 10,000 - 8500 BC. Scientists speculate that this cooling may have been caused by the release of fresh water trapped behind ice on North America into the North Atlantic Ocean. The release altered vertical currents in the ocean which exchange heat energy with the atmosphere. The warming resumed by 8500 BC. By 5000 to 3000 BC average global temperatures reached their maximum level during the Holocene and were 1 to 2 degrees Celsius warmer than they are today. Climatologists call this period the Climatic Optimum. During the Climatic Optimum, many of the Earth's great ancient civilizations began and flourished. In Africa, the Nile River had three times its present volume, indicating a much larger tropical region.

From 3000 to 2000 BC a cooling trend occurred. This cooling caused large drops in sea level and the emergence of many islands (Bahamas) and coastal areas that are still above sea level today. A short warming trend took place from 2000 to 1500 BC, followed once again by colder conditions. Colder temperatures from 1500 - 750 BC caused renewed ice growth in continental glaciers and alpine glaciers, and a sea level drop of between 2 to 3 meters below present day levels.

The period from 750 BC - 800 AD saw warming up to 150 BC. Temperatures, however, did not get as warm as the Climatic Optimum. During the time of Roman Empire (150 BC - 300 AD) a cooling began that lasted until about 900 AD. At its height, the cooling caused the Nile River (829 AD) and the Black Sea (800-801 AD) to freeze.

The period 900 - 1200 AD has been called the Little Climatic Optimum. It represents the warmest climate since the Climatic Optimum. During this period, the Vikings established settlements on Greenland and Iceland. The snow line in the Rocky Mountains was about 370 meters above current levels. A period of cool and more extreme weather followed the Little Climatic Optimum. A great drought in the American southwest occurred between 1276 and 1299. There are records of floods, great droughts and extreme seasonal climate fluctuations up to the 1400s.

From 1550 to 1850 AD global temperatures were at their coldest since the beginning of the Holocene. Scientists call this period the Little Ice Age. During the Little Ice Age, the average annual temperature of the Northern Hemisphere was about 1.0 degree Celsius lower than today. During the period 1580 to 1600, the western United States experienced one of its longest and most severe droughts in the last 500 years. Cold weather in Iceland from 1753 and 1759 caused 25% of the population to die from crop failure and famine. Newspapers in New England were calling 1816 the year without a summer.

The period 1850 to present is one of general warming. Figure 7x-1 describes the global temperature trends from 1880 to 2006. This graph shows the yearly temperature anomalies that have occurred from an average global temperature calculated for the period 1951-1980. The graph indicates that the anomolies for the first 60 years of the record were consistently negative. However, beginning in 1935 positive anomolies became more common, and from 1980 to 2006 most of the anomolies were between 0.20 to 0.63 degrees Celsius higher than the normal period (1951-1980) average.

In the 1930s and 1950s, the central United States experience two periods of extreme drought. In the seventeen year period from 1990 to 2006, ten of the warmest years in the last 100 years and possibly since the Little Climatic Optimum have occurred. Proxy and instrumental data indicate that 2005 was the warmest year globally in 1200 years of Earth history. Many scientists believe the warmer temperatures of the 20th and 21st centuries are being caused by the human enhancement of the Earth's greenhouse effect.

Causes of Climate Change

Figure below illustrates the basic components that influence the state of the Earth's climatic system. Changes in the state of this system can occur externally (from extraterrestrial systems) or internally (from ocean, atmosphere and land systems) through any one of the described components. For example, an external change may involve a variation in the Sun's output which would externally vary the amount of solar radiation received by the Earth's atmosphere and surface. Internal variations in the Earth's climatic system may be caused by changes in the concentrations of atmospheric gases, mountain building, volcanic activity, and changes in surface or atmospheric albedo. The work of climatologists has found evidence to suggest that only a limited number of factors are primarily responsible for most of the past episodes of climate change on the Earth. These factors include:

- Variations in the Earth's orbital characteristics.
- Atmospheric carbon dioxide variations.
- Volcanic eruptions
- Variations in solar output.

VARIATIONS IN THE EARTH'S ORBITAL CHARACTERISTICS

The Milankovitch theory suggests that normal cyclical variations in three of the Earth's orbital characteristics is probably responsible for some past climatic change. The basic idea behind this theory assumes that over time these three cyclic events vary the amount of solar radiation that is received on the Earth's surface.

The first cyclical variation, known as eccentricity, controls the shape of the Earth's orbit around the Sun. The orbit gradually changes from being elliptical to being nearly circular and then back to elliptical in a period of about 100,000 years. The greater the eccentricity of the orbit (i.e., the more elliptical it is), the greater the variation in solar energy received at the top of the atmosphere between the Earth's closest (perihelion) and farthest (aphelion) approach to the Sun. Currently, the Earth is experiencing a period of low eccentricity. The difference in the Earth's distance from the Sun between perihelion and aphelion (which is only about 3%) is responsible for approximately a 7% variation in the amount of solar energy received at the top of the atmosphere. When the difference in this distance is at its maximum (9%), the difference in solar energy received is about 20%.

The second cyclical variation results from the fact that, as the Earth rotates on its polar axis, it wobbles like a spinning top changing the orbital timing of the equinoxes and solstices. This effect is known as the precession of the equinox. The precession of the equinox has a cycle of approximately 26,000 years. According to illustration A, the Earth is closer to the Sun in January (perihelion) and farther away in July (aphelion) at the present time. Because of precession, the reverse will be true in 13,000 years and the Earth will then be closer to the Sun in July. This means, of course, that if everything else remains constant, 13,000 years from now seasonal variations in the Northern Hemisphere should be greater than at present (colder winters and warmer summers) because of the closer proximity of the Earth to the Sun.

The third cyclical variation is related to the changes in the tilt (obliquity) of the Earth's axis of rotation over a 41,000 year period. During the 41,000 year cycle the tilt can deviate from approximately 22.5 to 24.5°. At the present time, the tilt of the Earth's axis is 23.5°. When the tilt is small there is less climatic variation between the summer and winter seasons in the middle and high latitudes. Winters tend to be milder and summers cooler. Warmer winters allow for more snow to fall in the high latitude regions. When the atmosphere is warmer it has a greater ability to hold water vapor and therefore more snow is produced at areas of frontal or orographic uplift. Cooler summers cause snow and ice to accumulate on the Earth's surface because less of this frozen water is melted. Thus, the net effect of a smaller tilt would be more extensive formation of glaciers in the polar latitudes.

Periods of a larger tilt result in greater seasonal climatic variation in the middle and high latitudes. At these times, winters tend to be colder and summers warmer. Colder winters produce less snow because of lower atmospheric temperatures. As a result, less snow and ice accumulates on the ground surface. Moreover, the warmer summers produced by the larger tilt provide additional energy to melt and evaporate the snow that fell and accumulated during the winter months. In conclusion, glaciers in the polar regions should be generally receding, with other contributing factors constant, during this part of the obliquity cycle.

Computer models and historical evidence suggest that the Milankovitch cycles exert their greatest cooling and warming influence when the troughs and peaks of all three cycles coincide with each other.

ATMOSPHERIC CARBON DIOXIDE VARIATIONS

Studies of long term climate change have discovered a connection between the concentration of carbon dioxide in the atmosphere and mean global temperature. Carbon dioxide is one of the more important gases responsible for the greenhouse effect. Certain atmospheric gases, like carbon dioxide, water vapor and methane, are able to alter the energy balance of the Earth by being able to absorb longwave radiation emitted from the Earth's surface. The net result of this process and the re-emission of longwave back to the Earth's surface increases the quantity of heat energy in the Earth's climatic system. Without the greenhouse effect, the average global temperature of the Earth would be a cold -18° Celsius rather than the present 15° Celsius.

Researchers of the 1970s CLIMAP project found strong evidence in deep-ocean sediments of variations in the Earth's global temperature during the past several hundred thousand years of the Earth's history. Other subsequent studies have confirmed these findings and have discovered that these temperature variations were closely correlated to the concentration of carbon dioxide in the atmosphere and variations in solar radiation received by the planet as controlled by the Milankovitch cycles. Measurements indicated that atmospheric carbon dioxide levels were about 30% lower during colder glacial periods.

It was also theorized that the oceans were a major store of carbon dioxide and that they controlled the movement of this gas to and from the atmosphere. The amount of carbon dioxide that can be held in oceans is a function of temperature. Carbon dioxide is released from the oceans when global temperatures become warmer and diffuses into the ocean when temperatures are cooler. Initial changes in global temperature were triggered by changes in received solar radiation by the Earth through the Milankovitch cycles. The increase in carbon dioxide then amplified the global warming by enhancing the greenhouse effect.

Over the past three centuries, the concentration of carbon dioxide has been increasing in the Earth's atmosphere because of human influences. Human activities like the burning of fossil fuels, conversion of natural prairie to farmland, and deforestation have caused the release of carbon dioxide into the atmosphere. From the early 1700s, carbon dioxide has increased from 280 parts per million to 380 parts per million in 2005. Many scientists believe that higher concentrations of carbon dioxide in the atmosphere will enhance the greenhouse effect making the planet warmer. Scientists believe we are already experiencing global warming due to an enhancement of the greenhouse effect. Most computer climate models suggest that the globe will warm up by 1.5 - 4.5° Celsius if carbon dioxide reaches the predicted level of 600 parts per million by the year 2050.

Volcanic Eruptions

For many years, climatologists have noticed a connection between large explosive volcanic eruptions and short term climatic change. For example, one of the coldest years in the last two centuries occurred the year following the Tambora volcanic eruption in 1815. Accounts of very cold weather were documented in the year following this eruption in a number of regions across the planet. Several other major volcanic events also show a pattern of cooler global temperatures lasting 1 to 3 years after their eruption.

At first, scientists thought that the dust emitted into the atmosphere from large volcanic eruptions was responsible for the cooling by partially blocking the transmission of solar radiation to the Earth's surface. However, measurements indicate that most of the dust thrown in the atmosphere returned to the Earth's surface within six months. Recent stratospheric data suggests that large explosive volcanic eruptions also eject large quantities of sulfur dioxide gas which remains in the atmosphere for as long as three years. Atmospheric chemists have determined that the ejected sulfur dioxide gas reacts with water vapor commonly found in the stratosphere to form a dense optically bright haze layer that reduces the atmospheric transmission of some of the Sun's incoming radiation. In the last century, two significant climate modifying eruptions have occurred.

El Chichon in Mexico erupted in April of 1982, and Mount Pinatubo went off in the Philippines during June, 1991. Of these two volcanic events, Mount Pinatubo had a greater effect on the Earth's climate and ejected about 20 million tons of sulfur dioxide into the stratosphere. Researchers believe that the Pinatubo eruption was primarily responsible for the 0.8 degree Celsius drop in global average air temperature in 1992. The global climatic effects of the eruption of Mount Pinatubo are believed to have peaked in late 1993. Satellite data confirmed the connection between the Mount Pinatubo eruption and the global temperature decrease in 1992 and 1993. The satellite data indicated that the sulfur dioxide plume from the eruption caused a several percent increase in the amount of sunlight reflected by the Earth's atmosphere back to space causing the surface of the planet to cool.

Variations in Solar Output

Until recently, many scientists thought that the Sun's output of radiation only varied by a fraction of a percent over many years. However, measurements made by satellites equipped with radiometers in the 1980s and 1990s suggested that the Sun's energy output may be more variable than was once thought. Measurements made during the early 1980s showed a decrease of 0.1 percent in the total amount of solar energy reaching the Earth over just an 18 month time period. If this trend were to extend over several decades, it could influence global climate. Numerical climatic models predict that a change in solar output of only 1 percent per century would alter the Earth's average temperature by between 0.5 to 1.0° Celsius.

Scientists have long tried to also link sunspots to climatic change. Sunspots are huge magnetic storms that are seen as dark (cooler) areas on the Sun's surface. The number and size of sunspots show cyclical patterns, reaching a maximum about every 11, 90, and 180 years. The decrease in solar energy observed in the early 1980s correspond to a period of maximum sunspot activity based on the

11 year cycle. In addition, measurements made with a solar telescope from 1976 to 1980 showed that during this period, as the number and size of sunspots increased, the Sun's surface cooled by about 6° Celsius. Apparently, the sunspots prevented some of the Sun's energy from leaving its surface. However, these findings tend to contradict observations made on longer times scales. Observations of the Sun during the middle of the Little Ice Age (1650 to 1750) indicated that very little sunspot activity was occurring on the Sun's surface. The Little Ice Age was a time of a much cooler global climate and some scientists correlate this occurrence with a reduction in solar activity over a period of 90 or 180 years. Measurements have shown that these 90 and 180 year cycles influence the amplitude of the 11 year sunspot cycle. It is hypothesized that during times of low amplitude, like the Maunder Minimum, the Sun's output of radiation is reduced. Observations by astronomers during this period (1645 to 1715) noticed very little sunspot activity occurring on the Sun.

During periods of maximum sunspot activity, the Sun's magnetic field is strong. When sunspot activity is low, the Sun's magnetic field weakens. The magnetic field of the Sun also reverses every 22 years, during a sunspot minimum. Some scientists believe that the periodic droughts on the Great Plains of the United States are in someway correlated with this 22 year cycle.

El Nino, La Nina and the Southern Oscillation

El Nino is the name given to the occasional development of warm ocean surface waters along the coast of Ecuador and Peru. When this warming occurs the usual upwelling of cold, nutrient rich deep ocean water is significantly reduced. El Nino normally occurs around Christmas and usually lasts for a few weeks to a few months. Sometimes an extremely warm event can develop that lasts for much longer time periods. In the 1990s, strong El Ninos developed in 1991 and lasted until 1995, and from fall 1997 to spring 1998.

The formation of an El Nino is linked with the cycling of a Pacific Ocean circulation pattern known as the southern oscillation.

In a normal year, a surface low pressure develops in the region of northern Australia and Indonesia and a high pressure system cver the coast of Peru. As a result, the trade winds over the Pacific Ocean move strongly from east to west. The easterly flow of the trade winds carries warm surface waters westward, bringing convective storms to Indonesia and coastal Australia. Along the coast of Peru, cold bottom water wells up to the surface to replace the warm water that is pulled to the west.

In an El Nino year, air pressure drops over large areas of the central Pacific and along the coast of South America. The normal low pressure system is replaced by a weak high in the western Pacific (the southern oscillation). This change in pressure pattern causes the trade winds to be reduced. This reduction allows the equatorial counter current (which flows west to east - see ocean currents map in topic 8q) to accumulate warm ocean water along the coastlines of Peru and Ecuador. This accumulation of warm water causes the thermocline to drop in the eastern part of Pacific Ocean which cuts off the upwelling of cold deep ocean water along the coast of Peru. Climatically, the development of an El Nino brings drought to the western Pacific, rains to the equatorial coast of South America, and convective storms and hurricanes to the central Pacific.

After an El Nino event weather conditions usually return back to normal. However, in some years the trade winds can become extremely strong and an abnormal accumulation of cold water can occur in the central and eastern Pacific. This event is called a La Nina. A strong La Nina occurred in 1988 and scientists believe that it may have been responsible for the summer drought over central North America. The most recent La Nina began developing in the middle of 1998 and was persistent into the winter of 2000. During this period, the Atlantic Ocean has seen very active hurricane seasons in 1998 and 1999.

In 1998, ten tropical storm developed of which six become full-blown hurricanes. One of the hurricanes that developed, named Mitch, was the strongest October hurricane ever to develop in about 100 years of record keeping. Some of the other weather effects of

La Nina include abnormally heavy monsoons in India and Southeast Asia, cool and wet winter weather in southeastern Africa, wet weather in eastern Australia, cold winter in western Canada and northwestern United States, winter drought in the southern United States, warm and wet weather in northeastern United States, and an extremely wet winter in southwestern Canada and northwestern United States.

Prior to the 1980s and 1990s, strong El Nino events occurred on average every 10 to 20 years. In the early 1980s, the first of a series of strong events developed. The El Nino of 1982-83 brought extreme warming to the equatorial Pacific. Surface sea temperatures in some regions of the Pacific Ocean rose 6° Celsius above normal. The warmer waters had a devastating effect on marine life existing off the coast of Peru and Ecuador. Fish catches off the coast of South America were 50% lower than the previous year. The 1982-83 El Nino also had a pronounced influence on weather in the equatorial Pacific region and world wide. Severe droughts occurred in Australia, Indonesia, India and southern Africa. Dry conditions in Australia resulted in a 2 billion dollar loss in crops, and millions of sheep and cattle died from lack of water. Heavy rains were experienced in California, Ecuador, and the Gulf of Mexico.

Our understanding of the processes responsible for the development of El Nino is still incomplete. Scientists are able to predict the future development of an event by noting the occurrence of particular weather precursors. Researchers also now have a pretty complete understanding of the global weather effects caused by the formation of an El Nino.

6

PHYSICAL FEATURES

Geographical Set Up: India takes its standard time from the meridian of 82 30 E, which is 5 ½ hours ahead of Greenwich Mean time (0 longitude).Pakistan time is 5 hours ahead of GMT and Bangladesh time is 6 hours ahead of GMT. Significance of Location: Barring the plateau of Baluchistan (which form part of Pakistan), the two great ranges of Sulaiman and Kirthar cut it off from the west. Along the north, the great mountain wall formed by the Hindukush, Karakoram and the Himalayas, which is difficult to cross, cuts it off from the rest of the continent. Similarly, the southward of-shoots of the Eastern Himalayas separate it from Russia. The tropical monsoon climate of India, which ensures a fair supply of moisture and forms the basis of farming in India, is also a result of its location in the southern part of Asia. Since the opening of Suez Canal (1867) India's distance from Europe has been reduced by 7,000km. It thus bridges the space between the highly industrialized nation of the west and the semi-arid, and south-western Asia and the most fertile and populated regions in the south-east and far-east countries.

The Trans Himalayas or Tibetan Himalayas: The largest glaciers are Hispar and Batura (over 57 km long) of Hunza Valley and Biafo and Baltaro (60 km long) of Shigar Valley. The Siachen of Nubra Valley is the longest with a length of over 72 km.The Purvachal or the Eastern Hills: In the east after crossing the Cihang gorge the Himalayas bend towards south forming a series of hills running through Arunachal Pradesh, Nagaland, Manipur, Mizoram, Tripura and eastern Assam and form the boundary between India and Burma.

Physiographic Units of India

S. NO	UNITS	AREA KM (Sq) (appro)	% OF TOTAL AREA
01	Northern mountains	578,000	17.9
02	Great Plains	550,000	17.1
03	Thar Desert	175,000	5.4
04	Central Highlands	336,000	10.4
05	Peninsular Plateaus	1,241,000	38.5
06	Coastal Plains	335,000	10.4
07	Islands	8,300	0.3

Brahmaputra rivers divide Himalayas into three sections: the main Himalayas, the northwest Himalayas and the southeast Himalayas. The main Himalayas running from the Pamir Plateau in the northwest to Arunachal Pradesh in the southeast are the youngest mountains in the world. The highest peak of the word, the Mount Everst(8,884m, named after Sir George Everst). There are about 140 peaks in the Himalayas whose elevation is more than the Mount Blanc (4,810m),the highest peak of the Alps.

The three mountain ranges: the Himadri in the north(the greater Himalayas)the Himachal in the middle(the lesser Himalayas) and the Siwalik(the Outer Himalayas),facing thr palins of India.

The Himadri is of grat elevations (6,000m) which remains covered with everlasting snows. The Siwalik have some flat-floored structural valleys knowns as duns. Dehradun is well-known. Between the Himadri and the Himachal are some broad synclincal valleys. We also classify them as Punjab Himalayas, Kumayun, Assam Nepal and Northern.

Significance of Himalayas: (i) Physical Barriers (ii) Birthplace of Rivers (iii) Influence on climate (iv) Flora and Fauna (v) Mineral Resources (vi) Economic Resources (vii) Tourist

THE GREAT NORTHERN PLAINS

Lies between the great Himalayas in the North and the plateau of Peninsular India in the south. Nearly 2400 km long around 250-320 km broad, the most extensive plan indeed. It is said that this region was once a vast depression, filled with silt – brought down by the three Himalayas River, namely the Indus, the Ganga and the Brahmaputra and their numerous tributaries.

It contains some of the richest soils. The bhangar refers to the upland formed by deposition of older alluvium in the river beds and the Khadar are lowlands formed by deposition of detritus of new alluvium in the river beds.

Bhabar and Terai: Includes those regions where the Himalayas and other hilly regions join the plains. Coarse sand and pebbles are deposited. Bhabar lands are narrower in the east and extensive in the western and north-western hilly. Water converts large areas along the river into swamps known as Terai.

The Western or Rajasthan Plains: are known as Marusthali of Thar and the adjoining Bagar areas to the west of Aravalli. Luni whose water is sweet in the upper reaches and saltish by the time is reaches the sea.

The several salt lakes in the region such as the Sambhar, Degana, Kuchaman and Didwana; from which table salt is obtained. In most of the region shifting sand dunes occur.

The Punjab-Haryana Plain: These plains owe their formation to the Sutlej, the Beas and the Ravi rivers. Many low lying flood plains (called bets) are found here. The Bari Doab between Ravi and Beas rivers, the Bist Doab between the Beas and Sutlej and the Malwa plain are relatively more fertile plain.

The Ganga Plain: The Ganga-Yamuna Doab comprising the Rohilkhand and the Avadh Plain is the tile area that is drained by the tributaries of Ganga.

The North Bengal Plains: The Plains extending from the foot of Eastern Himalayas to the northern limb of Bengal basin cover an area of 23,000km2.

Brahmaputra Plains: This is a low level plain, rarely more than 80km broad, surround by High Mountain on all sides except on the west.

Significance of the Great Plains: Riverine region, Fertile soil, favorable climate, flat surface, constructions of roads, extensive system of irrigation.

The Peninsular Plateau: Oldest structure of the Indian subcontinent whose slow and steady movement towards north and north-east has been responsible for creation of the Himalayas and the Northern Plains in place of the Tethys sea of geological time. It is marked of from the Indo-Gangetic plain by the mountain and hill ranges such as the Vindhyas, the satpura, and Mahadeo, Maikal, and Sarguja ranges with the average height is usually divided into two major subdivisions with the Narmada valley as the line of demarcation. The region north of the Narmada valley is known as the Central Highlands and in south of the Narmada valley lies the Deccan Plateau.

THE CENTRAL HIGHLANDS

Old Aravalli Mountain on the west and the Vindhyas on the south. This region slopes northward to the Ganga plains. The western part of the Central highlands is known as the Malwa Plateau. The Central part has a number of small plateaus like those of Rewa, Baghelkhand and Bundlekhand. The eastern part of the Central Highlands comprises the Chotanagpur plateau.

The Deccan Plateau: The Deccan Plateau extends from the vindhyas to the southern tip of the Peninsula. This triangle plateau is at its widest in the north. The Vindhya Range and its eastern extension namely Mahadev hills Kaimuir Hills and Maikal Range from its northern edge. Western Ghats are known by different regional names such as the Sahyadris in Maharastra and Karnataka, the niligris in Tamil Nadu and Annamalai and the Cardamon hill along the Kerala and Tamil nadu border. The elevation of the ghats increases towards the south. The highest peak, Anaimudi (2,695 m) is in Kerala. The most important gap in the Western Ghats is the

Palghat gap which links Tamil Nadu with Kerala. The Bhorghat and the Thalghat are other gaps lying in Maharastra state.

Eastern Ghats: These hills rise steeply from the Coromandel coastal plain. The Eastern Ghats are well developed in the region between the Godavari and Mahanadi rivers. The Eastern Ghats and Western Ghats converge in the Nilgiri hills. Dodda Betta (2,637 m) is the highest peak in the Nilgiri hills.

Significance of Peninsular Plateau: (i) Geological richness (ii) Sources of Irrigation and hydroelectricity (iii) Agricultural Resources (iv) Forest Resources (v) Rich Fauna

THE COASTAL PLAINS AND ISLANDS

The Coastal plains: The Peninsular plateau is bounded by coastal plains on the east and west. There is wide difference between the eastern and western coastal plain. The west coast is narrower but wet. East coast much wider but relatively dry. A number of river deltas occur on the east coast. The deltas of east coast from the 'granary' of the five southern states- Andhra Pradesh, Tamil Nadu, Karnataka, Kerala and Pondicherry. The western coastal strips which have a large number of lagoons and back waters on other hand are noted for spices, areca nuts, coconuts palms etc.

Western coastal Plain: These lies between the Western Ghats and the Arabian seas and stretch from Kutch in the north to Kanyakumari in the south. The Gujarat plain is a broad and flat plain. The Kutch Peninsula, Gulf of Kutch, and the Gulf of Cambay. The Kathiawar Peninsula, also known as Saurashtra which lies to the south of Kutch, is also a plain level area except for some hills rising into Mount Girnar. Sun-divided regionally into the Konkan coast in Maharastra Canara coast in Karnataka and Malabar Coast in Kerala.

Eastern Coastal Plain: The eastern coastal low lands extend from the mouth of the Ganga to Kanyakumari. The northern half is called Northern Circars or Kalinga coast, while the southern half is known as the Coromandal coast. The border part is the Carnatic region, which is about 480 km wide. They are not suitable for harbours as their mouths being full of sit.

Significance of Coastal plains: (i) Harbours (ii) Specialized crops (iii) Fisheries and Navigation (iv) Economic Influence (v) Historical Importance

ISLANDS

Bay of Bengal Islands: The Andaman & Nicobar group of islands are separated by 10 Degree channel. These islands have been formed by extension of tertiary mountain chain of Arakan Yoma. The Andaman group of island is divided into 3 major groups' viz., North Andaman, Middle Andaman and south Andaman, collectively called Great Andamans. Little Andaman is separated from Great Andamans by Duncan passage. The Nicobar group of islands of which Great Nicobar is largest and southern most one. Saddle peak situated in Andaman Islands is the highest peak of Andaman & Nicobar group.

The Dhuliar peak is the highest peak of Nicobar group of islands.More habitable and different origin thanofArabian sea islands. Barran island is dormant volcano and Narcondam island is extinct volcano.

Lakshwadeep islands: Coral- More Muslim population and have fringing reefs. They are 25 small island groups. The island's north is known as Amindivi and spot is Cannonore island. Extreme south is Minicoy islands which is largest.

CLIMATE REGIONS

1. Tropical Rainy climate Region: This region has consistently even temperature, which stays above 18 C even in December, April, and May are the hottest months, the temperature varying from 18 C to 27 C. July and August are the coolest months, which copious rainfall. The average rainfall exceeds 250cm, which encourages wet evergreen forests. The western coastal strip, Western Ghats, south of Bombay, Meghalaya, western Nagaland and Tripura come in this climatic region.

2. Tropical Savanna Region: The chief feature of this climate is the long dry period. Temperature even in winter stay above 18 C, and in summer may even go up to 46 c. Rainfall, except in the southeastern parts, is in summer and averages about 100cm. In the south eastern parts, the retreating monsoons bring sufficient rains. A major part of the southern peninsula, except the arid tract lying east of the Western Ghats, northeastern Gujarat, south Bihar, major parts of Madhya Pradesh, Orissa, northern Andhra Pradesh, eastern Maharastra, and eastern TamilNadu coast come under this region.
3. Tropical Steppe Region: The average temperature is over 27 C, the lowest temperature being about 23 C April and May are the hottest months, when temperature may rise over 30 C. Average rainfall being less than 75cm, the region comprises a part of the famine zone of the country. The southwest monsoons bring rain to this region. The region comprises the rain shadow areas lying east of the Western Ghats and covers Karnataka, interior TamilNadu, western Andhra Pradesh and central Maharastra,
4. Sub-Tropical Steppe Region: The average temperature rises over 27 C and as high 48 C is recorded during summer. Rainfall from the southwest monsoon averages between 50 to 75 cm. It often fails, leading to widespread drought conditions. This region comprises tracts stretching and encompassing western Rajasthan and northern Gujarat.
5. Tropical Desert Region: The summer Temperature rises over 48 C, while in winter it goes down to 1 C. May and June are the hottest months. Average rainfall is 12.5 cm and very unreliable. Excessive evaporation during summer and intense cold during winter hinder crop production except through river irrigation. Western Rajasthan and parts of Kutch, which are purely sandy plains, come in this region.
6. Humid Sub-Tropical Region: Summer temperatures are 46 C to 48 C. Average rainfall, mostly from summer monsoons,

is about 62.5 cm, which increases to over 250cm in the east. Winters are virtually dry. This region is spread over the foothills of the Himalayas, eastern Rajasthan, plains of U.P, Bihar, northern Bengal, part of Assam and Arunachal Pradesh.

7. Mountain Region: Average temperature in June is 15 C to 17 C, in winter it goes below 8 C. On the northern slopes of the Himalayas, the rainfall is scanty, about 8-10 cm, but the western slopes enjoy a heavy rainfall of over 250 cm. The entire Himalayan belt comprising both the trans-Himalayas and the main Himalayas come under this region.

THE PENINSULAR PLATEAU

The Peninsula plateau is roughly triangular in shape with base coinciding with southern edge of the great edge of the Great Plains. It covers a total area of 160,000km 2. (About half of total land area of the country)

The Plateaus of Peninsular India

1. The Marwara Upland: It lies east of Aravali range made up of stand stone, shales and limestone of Vindhayan period. The upland is drained by Banas River originating in Aravali range.
2. The Central Highland: Also called the Madhya Bharat Pathar, lying in the east of Marwara upland and drained by Chambal and its tributaries.
3. The Bundelkhand Upland: To south of Yamuna river between Madhya Bharat Pathar and the Vindhyan scarap lands consists of granites and gneiss.
4. Malwa Plateau: Bonded by Aravali range in the west and Bundlekhand in east and Vindhayas in south. It is an extensive lava plateau in M.P. with black soil drained by a number of north flowing rivers like Betwa, Parbati, Kali Sindh, Chambal and Mahi.

5. Baghelkhand: East of Makal range and bounded by Son River on the north.
6. Chhotanagpur Plateau: It covers mostly Jharkhand adjoining eastern Madhya Pradesh and Purulia of West Bengal. This Plateau is composed mainly of Gondwana rocks with patches of granites ad gneisses and Deccan lavas. The highest general elevation is in the Midwest portion known as patlands (high level laterite plateau e.g. Netarhat). The Plateau is drained by numerous rives in a radial pattern such as Damodar, Subarnrekha, North Koel, South Koel and Barakar river.
7. Meghalaya Plateau: This Plateau has been separated from main block of the peninsular plateau by a gap called Ganu-Raj Mahal gap. From east to west the plateau comprises Gana, Khasi and Jaintia hills and Mikir hills. Shilong is the highest point of the plateau.
8. The Deccan Plateau: This is the largest unit covering an area of 5 lakh sq.km. It comprises Maharastra Plateau, Karnataka plateau and the Telengana plateau (Andhra Pradesh). The general slope is form west to east. Indicated by flow of major rivers like Mahanadi, Godwari, Krishna and Cauveri.
9. The Chhattisgarh Plain: It is the only plain worth the name in the vast stretch of plateau drained by upper course of Mahanadi. This saucer shaped depression lies between Makal range and Orissa hills.

HILL RANGE OF THE PENINSULA

- Aravali Range: Aravalis are the world's oldest fold mountain running in north east to southwest direction from Delhi to Palampur in Gujarat. Gurushikhar is the highest peak situated in Mount Abu. Barr, Piplighat, Dewair and Desuri passes allow movements by roads and railways.
- Vindhyan Range: It raises as an escarpment flauting the northern edge of the Naramada, Son-trough. The Vindhyas are continued eastward as the Bharner and Kaimur hills.

This range acts a s a water divided between Ganga system and river system of South India. The Makal range forms a connecting link between Vindhyan and Satpuras.

- Satpura Range: It is a series of seven (Sat) mountains running in east-west direction south of vindhyas and in between the Narmada and Tapi. Commencing from Rajpipla hills in the west through the Mahadeo hills it extends to Makal range in the east. Dhupgarh near Panchmarhi on Mahadeo hills is highest peak of Satpuras.
- Western Ghats (Sahyadris): The western Ghat run in north-south direction from Tapi valley to north of Kanyakumari. Along the Arabian sea-coast for about 1600 Km. these are Block Mountains due to the down warping of the land to the Arabian Sea. Sahyadris form the real water divide of the peninsula. All the important rivers rise from these hills and flow eastward. The Sayadris up to 16 north latitude are mainly composed of basalt. In this portion Kalsubai is the highest peak. South of Goa Sahyadris are composed of granites and Gneisses. In the Nilgiri hills, Eastern Ghats join the Sahyadris to form a mountain knot whose highest point is Doddabetta (2637 m). South of it is Palghat gap connecting Tamil Nadu with Kerala. South of Palghat there is mountain knot comprising Annamalai hills in north. Patni hills in the north-east and the Cardamon hills in the south. Anaimudi (2695 m) situated in the Annamalai hills is the highest peak of Sahyadri. Kodaikanal hill station is located on the Patni hills. There are 3 important passes in the Sahyadris: (a) Thalghat (b) Bhorghat (c) Palghat
- Eastern Ghat: It is a chain of highly broken and detached hills starting from Mahanadi in Orissa to Vaigai in Tamil Nadu. These are part of the very old fold mountains. It is only in the northern part between Mahanadi and Godavari that Eastern Ghats exhibit true mountain character comprising Maliya and Maduguala konda ranges, South of Godawari the broken hill ranges are Nallamalai, Palkonda,

and Javadi, Shavroy and Biligiri Rangan hills. Mahendragiri is the tallest peak of eastern Ghat.

SOILS

- COMPOSITION OF SOIL: Soil is the loose material which forms the upper layer of the mantel rock, i.e., the layer of loose fragments which covers most of the earth's land area. It has definite and constant composition. It contains both decayed plants and animals substances. The four main constituents of soils are;
  - (i) Silica: The chief constituent of sand
  - (ii) Clay: is a mixture of silicates and contains several minerals such as iron, potassium, calcium, sodium and aluminum. Particles of clay absorb water and swell.
  - (iii) Chalk: (calcium carbonate) provides calcium, the most important element for the growth of plants.
  - (iv) Humus: is not a mineral, it is an organic matter. It is formed by decomposed plant remains, animal manure and dead animals and is the most important element in the fertility of the soil. It helps retain moisture in the soil and helps the plant in absorbing materials from the soil for building its body. A soil looks dark on account of the presence of humus.
- TOP SOIL AND SUB SOIL: Two layers namely top soil and sub soil. Top soil(the upper layer) is of greater importance. Good top soil means good crops. It varies considerably in depth and also in character and ability to grow crops. It is only a few meters deep. Million of bacteria, insects and worms live in it. Top soils develop very slowly. It may take years to form top soil suitable for plants, but it can be washed away in a few years if proper precautions are not taken. Sub soils consist of the parent material from which soil is formed. It also contains plant food and moisture but it is not a s productive as top soil. It has to be converted

into soil and it may take years to convert sub soil into soil. Below the sub soil generally there is solid rock.

- FORMATION OF SOIL: The natural processes involved in the formation of soil are
  - (i) Weathering: process of disintegration of rocks into soil.
  - (ii) Deposition: process of progressive lying down of rock particles carried by rivers, ice, marine, currents wind or tides.
  - (iii) Biochemical processes

    Soil formation depends upon the following factors;

    *Nature of the parent rock, * Climate, * Natural Vegetation, * Topography, * Time
- GENERAL CHARACTERISTICS OF DIFFERENT SOILS
  - a) Sandy Soil (light soil): It contains more than 60% sand and les than 10% clay. It is easy to cultivate and is favoured for fruits and vegetables.
  - b) Clayey Soil: It has high proportion of clay. It becomes sticky when mixed with water. A soil very rich in clay is called 'heavy',
  - c) Loam: is rich soil and consist of a mixture of sand and clay. All loamy soils are good for farming and general gardening.
- MAJOR SOIL TYPES: The Indian Council of Agricultural Research (ICAR) classifies the soils of India into eight categories.
- ALLUVIAL SOIL: This is the most important and widespread group of soils. It covers about 15 lakh sq.km of the land area in Great Plains from Punjab to Assam and also in the valleys of the Narmada and Tapi, Mahanadi, Godavari, Krishna and Cauvery. These soils have been brought down and deposited by three great Himalayan rivers Sutlej, Ganga and Brahmaputra. These soils consist of varying

proportions of san, silt and clay. Khadar is the newer alluvium which is sandy, light coloured and occurs near river beds where deposition takes place regularly and bhangar or older alluvium. Alluvial soils as a whole are very fertile and therefore the best agricultural soils of the country. The regions of these of these soils constitute the' wheat and rice bowls' of India.

- BLACK SOIL: As the name indicates these soils are black in Colour and since they are ideal for growing cotton, they are also called cotton soil. These soils, covering an area of 5.46 lakh sq.km, are most typical of the Deccan trap (Basalt). The black Colour of regur is variously attributed to the presence of titaniferrous magnetite, compounds of iron and aluminum-Unsuitable for heavy irrigation. Ideally suited to dry farming. Suitable for cotton, cereals, oilseeds like linseed, castor and safflower, many kinds of vegetables and citrus fruits.
- RED SOIL: These soil occupy about 5-18 lakh sq.km over the peninsula reaching up to Rajmahal Hills in the east, Jhansi in the north and Kutch in the West. In North western peninsula is covered by the black soils and the remaining south-eastern half is covered by red soils- Entire black soil in the eastern part of Peninsula comprising of Chhotanagpur plateau, Orissa, east Madhya Pradesh, Telengana, the Niligris, Tamilnadu plateau and Karnataka. The soil have reddish colour due to iron compounds. It is suitable for rice, ragi, tobacco and vegetables.
- LATERITE SOILS: These soils occupying an area of 1.26 lakh sq.km- Found capping the flat uplands, and are spread in western coastal region receiving very heavy rainfall – Poor in nitrogen, phosphoric acid, potash, lime – suitable for rice, ragi, tapioca and cashewnuts.
- FOREST AND MOUNTAIN SOIL: These soils occupy about 2.85 lakh sq.km in the hilly regions of the country– described as soils in the making – found in the Himalayas

and the other ranges in the north and high hill summits in the Sahyadris, Eastern Ghats and Peninsula – poor in potash, phosphorous – Temperate fruits, maize, wheat and barley are grown in Jammu and Kashmir and Himachal Pradesh where soils are mostly podzols which are acidic in re-action.

- ARID AND DESERT SOILS: Northwestern parts of the country and occupy about 1.42 sq. km area in Rajasthan, south Haryana, north Punjab and Rann of Kutch. Thar Desert alone occupies an area of 1.06 sq. km. It contains high percentage of soluble salts and a low to very low organic matter.
- SALINE AND ALKALINE SOILS: These soils occupy about 170 lakh sq. km of arid and semi-arid areas of Rajasthan, Punjab, Haryana, Uttar Pradesh, Bihar and whole of Maharastra. Textually they are sandy to loamy sand. Saline soils contain free sodium. Crops grown on these soils include rice, wheat, cotton, sugarcane and tobacco.
- PEATY AND MARSHY SOILS: These soils cover an area of about 150 sq. km in the Kottayam and Allepey districts of Kerala. They are suitable for paddy cultivation.
- SOIL FERTILITY: The factor responsible for deficiency of Indian soils are: (i) loss of nutrients, largely brought about through the removal of harvested crops, (ii) leaching which occurs under heavy monsoonal rains, causes loss of nutrients, sandy soils are more subject to leaching than the heavier ones and bare soils are more than those covered by plants. Indian soils are mainly deficient in nitrogen, phosphorus and potash. These can be supplied to the soils by application of organic manures and fertilizers.
- SOIL EROSION: Soil erosion is the removal of soil particles by natural agencies such as water and wind and also as a result of human and animal interference.
- TYPES OF SOIL EROSION: Two types of soil erosion:

  (i) Water Erosion: The important types of this erosion are sheet, rill and gully. In sheet erosion thin layer of soil is removed by the water during heavy rains. If the erosion continues unchecked, numerous finger-shaped grooves may develop all over the area as a result of the silt-landen run-off. This is called rill erosion. The rills may deepen and enlarge into gullies.

(ii) Wind Erosion: Wind erosion is mainly confined to arid and semi-arid areas devoid of vegetation. Wind, particularly during sand-storms, lifts and carries away soil particles leaving behind a depression devoid of top fertile soil. Rajasthan and the adjoining areas of Haryana, Uttar Pradesh and Gujarat show this type of soil erosion.

- CONSEQUENCES OF SOIL EROSION: (i) heavy floods in rivers, (ii) lowering down of sub soil water level, (iii) reduction of soil fertility, (iv) silting of streams and water courses, (v) disappearance and downfall of civilizations.
- a) SOIL CONVERSATION: Soil conservation is an effort made by man to prevent soil erosion to retain the fertility of soil. It may not be possible to stop soil erosion entirely. b) Measures for Soil Conservation: (i) Planting cover crops, (ii) Adoption of correct farming techniques, (iii) Terracing the practice of cutting steps in hillside, to create level land for cultivation, (iv) Construction of check dams, (v) Creation of wind break, (vi) Controlling of grazing of pastures, (vii) Suspending cultivation for one season and more so as to help the soil recover its fertility.

THE EARTH'S CRUST

The earth is made up of several concentric layers. The outer layer of the earth's crust is called lithosphere, which comprises two distinct parts. The upper parts consist of granitic rocks and form the continents.

Its main mineral constituents are silica and alumina knows as Sial. It has an average density of 2.7. The lower part is a continuous zone of densers, basaltic rocks forming the ocean's floors. Comprising mainly silica, iron and magnesium known as Sima and has an average density of 3.0. The Sial and the Sima together form the earth's crust which varies in thickness 4.8 to 6.4 km, beneath the oceans and about 48 km under some o continents. Beneath the lithosphere is the mantle known as the mesosphere about 2880 kms thick. Composed mainly very dense rock rich in Olivine.

The interior layer is the core known as baryshpere about 2456 km in radius is made up mainly iron (Fe) and nickel (ni) known as nife. The temperature of core is as high as 2000 C and subject to extremely high pressure. The crust forms only 0.5% of the volume of the earth, 83% consist of the mantle and 16% makes the core that of the earth.

The mean radius of the earth is 6400 km. the average rate of increase temp 1 C for every 32 meters of descent. But in upper 100 kms, the increase is estimated at 12 C/kms. It is 2 C/Km in next 300 kms and 1 C/kms below it.

Name of the layer	Chemical Composition	Volume (Earth)	Mars (Earth)	Density	Physical Properties
CRUST (A) (i) Outer-part of lithosphere (ii) Inner part of Lithosphere	Sial	1% of the earth	10%	2.75 to 2.90	Solid
MANTLE (B) (i) Outer part of mantle (ii) Inner part of mantel	Silica with Sima Wholly Sima	83%	68%	3.10 to 4.75 4.75 to 5.00	Partly molten Close to melting point
CORE (C) (i) Outer part of Core (ii) Inner part of Core	NiFe	16%	32%	5.1 to 13	Plastic state Solid and rigid because of tremendous overlying pressure.

Composition of Earth's Crust

1) oxygen: 46.6% 2) Silicon- 27.27% 3) Aluminium: 8.13% 4) Iron- 5% 5) Calcium-3.63% 6) Sodium- 2.83% 7)Pottasium- 2.59% 8) Magnesium- 2.09% 9)Others- 1,41%

CLASSIFICATION OF ROCKS ACCORDING TO ORIGIN

IGNEOUS ROCKS: Igneous rocks are formed by the cooling and solidification of molten rock (magna) from beneath the earth's crust. They one normally crystalline in structure. They do not occur in layers and not contain fossils. Some rocks can form a high percentage of silica are said to be acid. E.g., Granite. Other rocks such as Basalt contain a high percentage of iron or Aluminium or magnesium oxides are called basic rocks. There are two main groups:

- Volcanic Rocks: These are mole nocks poured out of volcanoes as lavas. They solidify rapidly on the earth's surface and the crystals are small. E.g. basalt.
- Plutonic Rocks: These are igneous rocks solidified deep in the earth's crust and they reach the surface only by being exposed by erosion. E.g., granite, diorite and gabbros etc.,

SEDIMENTARY ROCKS: Sedimentary rocks are formed from sediment accumulated over long periods, usually under water and deposited usually in layers by water, wind or moving ice. They are non-crystalline and often contain fossils of animals, plants and other micro-organisms. There are three main groups;

- Mechanically-formed: (a) Wind-deposited e.g loess, (b) River-deposited e.g., clays, gravels, and alluviums, (c) Glaciers-deposited e.g., morains, sands and gravels and boulder clay, (d) Sea-deposited.
- Organically formed: (a) From animals e.g., chalk and coral, (b) From plants e.g., Peat, lignite, coal.
- Chemically formed: e.g., rock slat, borax, gypsum, nitrates, potash and certain limestone.

METAMORPHIC ROCKS: All those rocks whose structure and appearance have been changed by great heat or great pressure or both. Any rock can be changed into a metamorphic rock. In theses manner (a) State (from clay), (b) Marble (from limestone), (c) Quartzite (from sandstone), (d) Graphite (from coal), (e) Gneiss (from granite), (f) Schist (from shale).

STRUCTURE OF ATMOSPHERE

According to Petterssen, the atmosphere is divided into the following five layers:

TROPOSPHERE: The lowermost layer of the atmosphere is known as Troposphere and is the most important layer because almost all of the weather phenomena is occurred in this layer. E.g., Fog, cloud. Thunder, lightning, etc., occurs in this layer. It extends roughly to a height of eight kilometers near the poles and about 18 kilometers at the Equator. The thickness of the troposphere at the equator is the greater heights by strong conventional currents. Temperature decreases with increasing height at the rate of 6.5 C per 1000m. This rate of decrease of temperature is called normal lapse rate. This layer contains dust particles and over 90% of the earth's water vapour. The upper limit of the tropopause is called troposphere which is about 1.5km. Thick. Temperature ceases to fall with the air temperature at the troposphere is about-80 C over the equator and about -45 covers the poles. The word troposphere literally means zone or region of mixing whereas the word tropopause means where the mixing stops.

STRATOSPHERE: The Stratosphere begins at the tropopause which forms its lower boundary. The lower stratosphere is isothermal in character, i.e, the temperature in the lower part of this layer does not change with altitude.

The stratosphere extends up to a height of 50 km. Afterwards it gradually increases up to a height of 50 km because of the presence of ozone layer which absorbs the Sun's Ultra-Violet Rays. Clouds are almost absent and there is very little dust or water

Vapours. The air movement is almost horizontal. The upper boundary of the stratosphere is called Statopause. Above this level there is a steep rise in temperature.

MESOSPHERE: Over the stratopause there exists the third layer known as mesosphere. It extends up to a height of 80 kms. Temperature decreases with height again and reaches up to – 100 C at the height of 80 kms.

IONOSPHERE: Ionosphere is located between 80 km to 400 kms. It is electrically charged layer. Radio waves transmitted from the earth are reflected back to the earth by this layer. Temperature again starts increasing with height because of radiation from the sun. The ionosphere consists of the following ionized layers:

D – Layer: 60 -99 km

E – Layer: 90 – 130 km

Sporadic Layer: 110 km

E2 Layer: 150 km

F1 Layer, F2 Layer: 130 -1890 km

G Layer: 400 km and above.

EXOSPHERE: The outermost layer of the earth's atmosphere is known as the exosphere which lies between 400 and 1000kms. The atmosphere in this region is so rarefied that it resembles a nebula-hydrogen and helium gases predominates in this outermost region. The temperature becomes 5568 C at its outer limit but this temperature is entirely different from the air temperature of the earth's surface.

LATITUDE, LONGITUDE AND TIME

The earth is nearly a sphere and it has no edges. It presents some difficulties in positioning its surface features. To over come this problem, a network of imaginary lines is drawn on a globe or a map to help us locate places. The spinning of the earth on its axis provides – the North Pole and South Pole. They form the basis for the geographical grid. The grid consists of two sets of lines –

horizontal and vertical. The horizontal lines, running eat-west, are circular and parallel to each other.

The line drawn midway between the North Pole and the South Pole is called the equator. It is the largest circle and hence, is called a great circle. All other parallels get smaller in size in proportion to their distances form the equator towards the Poles. These imaginary lines running east-west are commonly known as parallels of latitude. The vertical lines, running north-south are halves of the great circle and join the two Poles.

They are called meridians of longitude. The latitudes and longitudes are commonly referred to as coordinates because they provide systematic network of lines upon which position of various surface features of the earth can be represented.

LATITUDES: The latitude of a place on the earth's surface its distance north to south of the equator measured along the meridian of that places as an angle from the centre of the earth. Lines joining places with the same latitudes are called parallels. The value of equator is 0 and the latitude of the poles are 90 N and 90 S.

If the parallels of latitude are drawn at an interval of one degree, ther will be 90 parallels in the northern and southern hemisphere each. The total number of parallels thus drawn including the equator, the letter N or S is written along with the value of latitude. If the earth were a perfect sphere – 23 ½ N –Tropic Cancer, 23 ½ S – Tropic of Capricorn, 60 ½ N – Artic, 60 ½ S – Antarctic, 1 of latitude (a one- degree arc of a meridian) would be a constant value i.e., 111 km – a degree of latitude changes slightly in length from the equator it is 110.6 km, at the poles it is 111.7 km. Latitude of a place may be determined with the help of the altitude of the sun or the Polar Star.

LONGITUDE: Unlike the parallels of latitude, which are full circles, the meridians of longitude are semi-circles touching the poles. Meridians intersect the equator at right angles. The meridian of longitude passing through the Greenwich observatory (near

London) has been adopted as the Prime Meridian by an international agreement and has been given the value of 0 degree. The numerical value of a longitude varies form 0 degree to 180 degree East or West– be 360 degree meridians.

LONGITUDE AND TIME: While rotating on its axis, the earth completes one circle (360 degree) in approximately 24 hours time. In other words, it move 15 degree longitudes per hour. As such the sun appears to be traversing 15 degree of longitude from east to west every hour or 1 degree of longitude in every 4 minutes. Thus, when it is 12 noon at Greenwich (Prime meridian), the time at 30 degree east of Greenwich will be 30*4= 120 minutes or 2 hours ahead of Greenwich time. In order to maintain uniformity of time as far as possible within the territorial limits of a country us taken as the standard meridian and its local time is taken as the standard time for the whole country. The standard meridian is selected in a manner that it is divisible by 15 degree or 7 degree 30' so that the difference between its standard time and the Greenwich Mean Time may be expressed as multiples of an hour or half an hour. The Standard meridian of India is 82degree30' E and the standard time is 5 ½ hours a head of Greenwich Mean Time.

7

GEOGRAPHICAL POSITIONS

The great continent of Asia divides in the south into three vast peninsulas; Arabia on the west, Indo-China on the east, and the southern half of India in the centre. India proper includes the whole of the central peninsula, and stretches northwards to the mountain ranges which separate it from Central Asia. The northern half is often called Continental India, to distinguish it from Peninsular India, the southern half. The Tropic of Cancer is, speaking roughly, the dividing line between these two. From this line Peninsular India stretches southwards for more than 15°, or over 1,000 miles; while Continental India extends almost as far to the north.

The natural boundaries of India are exceedingly well defined. The peninsula is separated from Arabia by the Arabian Sea, and from Indo-China by the Bay of Bengal. These two arms of the Indian Ocean give the peninsula a coast line of nearly 3,000 miles. In the north the Himalayas form an almost impassable barrier for 1,500 miles. On the north-west for 800 miles, and on the north-east for 400 miles are regions of more broken mountainous country stretching in ever diminishing altitudes from the extremities of the Himalayan wall to the sea. These give north-west and north-east frontiers, both of which are fairly well defined. As frontiers they are imperfect only in comparison with the mighty mountainous ramparts which protect the north. No other country, of equal extent, not being an island, is so completely isolated as India, or forms so true a geographical unity. This fact, more than any other single cause, has moulded its destiny and guided the development of its people.

In strict geographical usage the name INDIA should be applied only to this well-defined geographical whole. In common use, however, a wider sense is often given to it, making it synonymous with The Indian Empire.

The Empire of India extends beyond the natural boundaries of India proper, both on the east and the west. On the east it takes in Burma and on the west Baluchistan, both of which are frequently spoken of as provinces of India. This is convenient when political matters are under consideration. But it should not be forgotten that it is only politically that cither of these provinces belongs to India. In almost all the aspects with which non-political geography is concerned, both the Indo-Chinese peninsula and Baluchistan are widely different from India proper.

On the other hand the island of Ceylon, though politically separated from India, geographically belongs to it, being a part of the great land-mass which forms the Indian peninsula. Ceylon is a " continental island," standing on the " continental shelf." At one time the shallow strait which now separates Ceylon from the mainland did not exist; and a very slight elevation of the bed of the strait would make it a part of south India again. In all their physical conditions Ceylon and the southern part of the peninsula arc one, though the name India is never used to include the Island Colony.

SURROUNDING SEAS

The Indian Seas

The Indian peninsula is washed on the cast by the Bay of Bengal, and on the west by the Arabian Sea. If the level of these seas were reduced by but a few feet, Ceylon would be united with the mainland by a narrow isthmus. If it were reduced by 600 feet (or 100 fathoms) this isthmus would be 130 miles wide. The " hundred fathom line " is commonly taken as the boundary of the " continental shelf." The depth of the water increases slowly up to this point, and then the ocean bed drops rapidly to a depth of 1,000 fathoms or more. A glance at the map will show this. Around the peninsula of India the hundred-fathom line varies in distance from the coast from about 50 miles off Madras to 300 miles off the Gulf of Cambay. Where the coast is rocky the ocean bed often drops to a great depth with exceeding rapidity. This is the case to the east of Ceylon, where a depth of over 1,000 fathoms is reached within 25 miles of the shore.

If the level of the surrounding seas were reduced by about 100 fathoms the general contour of India would not be greatly changed. Ceylon would, as we have seen, be united with the mainland, and the whole of the peninsula would be considerably increased in width, particularly in the north. The Gulfs of Cambay and Cutch would disappear. Bombay would be 250 miles from the sea, and Karachi 80 miles; while Orissa and Chittagong would be united by land, except for one curious arm of greater depth, stretching in a north-easterly direction towards the mouth of the Ganges, which would still be claimed by the sea. But on the whole the general shape of peninsular India would be but little changed.

Far greater would be the changes wrought in the eastern and western peninsulas of southern Asia. In the west, the shallow Persian Gulf would be drained, and Arabia would no longer be a peninsula. In the east, Indo-China would stretch 1,000 miles south of Annam, and would take in the great islands of Sumatra, Java, Borneo, and the Celebes, which are all continental islands. The Andaman and Nicobar groups of islands would then each form one long and narrow island, and the two together would enclose between themselves and the mainland a deep and almost land-locked sea.

If the level of the sea were reduced by 1,000 instead of 100 fathoms, the further changes in the contour of the land would be trifling, for from 100 to 1,000 fathoms the depth increases everywhere with great rapidity. The hundred-fathom line, or the edge of the continental shelf, is thus the true continental boundary. It indicates, far more accurately than the coast line, the actual contour of the great land-mass that forms the continent.

The Natural Divisions of India

Sir William Hunter remarks that if we could view the whole of India from a balloon, we should see that it is divided into " three separate and well-defined tracts." In the north and north-west is the region of mountains, the vast Himalayan range with their allied systems. Immediately to the south is the almost equally vast region of plains, the soil of which has been deposited by the great rivers that drain the mountains. To the south again is the region of plateaux, which includes almost the whole of peninsular India. The plateaux are bounded by ranges of hills, broken along the north and east but more continuous on the west; and between the hills and the sea there is everywhere a narrow strip of alluvial land formed, like the great plains of the north, by the rivers that drain the higher land. To these three well-defined regions of India proper, we must now, if we speak of the Empire of India, add a fourth, viz., Burma—a region of alternate mountain ranges and valleys, with the great delta of the Irrawaddy towards the south.

The Himalayan Region

India, we are often told, is " bounded on the north by the Himalayas." But this great mountain chain is much more than a mere boundary. The vast system of highlands of which the Himalayas form the southern wall, is of such immense importance to India that it claims the most careful attention, and forms the natural starting point for any study of Indian Geography. From the Pamir Plateau which lies to the northwest of Kashmir, and from its great height is appropriately called in the native language, " the roof of the world," the Hindu Kush range runs in a south-westerly direction into Afghanistan. From the same centre, but running in an east-south-easterly direction, are the Muztagh or Karakorum Mountains, a range of great and sustained height. To the south of this range, and running at first almost parallel with it, is the western portion of the Himalayas proper.

The river Indus, rising in Tibet, flows in a north-westerly direction between the Karakorum and Himalaya ranges, breaking through the Ladakh Range on its course, and then, bending sharply to the south-west, divides the western extremity of the Himalayas from the spurs of the Hindu Kush. From this point the Himalayas, there called the Zaskar range, run first in a south-easterly direction, and then gradually bend round to the cast. The Brahmaputra rises near the Indus, north of the main range, and after flowing in an easterly direction for over 800 miles, rounds the eastern extremity of the Himalayas just as the Indus rounds the western. The entire range is thus held "within the gigantic arms" of these two mighty rivers. The length of the range is about 1,500 miles, and its width from 150 to 200 miles. In parts it is flanked on its southern side by low and detached parallel ranges of hills, wholly different in geological structure and history. But in most places the main range rises from the plains with considerable abruptness. Throughout its entire length one continuous range can be traced which contains most of the loftiest peaks, more than twenty of which exceed 24,000 feet in height.

The most westerly peak in the Himalayas proper is Nanga Parbat, which lies just within the angle of the Indus and rises to a height of 26,020 feet. About 150 miles to the north-east, and at the other side of the river. Mount Godwin-Austen (28,258) second, only to Mt. Everest, dominates a magnificent group of peaks in the Karakorum Range. Nanda Devi (25,661) is in Kumaon, south of the watershed that separates the Indus and the Tsan-pu. To the west are Dhaulagiri (26,826), Gosai Than (26,300), Everest, or Gaurisankar, the highest mountain in the world (29,140), Kinchinjunga (28,176),and Chamalhari (23,929). In many respects Kinchinjunga is the most notable of these great mountains. It has no rival near it, so that its mighty proportions are well seen. From Darjeeling the view is particularly fine, and is admitted by most travellers to surpass in sublimity and grandeur anything to be seen elsewhere.

The passes across the Himalayas are numerous, but of comparatively little account. Some are over 18,000 feet in height. Tlic Bara Lacha and Parang-la passes cross into Kashmir from the north-west corner of the Punjab. From Kashmir one of the best roads to Uiasa is via the Pangong Lake. Most of the trade between Northern India and Tibet has for centuries been by these routes. In the north of Kashmir the Karakorum and Muztagh passes, which cross the Karakorums respectively east and west of Mount Godwin-Austen, have been the chief routes of the trade with Central Asia. The Niti pass is north of anda Devi, near the source of the Ganges, and leads from Garhwal into Tibet. The No-la pass crosses the mountains in the north of Nepal, and the Jailep-la pass is south of Chamalhari, and east of Sikkim.

The Himalayas are, however, only the southern wall of a great mountain system which should be studied as a whole. Branching from the northern side of the Karakorum Range are the Kwen Lun Mountains which run at first due east, then bend slightly to the north, and further east to the south again. These form the northern boundary of the Plateau of Tibet. Between them and the Himalayas the elevation nowhere falls below 12,000 feet, and the average is probably over 15,000. The length of the Plateau from east to west is 1,600 miles, and its width from north to south varies from 200 to 600 miles. Its area is nearly half a million square miles. There is no other mountain-mass in the whole world at all to compare with. It is difficult to give any adequate idea of its size. The Alps of Central Europe do not cover one-thirtieth of its area, and are greatly inferior in average height. Its importance to India can hardly be over-estimated. It forms a northern rampart which no enemy has ever scaled, and with its great southern buttress, the Himalayas, exerts an influence upon the climate and rainfall of India which has done much to determine the character of the country and the development of its people.

The main chain of the Himalayas, though of much greater average height than any other continuous chain traversing the plateau, does not constitute the water- parting between India and Tibet, which is from 100 to 200 miles to the north of it. A second wall of the Himalayas has often therefore been assumed to run north of the trough of the Indus and Tsan-pu. Dr. Sven Hedin, the Swedish traveller, claims to have traced, during his travels in Tibet in 1907-8, a continuous chain running east and west at a distance varying from 130 to 300 miles north of the Himalayas and forming the true watershed. This range he names the Trans Himalaya. It is not, however, a part of the Himalayan system, but a more ancient range, and though it forms the watershed it does not rival the Himalayas. Geological evidence shows that the general lines of drainage as they exist to-day were established long before the upheaval of the main Himalayan range, and that the process of upheaval was slow enough for the rivers to maintain their ancient channels by their own erosive power. This is seen most clearly in Nepal, where the drainage is not to the Tsan-pu in the north, but southward through deep gorges in the vast Himalayan chain, gorges which the streams themselves have cut.

Geological evidence also shows that the eastern Himalayas are far more ancient than the western, but the entire range is young in comparison with the Aravallis or the Eastern Ghats, both of which are of great geological antiquity. There was, doubtless, a time in very remote geological ages when what now forms the Indian peninsula was joined to South Africa by a broad stretch of land, of which we still have remnants in the Maldives, the Laccadives, the Seychelles, and Madagascar. In those early days the Eastern Ghats constituted the eastern boundary of the land, while the Aravallis bounded it on the west. Long ages of erosion have worn these two ranges down till they are now, probably, but a shadow of what they once were. At that time the Aravalli peaks looked out over a vast north-western sea, which appears to have been entirely cut off from the southern ocean. The rocks which now compose the mountain systems west and north of the Indus, as well as most of the great Tibetan Plateau, were then being slowly formed at the bed of the sea. There is also abundant evidence that in subsequent ages they were repeatedly thrust upwards and again submerged, existing alternately as dry land and sea bed, until the final upheaval began which slowly raised them to their present altitudes.

The Eastern Ghats were apparently also at one period connected by an unbroken chain of hills with the eastern Himalayas, a connection which continued till a comparatively recent geological age. The whole southern drainage of the Himalayas consequently, being cut off from the eastern seas, found its way across the continent and reached the sea by the Indus valley. The gradual subsidence of a vast tract, including probably the whole of Bengal as well as a long stretch to the west, established an easterly drainage and diverted the Himalayan rivers to the Bay of Bengal. But that the main drainage of the Himalayas has from the very earliest ages been towards the south is clearly shown by the character of the beds that form the Siwaliks and other parts of the sub-Himalayan range of hills. These are all composed of fresh water deposits, which were laid down by the age-long action of rivers that drained the adjacent mountains, and then thrust upwards by much later earth-movements.

Mountains of the North-West

Just as on the north the Himalayas separate India from the Plateau of Tibet, so on the north-west lower and more irregular ranges separate it from the great Plateau of Iran, which includes almost the whole of Afghanistan, Baluchistan, and Persia. The Iranian Plateau is of much inferior altitude to the Tibetan, varying from 3,000 to 5,000 feet above sea level.

It is also more broken by mountains, and in the centre contains a large oval depression, the inland basin of the Helmandi a desert tract with an average elevation of about 1,500 feet. The ranges that divide 'the plateau from India run almost parallel to the river Indus, and from 50 to 150 miles west of it. They are broken and irregular, fairly high in the north, but decreasing in altitude as they approach the sea.

From the Pamir Plateau the Hindu Kush, a flatbacked ridge of great elevation runs in a south-westerly direction, forming the watershed between the systems of the Indus and the Oxus. Branching from the Hindu Kush the short but lofty Safed Koh range runs in an easterly direction south of the Kabul river. From this range rugged and broken extensions stretch south as far as the river Gomal. South of the Gomal are the Sulaiman Mountains running north and south, of lower elevation, but culminating in the north in the lofty peak of Takht-i-

Sulaiman, over 11,000 feet high. Towards the south the folds of the Sulaimans open out, and, in steadily decreasing altitudes, bend round to the west. Further to the south again, and further west, are a number of still lower ranges, running in almost parallel ridges at first in a southerly direction, and then, like the Sulaimans, bending gradually round to the west. The most easterly of these, the Khirthar range, maintains its southern direction almost to the sea.

These various mountain ranges form the natural north-west frontier of India proper. The frontier line, as in the old Sikh days, is the extreme limit of cultivation on the eastern slopes. Theoretically this is still the boundary of British India. But partly for the sake of frontier defence, and partly to bring under effective control the turbulent mountain tribes that were a constant menace to the frontier provinces and trans-frontier trade, British influence has been steadily pushed beyond the frontier. The North Western Frontier Province lies chiefly, and Baluchistan wholly beyond it. But even the latter is now practically within the boundaries of the Empire.

Across this frontier, which extends for nearly 850 miles, numerous passes over the mountains provide gateways between India on the east and Afghanistan and Baluchistan on the west. The passes across the Himalayas into Tibet are of comparatively little moment, being only the laborious routes of a small and uncertain trade. Very different is it with the passes across the North West Frontier. Every invading host that has ever penetrated into India by land has forced its way through one or other of these northwestern passes. Through one or other of them also each of the successive swarms of immigrants who have helped to people India have found their way into the northern plains. As trade routes the north-western passes are greatly more valuable than those of the Himalayas; but their chief importance lies in the fact that most of them are possible military roads (or might easily be made such) through which an invading foe might again force his way. The safety of India on the north-west is only secured by the strength with which the passes are held. Until comparatively recent years almost all the passes that were regarded as of primary importance were situated to the south of the Kabul river. But now those which give communication between India and Central Asia via Chitral are receiving almost greater attention than any others. These are the Malakand Pass in the east of Chitral, and the Barogil and Dorah passes over the Hindu Kush. The present importance of these passes is due to the fact that they are within loo miles of the nearest Russian outpost. To the south of the Kabul River the most important of the passes are the Khyber, the Kuram, the Tochi, the Gomal, and the Bolan.

The Khyber Pass is over the eastern spurs of the Safed Koh, twenty-five miles west of Peshawar, on the road which leads from Peshawar to Kabul. This is by far the most important line of communication between India and Afghanistan. It is an important trade route and a still more important military highway. A portion of the Khyber route west of the pass is along the valley of the Kabul, but the pass itself is considerably south of the river, as in the eastern part of its course the Kabul river flows through impassable gorges. The Kuram Pass is on another route to Kabul by the valley of the Kuram river.

The pass itself crosses the western spurs of the Safed Koh at a height of nearly 12,000 feet. The Tochi Pass is on the road from Bannu to Ghazni, once the capital of Afghanistan. The road follows the valley of the Tochi, a tributary of the Kuram, and then crosses the mountains south-east of Ghazni at a height of 11,500 feet. The Gomal Pass is 30 miles north of Takht-i-Sulaiman on the road passing up the valley of the Gomal to the plateau of Afghanistan. The Gomal marks the boundary between Afghanistan and Baluchistan. The Gomal Pass is the oldest of all the passes, and has for many centuries been the route by which the caravan trade from Persia through the valley of the Helmand has reached India. The Bolan Pass, which lies to the west of the southern Sulaimans, is now traversed by a railway which connects Quetta with India, and runs beyond Quetta to the frontier of Afghanistan.

The North-Eastern Frontier and the Mountains of Burma

The eastern extremity of the great Himalayan wall is, like the western, flanked by a series of lower chains running for the most part in a southerly or south-westerly direction. To the north-east of the bend of the Bramaputra these ridges are arranged in almost concentric arcs curving round to the south, and the inner one to the southwest. Geologically they are of much later formation than the Himalayas, and their upheaval diverted the Brahmaputra from its original course to the east and turned its enriching flood into Assam and Bengal. These ranges form an effective boundary to Eastern Bengal and Assam, and constitute the natural north-eastern frontier of India proper. This frontier is, however, of little importance compared to the north-western. In the past there has been considerable Mongolian immigration into India across the mountain barriers, but India has been peopled almost exclusively from the west. And though the Burmese have occasionally raided parts of Assam, no great conquering host has ever penetrated into India on this side. Now that Burma is a Province of the Empire, the geographical frontier is no longer of imperial, but only of provincial, moment. But it nevertheless separates two parts of the Empire that are widely and essentially different.

Three main chains can be traced, which start from the bend of the Brahmaputra and continue their coarse far to the south. The chain nearest to the river bends sharply to the south-west and under the name Patkai Hills shuts in the Brahmaputra valley on the south. The Naga and Lushai Hills continue the chain, bending gradually to the south again. From the Nagas, but separated from them by a narrow valley, the Khasi Hills stretch in a westerly direction into Bengal. South of the Lushais the main range takes a south-south-easterly course, and is then known as the Arakan Yoma. It becomes narrower and lower as it passes south and bends slightly to the west again. At Cape Negrais it dips into the sea, and continues as a well-defined submerged range for over 500 miles, cropping up at the Coco, Andaman, and Nicobar Islands, and finally emerging as the island of Sumatra. The second main chain runs south from the northern highlands, marking the watershed between the Irrawaddy and the Salwin. East of Bhamo it spreads out into a broad belt of highlands, known as the Kachin Hills in the north and the Karenni Hills in the south. Further south it narrows into the Poung-loung range which divides the Sittang basin from that of the Salwin. Between these two main ranges in the south is a short and low range, known as the Pegu Yoma, It divides the basins of the Irrawaddy and the Sittang, but is nowhere over 2,000 feet in height. The third main range, the Tanen- Taung - Gyi Mountains, bounds the Salwin basin on the east. It maintains a lofty elevation further south than either of the other ranges, and, as the Tenasserim Yoma, runs down the narrow arm of the peninsula, as far as Cape Victoria. These three Yomas, or ridges, give a configuration to Lower Burma totally different from anything to be found in India. They are all fairly regular and continuous, decreasing in elevation towards the south. They divide the country into narrow valleys along which the rivers take almost parallel courses to the sea.

The Indo-Gangetic Plain

Immediately south of the great mountain wall, the general curves of which it closely follows, lies the great plain of the Indus and the Ganges. The drop from the high ranges to the plain is made with comparative abruptness, and then the plain extends southwards, with a width varying from 100 to 300 miles, till it meets the broken highlands that form the northern boundary of the Deccan. The plain is entirely alluvial, being formed of the silt brought down by the great rivers which traverse it. The thickness of the alluvial deposit does not appear to be anywhere less than 600 feet, and in the delta of the Ganges there is reason to believe that it is three times this thickness. Geologically the plain is older than the Himalayas. There are also many indications that the plain has been subjected to steady depression, acting slowly through long ages. Geologists believe that the great forces that upheaved the Himalayas also reduced the level of the plain, and that the two processes went on together, both being parts of the same great earth-movement. The eastern part of the plain was in later ages subjected to a further depression. Originally the entire plain sloped towards the west, and the whole drainage was, as we have seen, into the Arabian Sea. The later subsidence of the eastern part of the plain changed the course of the rivers, and for ages the entire drainage from the Jumna eastwards has been to the Bay of Bengal.

The area of the plain is about 300,000 square miles. It includes almost the whole of the basins of the Indus and Ganges, and thus stretches without a break from the Arabian Sea to the Bay of Bengal. The watershed between these two basins is slightly to the west of the city of Delhi, where the plain reaches its greatest height, 924 feet above sea-level. From that point to the mouth of the Indus is 850 miles, and to the mouth of the Ganges 1,050 miles. The slope towards the sea is thus extremely gentle on both sides, and the rivers consequently flow slowly, depositing their silt as they go. The northern and eastern portion of this great plain is the most fertile and populous part of India. The rainfall, especially towards the east, is ample, and the river deposits greatly enrich the soil. In the east of the plain the Brahmaputra mingles its waters with those of the Ganges, and it has been estimated that the two rivers bring down annually more than 40,000 million cubic feet of solid matter to enlarge and enrich their common delta. In the west a large part of the plain—that lying south-east of the Indus and at a little distance from the river—is comparatively barren. The soil is sandy and the rainfall scanty. From 50 to 80 miles east of the Indus the waters of the river are made available, either by irrigation works or by the annual overflow, but beyond that the land is desert.

Peninsular India

South of the Indo-Gangetic Plain a belt of highlands, fairly well defined in the west, but broken and irregular in the east, runs right across India, separating the northern plains from the plateaux of the Deccan. This belt of hills runs, roughly speaking, along the Tropic of Cancer, so that the whole of central and southern India lies within the Tropics. Starting from the west we have first of all the Vindhya Range running almost due east from the Gulf of Cambay. The Vindhyas are the lowest of the ranges that form this belt of highlands, and exceed 2,000 feet in height only in one or two places. They are separated from the Satpura Range to the south by the narrow and beautiful valley of the Narbada. North of the western extremity of the Vindhyas, but separated from them by the valley of the Mahi, are the southern spurs of the Aravallis, a low and broken range, which stretch in a north-easterly direction into the northern plain. The highest point in the

Aravallis is Mount Abu in the south-west, which attains a height of 3,900 feet. The Aravallis are, as we have seen, by far the most ancient of all the mountains in the west of India. What we see now is but the remnant of a mighty range that has survived the ravages of countless ages. The Satpuras are a shorter range than the Vindhyas, but of considerably greater height. They form the northeastern boundary of the Deccan proper. East of the Satpuras and Vindhyas, the Mahadeo Hills, the Maikal Range, and the hills of Chota Nagpur, continue the belt of highlands right across the peninsula to the plains of Bengal.

South of this belt lies the great Plateau of the Deccan, which constitutes the central core of the peninsula. Except where broken in the east by the great rivers which flow into the Bay of Bengal, this plateau maintains an elevation of from 1,500 to over 3,000 feet. It is highest in the south and west, and slopes very gradually to the north and east.

The Plateau is bounded on the west by the Western Ghats, or Sahyadri Mountains. The northern extremity of this range is separated from the Satpuras by the valley of the Tapti. From this point the Western Ghats run southwards nearly parallel to the coast, and at no great distance from it, almost to the southern point of the peninsula.

The range is fairly continuous, but there are four important breaks. Two of these are near Bombay, another near Goa, and the fourth is the Palghat Gap, 200 miles further south, where the elevation drops swiftly from over 6,000 ft. to little more than 1,000 ft. Through all these openings in the hills railways now pass, connecting the west coast with other parts of India.

In the south the Western Ghats attain to much greater altitudes than in the north. Indeed, the highest peaks to be found south of the Himalayas lie immediately north and south of the Palghat Gap, where, in sharp contrast to the Gap itself, elevations of over 8,000 ft. are reached. The Nilgiri Hills lie to the north of the Gap, the Anamalais to the south. Eastward of the Anamalais are the Palnis, and to the south stretch the Cardamom Hills, maintaining an altitude of over 4,000 ft. to within 25 miles of Cape Comorin. On their western side, throughout their entire length, the slope of the Western Ghats is fairly steep, and between the foot of the hills and the sea is a wellwatered and fertile strip of alluvial plain varying in width from three or four miles in its narrowest part to thirty miles in the south, where the mountains recede somewhat from the sea. On their eastern side the slope is less rapid, and the elevation drops gradually to that of the plateau.

The eastern boundary of the plateau is a broken range of highlands stretching southwards from the hills of Orissa till their southernmost spurs, the Shevaroy Hills, almost meet the eastern spurs of the Nilgiris. The eastern highlands, though commonly called the Eastern Ghats, have little in common with their western namesakes. They are comparatively low, seldom exceeding 3,000 ft., as well as irregular and broken, and are separated from the sea by a much broader alluvial plain. Like the Aravallis, the Eastern Ghats are the remnants of a very ancient range, worn down by long ages of "weathering." The Western Ghats, on the other hand, are of comparatively recent elevation. This, together with the fact that almost the whole drainage of the plateau is to the east, accounts for the greater breadth of the alluvial plain, which varies from 50 to 150 miles in width, and stretches far inland where the great rivers force their way to the sea.

The plateau itself is highest in the southern angle formed by the converging eastern and western ranges. In that angle lies the

State of Mysore, a large part of which maintains an altitude of over 3,000 ft. In the west the plateau is almost everywhere well over 2,000 ft. From these higher levels it slopes gradually, and almost imperceptibly, in an easterly and northerly direction till it meets the Western Ghats, the low crests of which seldom rise to more than 1,000 ft. above it.

The Great Rivers and their Basins

Most rivers begin their course as mountain torrents, and this is particularly the case in north India, where almost all the chief rivers rise at exceptionally high altitudes, and before they emerge from their mountain bed have become streams of considerable volume. Most of the Himalayan rivers take their rise at elevations varying from 10,000 to 17,000 ft., and fall swiftly almost to the level of the plains through rocky channels which they have cut out for themselves. Their fall being rapid their flow is swift, and their erosive power proportionately great. Many of them flow at the bottom of steep ravines of their own making many thousands of feet deep. Mountain torrents cannot, therefore, change their course, but retain it from age to age, confined by the rocks through which they have cut their way. Such mountain torrents bring down a vast amount of solid matter to the level of the plains. The steep sides of their ravines are continually crumbling, and the disintegrated matter is washed into the bed of the torrent by which it is continually being carried down to lower and lower levels. If the rapidity of flow is checked at any point in the descent, so that a lake is formed, this solid matter is deposited, and in course of time a fertile valley is the result, through which the stream flows placidly to recommence its swifter descent further on. Many such valleys have thus been formed in the Himalayas, the beautiful Vale of Kashmir being one.

When such a river reaches the plains, it enters upon what we may call the second stage of its life. Its flow becomes slower in proportion to the flatness of the plain, and the silt which it has brought down is rapidly deposited on its banks and bed. In seasons of flood these deposits are again disturbed and carried further down. Sometimes such a river will build up its bed to a level above that of the surrounding plain. Or sometimes, having half filled up its channel, it will, in a season of great flood, overflow its banks; and as these banks are soft and easily destroyed, they are soon washed away, and the river cuts out a new, or auxiliary, channel for itself. As it approaches its mouth the flow becomes still slower, till in its estuaries it meets and mingles with the tidal waters of the sea. Here the final deposit of its solid matter takes place, and the land steadily encroaches on the sea. The old channels, or distributaries, of the river are continually being partially blocked up with silt, and in periods of flood its waters overflow and cut out new channels for themselves by means of which they reach the sea. Much of the silt brought down by such a river when in flood is washed out to sea. There it gradually settles, and the bed of the sea is raised around the river's mouth, or the numerous mouths of its distributaries. Mud islands presently appear, which in course of time are joined to the mainland, and others further out are formed. So the "delta " is always being slowly enlarged, and the land pushed further and further out.

Such is the character of almost all the rivers of India. In one point, however, the rivers of the north contrast sharply with those of the peninsula. The former are snow-fed, the latter are not. The great mountains of the north are a vast storehouse of water in the form of snow. The line of perpetual snow is at a height of about 16,000 ft. on the south side of the Himalayas, and at about 18,000 to 19,000 ft. on the north side and on the mountains of the north-west. In the winter the snow does not melt, and the northern rivers are, therefore, lowest in the early months of the year, when the effect of the monsoon rains is past, and the melting of the snow has not yet begun. But as soon as the warmer weather sets in the snows begin to melt, and then for several months there is a steady supply of water to all the rivers of the north. This is greatly increased when the rains set in, and in July the Himalayan rivers are in full flood. But the flow from the snows continues long after the monsoon rains have ceased. The rivers of the peninsula have no such supply, for there are no mountains south of latitude 27° N. high enough to reach the snow line. The southern rivers, therefore, being dependent upon the rains alone, are subject to much greater variation in volume than those which come down from the north and water the great plain.

The great rivers of the north, the Indus, the Brahmaputra, and the Ganges, drain the main slopes of the Himalayas both north and south; and the Indus and Brahmaputra bring the drainage of the north round the western and eastern extremities of the mountain chain. Some of the greater tributaries of these rivers rise north of the main chain, and make their way across the chain through deep gorges between the mountains. The Indus, its main tributary, the Sutlej, the Brahmaputra, and the Gogra, one of the chief tributaries of the Ganges, take their rise within 100 miles of each other, near Lake Manasarowar in Tibet, at an elevation of over 16,000 ft. The Ganges and another of its tributaries, the Jumna, rise in the mountains to the west of this lake. Manasarowar is thus the great hydroKraphic centre of North India.

The Indus. Rising in Tibet, the Indus flows first in a north-westerly direction for 800 miles, passing through Kashmir between the Himalayas and the Karakorums, and receiving the drainage of both these chains. Rounding the sea. Just at its bend it receives the waters of the Gilgit river from the west. Two hundred miles further on, near Attock, it is joined by the Kabul river, which, with its tributaries the Swat, the Panjkora, and the Chitral, drains the eastern slopes of the Hindu Kush and the Chitral Hills. Other important affluents from the west are the Kuram, with its tributary the Tochi, and the Gomal.

But the great affluents of the Indus are from the east. They are five in number, and, watering the Punjab, give that Province its name Panj-ab, five rivers. The Jhelum is the most westerly of these, and pours its waters into the Chenab, which, further down, also receives the waters of the Ravi. All these take their rise in the Himalayas, and, like the Indus, flow at first in a north-westerly direction. The Sutlej, the most easterly of the five rivers of the Punjab, flows from Rakas Tal, a lake to the west of Manasarowar, and, breaking through a gorge in the Himalayas north of Simla, enters the Punjab from the east. When half way on its course to the Indus it is joined by the Beas, which rises on the southern slopes of the hills not far from the source of the Chenab. At this point the Sutlej changes its course, which has hitherto been almost westerly, and after flowing for 300 miles in a south-westerly direction, joins the Chenab. One channel, called the Panjnad, thus carries the water of all five rivers to the Indus.

All these rivers being fed by the melting snows, as well as by the monsoon rains, are in flood in the late summer. After their emergence from the hills their course lie across an almost level alluvial plain composed for the most part of a soft loam. They therefore carve for themselves numerous wide and shallow channels, which they constantly tend to change. This is true also of the Indus in many parts of its course, as well as of most of the tributaries of the Ganges. In the broad plain there are no hills to confine them, and the soft earth of which their banks are composed is unable to withstand the erosive action of their flood waters.

From its confluence with the Panjnad the Indus flows midway between the frontier hills of Baluchistan and the region of the scantiest rainfall in India, the Thar or Indian Desert. It has, therefore, no further affluents of importance and in the lower part of its course gives more water than it receives. It does for Sind precisely what the Nile does for Egypt, watering and fertilizing the land for many miles on both sides. By the vast amount of silt which for ages it has brought down from the mountains it has built up for itself a bed higher than the surrounding country. Streams therefore flow from it instead of into it. This makes irrigation from the Indus for the most part exceedingly simple and easy, but at the same time it increases the danger of disastrous floods. The same force which has built the broad soft banks can also destroy them. When the river is in flood the swirling waters often make vast beaches in thoni, and widespread inundations with great loss of life and property are the result. Occasionally, also, the river will in consequence change its course, or make for itself a subsidiary channel often at a considerable distance from the main stream. At Sukkur, about 300 miles from its mouth, the river narrows into a rocky channel, and is spanned by a great railway bridge. Two hundred miles further south the Delta begins, and the river pours its waters into the Arabian Sea by many ever-shifting distributaries.

The Brahmaputra. This river, called the Tsan-pu north of the Himalayas, enfolds the eastern portion of the great mountain chain just as the Indus enfolds the western. Rising in the neighbourhood of Lake Manasarowar, it flows almost due east for a distance of almost 700 miles; then, bending sharply round the mountains, takes an almost westerly course through the narrow valley of Assam. On its way it receives the southern drainage of the Himalayas and the northern and western drainage of the Patkai and Khasi Hills. West of the Khasis it turns south, and almost immediately begins to throw off distributaries. About 100 miles from its mouth its main stream unites one of the chief distributaries of the Ganges. Their united waters reach the Bay of Bengal through two main channels known as the Pudda (or Padma) and the Arialkhan rivers. Two of the larger distributaries of the Brahmaputra, thrown off before its junction with the Ganges, flow into the Meghna, a river which drains the southern slopes of the Khasi Hills, and the western slopes of the Nagas and Lushais. The Meghna then unites with the Pudda fifty miles from the sea. Throughout its whole course from the north-east of Assam the Brahmaputra cuts for itself a multitude of channels, spreading itself in parts over a width of many miles and forming numerous river islands, most of which are covered with verdure in the dry season but completely submerged when the river is in flood.

The Ganges

The Ganges system is by far the most important river system in India. Not only is its basin the largest, but it includes the richest and most populous provinces of the Empire, provinces whose wealth and prosperity are in great part the gift of the river. The Ganges proper is formed in Garhwal by the union of two rivers, the Bhagirathi, which rises among the glaciers of Gangotri and is often called the Ganges, and the Alaknanda, which rises to the north-west of the great peak Nanda Devi and breaks through the Garhwal Himalayas. The Alaknanda is much the larger of these confluents. The river thus formed flows for 50 miles in a south-westerly direction, and then gradually bends round to the south and south-east, maintaining the latter direction till it has passed Allahabad. On its eastern and northern side it receives many tributaries, the chief of which is the Ramganga, which also rises in Garhwal. From the west and south it receives no tributary of importance till it reaches Allahabad, where it is joined by the Jumna.

The Jumna also takes its rise north of Garhwal and west of the Bhagirathi. In its course it describes a curve similar to that of the Ganges, and for the greater part of its way to Allahabad maintains a distance of from 50 to 80 miles west of that river. Unlike the Ganges, however, its main affluents are from the west and south. The most important of these is the Chambal which drains the northeastern slopes of the Aravallis and Vindhyas.

From Allahabad the Ganges flows eastwards, passing Benares, and a few miles further on is joined by the Gumti, which descends from the frontiers of Nepal. A hundred miles lower down it receives the waters of the Gogra, which rises near Lake Rakas Tal and breaks through a gorge in the mountains. On its way the Gogra receives the waters of the Sarda and the Rapti, and by the time it reaches the Ganges it rivals it in volume. Within the next 30 miles the Ganges is joined by the Son from the south and the Gandak from the north, and when north of the Rajmahal Hills it receives the Kiisi from the north.

Both the Gandak and the Kiisi rise north of the Himalayas and break through the mountain chain, while the numerous feeders of the Son drain the rocky highlands of the Central Provinces and Chota Nagpur. After passing the Rajmahal Hills the Ganges bends toward the south-east, and soon begins to throw off its distributaries to the south. The first of these is the Bhagirathi, which lower down becomes the Hooghly, and the point at which the Bhagirathi branches off is the beginning of the delta. The main stream still continues in a south-easterly direction, till south of Pabna it divides into two almost equal streams, one of which, the Madhumati, or Haringata, takes a more southerly course to the sea, and the other, the Pudda (or Padma) follows a more easterly course to Goalanda, where it unites with the Brahmaputra.

The northern and southern tributaries of the Ganges differ greatly in character. The former are fed, as we have seen, not only by the heavy rains which fall on the Himalayan slopes, but also by the melting snows. They are therefore much more constant than they would be if dependent on the rains alone. Though in flood in July and August they continue to bring down a fair quantity of water through the greater part of the year.

The southern tributaries have no snow reservoirs to draw upon. Their basins have also a much smaller rainfall than the Himalayas, particularly in the west. The ground they drain is also for the most part rocky, off which the water flows with great rapidity. The rivers, therefore, rise rapidly as soon as the summer monsoon brings its store of rain, and fall almost as rapidly when the rain ceases. When in flood they rival the northern rivers in volume, but for the greater part of the year they are little more than rivulets. For this reason they are of much less value for irrigation purposes than the Himalayan rivers. While (as we shall presently see) there are vast irrigation systems that draw their supplies from the latter, the systems dependent on the southern tributaries are few and small. The Ganges is also of immense value as the chief waterway of north India. Its volume is always sufficient to bear upon its bosom a vast host of boats of every description. At the various registering towns along its course over 130,000 river boats of various kinds are licensed to ply upon its waters. The river thus brings down a large part of the immense produce of the rich provinces which it traverses.

The Rivers of the Peninsula

Most of the great rivers of the peninsula pour their waters into the Bay of Bengal. In the map on page 28 the water-parting between east and west is shown by a line of heavier dots extending from north of the Himalayas to Cape Comorin.

It will be noticed that from the southern point this line follows the Western Ghats, till, from the northern extremity of this range, it strikes sharply westwards where the narrow basins of the Tapti and Narbada stretch far across the peninsula, the latter nearly two-thirds of the way to the Bay of Bengal. With these two exceptions the rivers which flow westwards are small and of little moment. The great rivers of the peninsula, though rising as a rule within a few miles of the west coast, make their way eastwards, gathering volume as they go.

The Narbada, rising near Mount Amarkantak, in the north of the Central Provinces, and a little to the east of Chota Nagpur, takes an almost straight course to the Gulf of Cambay. It receives few tributaries, and no large ones.

Like the Ganges it is a sacred river of the Hindus, and from its source to its mouth it is by very far the most beautiful river in India. "Of all the rivers in India," says Sir Lepel Griffin, "there is none which is surrounded by more romance and mystic interest; whilst for strange and fantastic beauty it takes high rank among the celebrated rivers of the world."

The Tapti rises south of the Mahadeo range of hills, and flow westward along the northern valley. Debouching through a gorge at their western extremity it is joined by the Piirna which drains the southern slopes of the same hills.

Like the Narbada, from which it is separated by the Satpura range, the Tapti flows westwards and empties itself into the Gulf of Cambay, a little to the north of the ancient port of Surat. The four great rivers of peninsular India which discharge into the Bay of Bengal are the Mahanadi, the Godavari, the Kistna, and the Cauvery.

The Mahanadi

The basin of the Mahanadi meets that of the Narbada, and one of its tributaries takes its rise, like that river, on the slopes of Mt. Amarkantak. The Mahanadi itself rises on the northern slopes of the hills that form the northern boundary of the State of Bastar in the Central Provinces.

It flows at first in a northerly direction till, having received its chief tributary, the Seonath, from the west, it turns to the east and flows east and south, past Sambalpur. Its numerous affluents drain a large tract of hilly country, and in the rainy season the river is of unusual volume for its length. When in flood it almost equals the Ganges. But, like all the Vindhyan rivers, it rises quickly and quickly falls again. The Mahanadi breaks through the hills by a gorge 40 miles long and of great beauty, and, after passing Cuttack, divides into the numerous channels of its delta. The river brings down a very large quantity of silt, and the delta is extensive and rapidly increasing.

The Godavari rises in the Western Ghats a little north of Bombay. It flows through the Nizam's Dominions, and for more than 350 miles its various tributaries form the northern boundary of that State. The general course of the Godavari is west-south-west for the first two-thirds of its length, then it turns to the south-west and maintains that direction till it reaches the sea. Its main tributary on the south is the Manjira, which rises in the Bhir country on the borders of Bombay. From the north, just at the point where it bends more to the south, it receives the waters of the Pranhita, a river almost as large as itself.

The Pranhita is formed by the union of three rivers, the Painganga from the west, the Wardha from the north-west, and the Wainganga from the north. Further on it receives from the north-east the Indravati, which rises on the western slopes of the Eastern Ghats and drains the unhealthy jungles of Bastar. In their passage through the Ghats the waters of the Godavari are confined for 20 miles within a deep and narrow channel, and the scenery on both sides is wild and grand. Shortly after its emergence from the Ghats it broadens into a vast and noble river, and at Rajahmundry it is crossed by a railway bridge if miles long. At Dowlaishweram, the apex of its delta, the river divides into three main distributaries and many smaller ones, and so reaches the sea.

The Kistna and its tributaries receive the eastern drainage of considerably more than one-half of the whole length of the Western Ghats. The Kistna basin, unlike that of the Godavari, is broadest towards the west, and gradually narrows as it approaches the Bay of Bengal. The Kistna rises near Mahabaleshwar ard flows first in a southerly direction. It has two great tributaries, the Bhima from the north and the Tungabhadra from the south. The Bhima rises to the north of Poona, and after flowing south-east through Bombay and the Nizam's Dominions, joins the Kistna a Uttle to the north of Raichur.

The Tungabhadra is formed by the union of two rivers, the Tunga and the Bhadra, both of which rise in the west of the Mysore State. They unite within the boundaries of that State, and, flowing in a north-easterly direction, separate the Presidency of Madras first from Bombay and then from Hyderabad. After receiving the waters of the Tungabhadra the Kistna turns to the north-east and continues its flow in that direction till it has passed the Nallamalai Hills, which cut it off from the plain of the eastern sea-board. Then it turns sharply to the southeast and so reaches the sea.

The Cauvery and its tributaries drain the whole of southern Mysore, the eastern slopes of the Nilgiris and Anamalais, and the northern and eastern slopes of the Palnis. It flows through some of the most productive and populous districts of South India, notably Tanjore, which it waters by means of extensive and ancient irrigation works. After passing Trichinopoly its delta begins. The river divides into two arms, the smaller of which, still called the Cauvery, flows almost due east, and divides again into several channels before it reaches the sea. The larger, called the Coleroon, flows in a north-easterly direction, and empties itself into the sea half way between Pondicherry and Negapatam.

A few miles from the city of Mysore the Cauvery divides, and the two arms, uniting again lower down, enclose the river island of Seringapatam, the famous stronghold at which Tipu Sultan made his last stand. Further down, two similar islands are formed, both held to be of great sanctity by Hindus. These are the island of Sivasamundram, at the southern frontier of Mysore, and the island of Srirangam, near Trichinopoly, the site of one of the largest and most famous Hindu temples.

The peninsular rivers depend for their supply of water upon the rainfall alone. For the most part also they traverse rocky land with a comparatively shallow soil into which little of the water sinks. During the dry season the river beds are, as a rule, nothing but vast expanses of sand, with a few sluggish and shallow rivulets.

But when the rains begin, these rivers rise with extraordinary rapidity, coming down from the hilly country in vast and ever increasing volume and with a swift and irresistible flow. Sometimes the "freshes " come down with such suddenness, and in such volume, as to overwhelm travellers who may be crossing their broad bed. Breaking loose from their banks these rivers often flood the country for many miles around.

But, except in their delta stage, they do not tend, like the rivers of the great northern plain, to change their course or cut for themselves new channels. When the flood subsides they sink again into their old beds. Because of the violence of their floods their action on the land is unusually great. Their flood waters are thick and muddy, and often discolour the sea for many miles from their mouths. Where the speed of their current is checked this mud, the washings of the inland hills, is deposited. Along the eastern coast this process has been going on for countless ages, for the Eastern Ghats, as we have seen, share with the Aravallis the honour of being the oldest hills in India. In the course of ages these hills have been worn down, and with their washings the rivers have built up a broad and fertile alluvial plain along the sea-board, which they are ever increasing and enriching.

The River Systems of Burma

We have seen that the mountains of the Indo-Chinese peninsula run from north to south, stretching southwards in almost parallel ranges, and in ever diminishing altitudes, from the great mountain systems of the north. Consequently, the great rivers of Burma which separate these ranges all take a southerly course. They are the Irrawaddy, with its great tributary the Chindwin, the Sittang, and the Salwin.

The Irrawaddy drains the greater part of Burma. It is a noble river, navigable by light draught steamers as far as Bhamo, 700 miles from the sea. and by smaller craft still further. Being snow fed it rises and falls, but is never very low. Till railways were constructed it was almost the only highway of commerce between Upper Burma and the coast, and it is still the chief. The Irrawaddy rises in the rugged mountains east of the Brahmaputra, and with the exception of about 60 miles after passing Bhamo, and again for a similar distance after passing Mandalay, when it turns in each case to the west, its general course is almost due south. At a distance of 800 miles from the sea it is more than half a mile wide, and it maintains a width of from, half a mile to a mile and a half all the way to its delta, except in four places where it breaks through defiles in the mountains, and, amid scenery of surpassing beauty, narrows into deep rocky channels. In one of these the river is only 600 ft. wide, but over 1,000 ft. deep. A little below Mandalay the Irrawaddy is joined by the Myitnge which drains the Shan Hills to the north-east. Thirty miles further down it receives the waters of its main tributary, the Chindwin. Rising, like the

Irrawaddy itself, east of the bend of the Brahmaputra, the Chindwin drains the eastern slopes of the Patkai and Naga Hills, and the Arakan Yoma. In its lower course, before its junction with the Irrawaddy, it waters a broad and fertile valley. A little below the point of confluence the Irrawaddy bends gradually to the south again. More than 100 miles from the sea the delta begins, and the river finds its way to the Gulf of Martaban through fourteen channels. On the most easterly of these distributaries stands the port of Rangoon, the chief port of Burma, and on the most westerly, the smaller port of Bassein.

The basin of the Sittang is separated from that of the Irrawaddy on the west by the Pegu Yoma, and from that of the Salwin on the east by the Poung-loung Hills, both of them fairly Continuous, though low, ranges, which run north and south, and enclose a rich and fertile valley from 50 to 90 miles in width. A glance at the map will show that the basin of the Irrawaddy meets that of the Salwin, about 100 miles south of Mandalay. The Sittang is, therefore, a comparatively short river, and being shallow at its mouth it is useless for navigation. It is subject also to a severe tidal bore. The tidal wave, concentrating in the apex of the gulf, rushes up the broad estuary as a wall of water, often from fifteen to twenty feet in height. The Sittang valley is fiat, and provides an excellent route for the railway to Mandalay.

The Salwin, like so many of the rivers of North India, rises amid the snows of Tibet. Bending to the south, 200 miles east of the Brahmaputra, it makes its long journey to the Gulf of Martaban between ranges of hills which in the north narrow its basin to a few miles. Throughout its whole course it has a rocky bed. At seasons of flood, when the Tibetan snows are melting, the Salwin brings down more water than the Irrawaddy. But numerous rocky rapids on its course make navigation impossible for more than 100 miles from its mouth.

Coast Line and Harbours

The total coast line of India and Burma, from Cape Monze on the western point of Sind to Victoria Point in the south of Tenasserim, is slightly over 4,800 miles in length. Seeing, however, that the peninsula of India stietches southwards from Latitude 25° N. for nearly 1,200 miles forming almost an equilateral triangle with that parallel as its base, and that Burma stretches about the same distance to the south on the other side of the Bay of Bengal, this long coast line is relatively short. It is comparatively uniform and regular, and is broken by few indentations of any magnitude. For the greater part of its length a sandy and almost level coast strip is washed by shallow seas. The waves, rolling in unbroken from the open ocean, break in the shallow water in long lines of surf, which even in fine weather are a difficulty and danger to small boats, and in stormy weather lash the shore with almost irresistible fury and make it impossible of approach. This is particularly the case on the south-east coast, but is more or less true all round the peninsula. In natural harbours India is unusually poor. Vast stretches of coast present no convenience or shelter whatever for shipping, neither land-locked bays nor navigable estuaries. India could therefore never become a great maritime country, and all her foreign sea-borne trade is carried in the ships of other nations.

Both the east and the west coasts of India are greatly affected by the surface currents, or drifts, in the surrounding seas, which are induced by the steady seasonal winds. During the south-west monsoon the currents run along the west coast of the peninsula from north to south, and along the east coast from south to north. During the north-east monsoon these directions are reversed. These currents exercise considerable erosive power, and at the same time they wash up, and move along the coast, vast quantities of sand, which is deposited wherever the force of the current is checked by its entry into a bay, or by its conflict with the river currents prolonged into the sea. The influence of these drifts is thus twofold. Where they beat upon an exposed promontory they gradually eat into the land. When they flow into a confined bay they wash more sand in than they can wash out, and slowly tend to fill the bay up. Striking examples of these two effects are to be found on the west coast, where the currents exert on the whole a more powerful influence than on the east. The extreme north-western point of Kathiawar, which is exposed to the full effect of the southwest monsoon drift as it bends round the north of the Arabian Sea, is being rapidly worn away, and the sea is steadily encroaching on the land. On the other hand, the Gulfs of Cutch and Cambay are rapidly silting up. One curious result of these drifts, seen almost equally along both coasts, is the formation of long banks of sand and mud, or bars, as they are called, a little distance from the mouths of all rivers. These bars are just beyond the scouring power of the flood water of the river, and they constitute an effectual barrier to navigation.

Beginning at the extreme west of India we have the excellent harbour of Karachi, a natural bay formed by a projecting ridge of rock and greatly improved by an extensive breakwater. Karachi is about 12 miles west of the most westerly outlet of the Indus. Being the nearest Indian port to Europe, and having direct railway communication with north India (by a bridge across the Indus at Sukkur), it attracts to itself the greater part of the sea-borne trade of Rajputana and the Punjab, and is a rapidly-growing port. Owing to the steady silting up of the entrance, however, the channel has to be incessantly dredged.

For 1 20 miles southeast of Karachi extends the delta of the river Indus, the shifting channels of which are navigable only by small craft. At one time the chief channel of the Indus discharged its waters into the Great Rann of Cutch, which separates the island of Cutch from Sind. Between Sind and the promontory of Kathiawar on the south are the Little Rann of Cutch and the Gulf of Cutch. The Ranns arc shown as arms of the sea on all maps, but they are no more than vast salt morasses, covered with shallow water only in the wet season, and in the dry months for the most part baked dry and hard.

They are the haunt of wild asses, which wander about in herds of 50 or 60, and are so timid and fleet that they can seldom be approached. The Ranns are sea-swamps in process of natural reclamation. The Gulf of Cutch is also exceedingly shallow, and when the tide is low much of it is bare sand. South-east of Kathiawar is the Gulf of Cambay, which, as we have seen, is gradually silting up. The port of Cambay at the north of the Gulf has lost almost all its sea trade, and the more famous ports of Broach, on the Narbada, and Surat, on the Tapti. are yearly being rendered more difficult of access from the same cause. Surat was at one time the wealthiest and most famous port in India.

About 150 miles south of the Gulf of Cambay is the excellent natural harbour of Bombay. It is protected by the islands of Bombay and Salsette, and offers abundant and safe anchorage. But owing to the constant deposit of silt at its entrance great care has to be taken to keep it open, and the largest vessels have to enter with caution. Bombay is admirably situated as the principal port for communication with the west, and is the chief mail route. It is almost equidistant from the north, south, and east of India, and is accessible by rail from all parts. 68. From Bombay south to Cape Comorin, though there are many small seaports, there are only two harbours that offer a safe anchorage in bad weather for vessels of large size. These are Goa and Karwar. The former is now served by the Southern Maratha Railway, and is growing in importance. The rest are "fair weather ports " only, and many of them are quite unapproachable when the south-west monsoon is blowing in force. Near the south of the peninsula there is an extensive system of backwaters or lagoon separated from the sea by broad banks of sand through which occasional openings give an outlet for flood water in the rains, and an inlet for the sea. In ancient days it is probable that these channels, as well as the lagoons themselves, were of much greater depth, and admitted ships of fair size. Now, however, though of inestim Bombay islands and Harbourable value as inland waterways, these lagoons are useless for seafaring purposes. Rounding Cape Comorin we enter the Gulf of Manar, on the western shore of which stands the small port of Tuticorin. The water is exceedingly shallow, and steamers have to anchor some miles out. but in spite of this Tuticorin has come to be of some importance as the chief peninsular port for communication with Ceylon. Northwanl are the Palk Straits, almost blocked by the islands of Rameswaram on the west and Manar on the east, and a long sand bank which almost unites the two.

On the landward side of the two islands arc shallow passages known as the Manar Passage and the Pamban Passage. Till a fcw years ago neither of them was more than six feet deep, and although they have recently been deepened and widened, they offer no route for large ocean steamers, which have to pass round the south of

Ceylon. The west coast of Ceylon, like that of the peninsula itself, is low and sandy, and is subject to the same silting.

There are extensive backwaters, in many respects similar to those on the west coast of India, and, like them, of great value for boat traffic. The port of Colombo, nearly 100 miles from the most southerly point of the island, is rapidly becoming one of the most important ports of call in Asia. It has a fair natural harbour, which has been very greatly improved by the construction of a long breakwater. As a port of call, and the point where almost all the great steamship lines traversing the Indian Ocean converge. Colombo has superseded Galle in the south of the island, though Galle Bay forms an excellent and fairly safe harbour.

The east coast of Ceylon contrasts sharply with the west, as well as with the entire coast of the peninsula, being everywhere rocky and descending quickly to the sea. The depth of water increases with unusual rapidity, a depth of 12,000 ft., or over 21 miles, being reached within 50 miles of the shore. There are several excellent and safe natural harbours, the chief of which is Trincomallee Bay, large enough, it is said, to accommodate all the navies of the world, and to be a safe refuge for ships of the largest order. Trincomallee is a British naval station; though in this respect it is of comparatively little moment, being off the main lines of sea-communication.

The east coast of India, from Pamban northwards to the Hooghly, has not a single natural harbour of any kind, and offers no shelter whatever to shipping in the furious storms that at particular seasons prevail in the Bay of Bengal. It is an unbroken stretch of inhospitable surfbeaten sands, or low, deltaic, mud islands. Across the mouths of all the great rivers bars stretch, which effectually close them to everything but boats of low draught. There are several ports along the coast at which there is a fair amount of shipping trade, but coasting steamers have to anchor far out to sea—in some places five or six miles and in bad weather the open sea is their only refuge. At Madras vast breakwaters have been constructed of solid blocks of concrete which enclose a portion of the roadstead. In good weather these secure for ships a smooth-water anchorage where they can load and unload without the inconvenience that they previously suffered from the restless waves. But as a place of refuge from bad weather the harbour thus made is useless, or worse than useless. The action of the surface drifts on the east coast is similar to that on the west, but as a rule not quite so powerful. In some places the land is gaining at the expense of the sea through the piling up of sand, and at others is being worn away by steady erosion. A remarkable instance of both these effects has been seen at Madras since the erection of the breakwaters. On the south side of the harbour the coast line is being pushed out to sea, while on the north side the sea is eating into the land.

Of the many distributaries that bring the waters of the Ganges to the sea, the only ones that are navigable for anything larger than river boats are the Hooghly and the Mutla. About 80 miles up the Hooghly stands Calcutta, the metropolis and premier port of India. The river is, however, exceedingly difficult to navigate, and in one part perilous.

At the bend in its course, where it receives the waters of the Kupnarayan, the James and Mary Sands have been formed. This is the most dangerous bank of quick-Long 90 of sands in the world. Vessels that strike it are swallowed up with appalling rapidity. Calcutta, therefore, holds its position as the chief port of India more because it taps the richest and most productive of all the Indian Provinces than by reason of its excellence as a seaport, in which respect it is far surpassed both by Bombay and Karachi.

In olden times the ships of the East India Company used to go no further up the river than Diamond Harbour, which still enjoys a certain amount of trade, and is now connected with Calcutta by railway. About forty years ago an attempt was made to relieve Calcutta of some of its shipping, which often greatly crowds the river, by opening a new port, called Port Canning, on the Mutla river, a channel of the delta, about 25 miles east of the Hooghly. Port Canning also is connected by rail with Calcutta, from which it is distant about 20 miles, but as a port it has not developed as was at first confidently expected.

From the Hooghly for a distance of 200 miles to the eastward stretch the low mud islands of the delta. In many parts, particularly in the east, these islands are cultivated, but they are mostly covered with low trees and shrubs, and are infested by tigers and crocodiles. The entire district is known as the Sandarbans, and is subject to disastrous floods both from the waters of the rivers and from storm waves.

One such wave which swept over the Sandarbans about thirty years ago caused an immense loss, both of life and property, no fewer than 100,000 people being drowned. None of the channels of the delta are navigable, save for river boats, till we come to the Meghna in the east, which will allow of the passage of river steamers at all times, and is an important waterway to Dacca. The Meghna is, however, subject to a severe tidal bore which makes its navigation difficult and dangerous. The Hooghly is subject to the same phenomenon, but not to so serious a degree as the Meghna.

The eastern shores of the Bay of Bengal are totally different from the western, being fringed with innumerable small rocky islands, mostly volcanic in origin. The sea bed immediately adjacent to the land being in most places rocky, the river mouths are not so greatly blocked with sand bars as is the case almost all round the Indian peninsula.

The rivers are therefore more open to sea traffic. For example, the comparatively small river Kaludan, at the mouth of which is the safe and well-protected port of Akyab, is freely open to the sea, in spite of a small bar. and can be navigated for over 50 miles by vessels of 400 or 500 tons burden. Akyab is the only port of any consequence north of Cape Negrais. Bassein and Rangoon are on channels of the Irrawaddy delta, and Moulmein is at the mouth of the Salwin. All these are easily accessible, and give safe anchorages to the largest vessels. This is also true of the smaller ports on the Tenasserim coast, Amherst Tavoy, and Mergui.

ISLANDS

With the exception of Ceylon, which does not belong to the Indian Empire and will be treated separately, the Islands of India are of comparatively little moment. They are, however, exceedingly numerous, especially off the coast of Burma, and though small, their united coast-line exceeds 3,000 miles in length. The total coast-line of the Indian Empire is 8,415 miles.

Salsette and Bombay are now connected with the mainland by a causeway, and can hardly be considered islands. Elephanta and Trombay are within the harbor of Bombay. Other smaller islands, mostly composed of volcanic rock, belong to the same group. The Laccadive and Maldive Islands are, as we have seen, remnants of the broad belt of land which, in far back geological ages, united India and South Africa. Or, more accurately, they are coral structures raised slowly by the coral polyp (which can only live comparatively near the surface of the water) upon the gradually submerging land. The Laccadives are about 200 miles west of the Malabar coast, and belong to India. The Maldives are 300 miles south-west of Cape Comorin, and are under a Sultan tributary to Ceylon. Nine of the Laccadive Islands are inhabited, and seventeen of the Maldives, the population being respectively about 10,000 and 30,000. Rameswaram and Manar are two islands lying between Ceylon and India, the former belonging to India, the latter to Ceylon. Rameswaram is a noted place of Hindu pilgrimage. Of the many low islands at the mouths of the Ganges, Brahmaputra and Meghna, the only ones of any moment are Saugor island in the west, and Shahbazpur and Sandip islands in the east.

The islands off the Burmese coast are totally different from those to the north of the Bay of Bengal, being mostly rocky, and volcanic in their origin. They differ also from the Laccadives and Maldives, inasmuch as, with the single exception of some of the Coco Islands, there is hardly any coral formation to be found among them. North of Cape Negrais the only islands of any moment, among the many hundreds with which the coast is studded, are

Barongo and Savage Island, which protect the port of Akyab, and the larger islands of Ramri and Cheduba a little further to the south. From Cape Negrais a well-defined submarine ridge runs southwards to Sumatra. About 75 miles south of the cape it crops up in the Preparis Isles, a group of minute volcanic peaks. Fifty miles further south are the Coco Islands, similar in every way except that they contain a minute volcano that is still very slightly active. Thirtyfive miles south of the Cocos the Andaman Islands begin, a beautiful and in many ways

important group, consisting of four large islands and many small ones, and stretching from north to south for a distance of over 200 miles. Further south again are the Nicobars. The Andamans and Nicobars constitute a Chief-Commissionership, and They have many excellent will claim attention later. natural harbours, well protected and with good anchorages. The same is also true of the Mergui Archipelago, which consists of many hundreds of rocky islands skirting the whole length of the Tenasserim coast.

8

CLIMATE OF INDIA

Blanford remarks that we may speak of the climates but not of the climate of India, for "the world itself affords no greater contrast than is to be met with at one and the same time within its limits." It would be a vain task to describe the climate of every part of India, and any attempt to do so is unnecessary. Climate is everywhere the result of certain conditions whose influence is well understood. The presence or absence of these conditions enables us readily to explain and understand all climatic differences.

Temperature

The Tropic of Cancer crosses India almost midway between its northern and southern points. Passing through Cutch on the west and the Gangetic Delta on the east, it very nearly marks the division between peninsular and continental India. The whole of the peninsula is within the tropics, and Cape Comorin is just over 8° north of the equator. The Indo-Gangetic plain, on the other hand, lies outside the tropics, but near enough to be within the region of greatest solar radiation in the summer months.

In the absence of all other modifying causes, therefore, we should expect the south of the peninsula to have the highest mean annual temperature, and the lowest annual range. Passing north we should expect the mean annual temperature steadily to diminish, and the mean annual range to increase; while from 2° south of the Tropic to 6° or 8° north of it we should expect to find the summer maxima higher than in any other part of India. In the main this is the case, but in India, as in all other countries, the presence or absence of water, the prevailing winds, the proximity of mountain chains, elevation and aspect often make the ordinary temperature of places in the same latitude totally different. It is easy to see how very greatly the climate of India is moderated by these various causes. Water in all its forms is the great moderator of heat and cold. Happily the greater part of the country is, as a rule, sufficiently well supplied with water to render extreme day and night temperatures impossible, and in many parts the climate is remarkably equable. The influence of the sea is also felt far inland all round the peninsula. In Rajputana, Sind and Baluchistan, however, the daily range is often so great as to be extremely trying to all but the most robust. In the highlands of Baluchistan during the late summer or early autumn a day temperature of 80° F. is often followed by a night minimum of 10° F. The air is exceedingly dry, the ground a mixture of rock and sand, and radiation proceeds with amazing rapidity.

It is in this connection that the nature of the soil, and the presence or absence of vegetation, exercise a powerful influence on climate. Some soils are shallow and porous and rest upon a bed of impenetrable rock, so that the rainfall quickly flows away and they are soon dry. Such is the character of the greater part of the east and south of peninsular India. Other soils have a remarkable power of absorbing and retaining the rain that falls upon them.

The black "cotton soil " that prevails over the greater part of the north-west of the peninsula and Kathiawar, and the mixture of clay and loam which forms the eastern part of the Gangetic plain, are both of this nature. From such soils there is always a large amount of evaporation, even when their surface seems quite dry, and they neither heat nor cool rapidly. The sands of Sind and Rajputana on the other hand retain no moisture. What little rain they receive soon dries up, and in the hot weather they are perfectly dry for several feet below the surface. Under the summer sun, therefore, they heat with great rapidity and to a very high degree; so much so that it is said often to be possible to cook an egg by simply laying it on the sand in the sunshine at noonday. Winds almost always blow from colder to warmer regions, and are one of nature's chief ways of equalising temperature. How much India owes to seasonal changes of wind we shall see presently. We may notice here, however, a common diurnal change which greatly mitigates the summer heat along the coasts of the peninsula. During the early part of the day the air over the land is warmed by the sun's rays far more than that over the sea. In the course of the afternoon, therefore, a cool and refreshing breeze sets in from the sea which attains its greatest strength a little before sunset and is felt for many miles inland. The hotter the day and the drier the air, the sooner does the sea-breeze begin and the stronger floes it blow. A few hours after sunset it dies down, and then, if the night be clear the air over the land cools more rapidly than that over the sea, so that towards morning a land-wind is established blowing out to sea. The sea breezes which blow daily in the hottest weather greatly moderate the heat along the Coromandel coast.

That elevation reduces temperature is a very familiar experience in India, where cool refuges from the heat of the plains are found at a multitude of hill stations. The extent of this reduction is about 1° F. for every 270 feet of vertical ascent. The plateau of Mysore, being over 3,000 feet in height, is always from 10° to 12° F. cooler than the adjacent plains. The same cause greatly moderates the heat all over the Deccan. 85. Hills or mountain chains exercise in other was also a powerful influence on climate. The slope of the hills turned towards the sun is always much warmer than the slope that looks away from it. Mountain chains also often intercept winds, increasing, or sometimes, though more seldom, reducing, the temperature of the protected plains as a result. The Himalayas protect the Gangetic plain from the keen and icy north winds that blow in winter across Tibet. On the other hand, during the south-west Monsoon, the Western Ghats keep both wind and rain from the plains immediately to their east, where both would be more than welcome. In the light of the foregoing paragraphs we may now illustrate the prevailing temperatures of India by a series of isothermal charts. In the following charts the recorded temperatures are reduced to sea-level, i.e.. they are increased by 1° F. for every 270 feet of elevation. The approximate temperature of any place can therefore easily be found by dividing its elevation in feet by 270 and deducting that number of degrees from the temperature. It will be observed that in December, the coolest month of the year, the hottest part of India is a small tract inland from Goa, almost half way between Cutch and Cape Comorin, where the mean temperature is over 80° F. Next come the southern and western parts of the peninsula, then the eastern as far north as a line stretching from north of Bombay to Vizagapatam. From this point the isotherms stretch irregularly from east to west across India, colder temperatures prevailing as we pass further and further north. By March the sun has come north to the equator and the temperature has increased all over India, but the peninsula is still the hottest part. Along the coast the temperature is from 80° to 85° F., but a large interior tract is over 85° F., and within that is a smaller tract over 90° F. Taking India as a whole, May is the hottest month of the year, the sun being well on his way to the Tropic of Cancer and the south-west monsoon as yet hardly felt. The region of greatest heat, over 95° F., is in Central India, with a large tongue stretching into Rajputana. The surrounding area, from 90° to 95° F., keeps clear of the coast except in the north-west, and stretches into Baluchistan. The coolest parts of India are a strip along the west coast and the whole region north and east of the Bay of Bengal. By August the full cooling effects of the monsoon have been felt, and it will be seen that the area of high temperature has moved away to the north-west, to a region untouched by the monsoon currents.

The Monsoons and Rainfall

The Monsoons are the seasonal winds that prevail in India and blow alternately from the south-west and north-east, bringing the abundant rains upon which the fertility and wealth of the country depend. The southwest monsoon, which in ordinary years reaches the southwest coast in May and blows in full force in the northern Provinces by the end of June, is by far the most important. It is emphatically the monsoon. It brings to five-sixths of peninsular and continental India and the southern slopes of their mountain wall their main supply of water. The north-east monsoon, though of less moment to the country as a whole, is of great importance to the south-east of the peninsula and the north of Cealon. These parts receive but little rain from the south-west, and the northeast monsoon makes up the deficiency.

The causes of the monsoons are not difficult to understand. We have seen that winds always blow from regions of higher to regions of lower pressure, and that regions of high temperature are also regions of low pressure. Winds therefore blow on the surface of the earth from colder to warmer regions. If the surface of the earth were all water, winds would blow in both hemispheres towards the equatorial belt, which would constitute a permanent zone of low pressure. By the rotation of the earth such winds would be diverted towards the west, and therefore north-east winds would prevail in the northern hemisphere and south-east winds in the southern hemisphere, and in each case these winds would be strongest when the sun was at the other side of the equator. As the southern hemisphere is mainly water, south-east winds do actually prevail over the greater part of its surface. But the northern hemisphere has more land than water, and therefore, owing to the different degrees in which land and water are heated by the sun's rays, the areas of lowest pressure are sometimes far removed from the equator, and the direction of the prevailing winds are changed. The winds in the northern hemisphere are therefore not characterized by the comparative uniformity that prevails in the south, and sometimes—as in the case of the south-west monsoon in India—the primal conditions are completely reversed.

By March 22nd the sun has passed the equator on his way north, and the whole of India, then everywhere fairly dry, is rapidly increasing in temperature. During that month the average pressure falls over the entire country. By the end of April an area of deeper depression has been formed over the United Provinces and Central India, and already over a considerable part of the peninsula light south-west winds have begun. These do not come from the sea, however, and so bring no water with them. By the middle of May the depression has largely increased in extent and its centre has become deeper. Its influence is consequently felt over a wider area, and as far south as the equator the winds are now mainly south-west. They strike the west coasts of India after travelling over warm oceans for many hundreds of miles, and come laden with moisture.

By the end of June the depression has increased enormously in extent, and has still further deepened over northern India. The monsoon is now fully developed, and south-west winds prevail for 30° north of the equator and from the coast of Africa to the Philppines. In July the depression is still larger and its centre of greatest depth is over Baluchistan. During August and September the depression gradually diminishes and moves to the south-east. The charts on page 55 illustrate the formation of the low pressure system and indicate the prevailing winds. By September 22nd the sun has passed south of the equator, and the vast dry highlands of Asia are cooling with extraordinary rapidity. The conditions of Central Asia as to pressure are therefore soon totally reversed. By the middle of October a large system of moderately high pressure has been formed, extending from the Caspian Sea to China. That remains of the old depression, greatly reduced, is now over the Bay of Bengal. North-east winds have begun to blow in the north of the Bay, though south-west winds still prevail in the south and east. Now winds blowing from the north-east come from colder and comparatively dry latitudes. They bring little moisture with them, and though they would take up a considerable quantity from the Bay of Bengal, they could give little rain to the east coast of India, upon which they blow. For they are travelling from colder to warmer latitudes, and, growing warmer as they go, are ever increasing their water-bearing power.

But south-west winds are still blowing in the south and east of the Bay of Bengal, and these coming from the warmer southern oceans are laden with moisture. Meeting the north-east winds this southerly current is bent round in the north of the Bay, and, chilled by the colder current which turns it back, it sheds its moisture in a fertilising flood on the east coast of the peninsula and far inland. It is for this cause that the north-east monsoon is sometimes called the "retreating monsoon," for its rain-giving power depends upon the south-west winds which it meets and overcomes. The rains of the north-east monsoon are, however, soon over, for by the end of November, the high pressure area having increased in intensity, north-east winds prevail over the whole Bay and the warm water-bearing currents are turned back long before they reach the latitude of India. The charts on the preceding page show the formation of the high pressure system over Central Asia, and the prevailing winds for October and December.

Though we speak of the "South-West Monsoon" and the " North-East Monsoon," thereby indicating the general direction of the wind, it must not be supposed that the winds actually maintain these directions in every part of India. They do not. They are diverted from their original direction to some extent by local variations of pressure, and to a much greater extent by the configuration of the country. The decline in barometric pressure from west to east during the south-west monsoon bends the south-west winds round towards the east, and they strike the coasts of Bombay as westerly winds. The opposite is the case in the north of Burma where the rapidly decreasing pressure to the north-west bends the winds round towards the north and then to the north-west. This influence is greatly intensified by the northern mountain wall, across which they cannot pass. The south-west monsoon current in the Gangetic plain blows, therefore, from the south-east, travelling from Bengal up the plain to the Punjab and then bending north again. For similar reasons the north-east monsoon in the Gangetic plain is a north-west wind, travelling from the Punjab to Bengal, where it bends round to the south. Blowing from the north-east in the northern part of the Bay, it' skirts the area of depression, bending gradually towards the south.

We must now follow the course of these winds and mark the conditions which determine the deposit of their life-giving store of water. The south-west winds, striking the west coast, are at once checked by the Western Ghats. To pass these the current is forced upward to colder altitudes, and at once a large part of its vapour is condensed, and heavy and continuous rains are the result from beyond the summit of the mountains to the sea. The rainfall is great all along the western coast during the whole of the south-west monsoon, but more particularly in the south, where it commences earliest. East of the Ghats the rainfall rapidly declines, for the current descends to warmer regions. In the month of July, when rain is falling heavily all along the Western Coast the winds reach Madras as hot and scorching blasts.

Towards the north the Western Ghats decline in height, and thus present less hindrance to the monsoon current. North of the Ghats are the long valleys of the Tapti and the Narbada. Up these the current sweeps, depositing a portion of its water as it goes, but reserving the bulk of it for the broken highlands of the Central Provinces and Chota Nagpur, where during the month of July the rainfall is very abundant. Further north again Kathiawar and Cutch get comparatively little, and Sind and the Indus valley very much less. The land is hot, and there are no mountains to force the current upwards, and so the winds sweep past, carrying their moisture with them till it is condensed on the slopes of the western Himalayas.

On the eastern side of India the south-west monsoon first gives a heavy rainfall to the south and west of Ceylon, but leaves the northern and eastern part of the island almost untouched. Sweeping up the Bay it strikes the coasts of Burma. Tenasserim receives a very copious watering, as also does the Arakan coast west of the Yoma. Fairly heavy rains, indeed, prevail for a couple of months over almost the whole of Burma, except a central area a couple of hundred miles north and south of Mandalay, which is comparatively dry. It is a warm and sheltered region consisting of plains and low hills, and the monsoon current, having deposited much of its water in the south and west, passes over it without shedding much more of its moisture till it meets the colder mountains of the north.

North of the Bay of Bengal, and in the valley of Assam, the rainfall is very heavy. Cherrapunji, on the southern edge of the Khasi Hills, has a fall far in excess of that of any other place in the world, receiving as a rule over 600 inches of rain in the year. This phenomenal fall, which extends only over a very small area, is due to a combination of causes. The clouds have swept up over many hundreds of miles of the warm bay and the Ganges delta, and the air is completely saturated with moisture. The slopes of the hills are sharp, and the current is swiftly diverted upwards. But this alone would not account for such a fall. Just at that point the current that is diverted toward the west by the frontier hills of Burma, meets that coming up direct from the bay, and it is probable that an upward swirl is caused that carries vast volumes of saturated air to cooler heights, ridding it thus of almost all its moisture. From the Khasis one branch of the southwestern current is diverted in a north-westerly direction along the southern slopes of the Himalayas and the great plain, and the other, turning to the east, passes up the valley of the Brahmaputra. Both these branches yield abundant rain, and the Provinces which they traverse are among the best watered tracts in India.

During the north-east monsoon the rainfall is chiefly on the east coast, extending inland in the south right across the peninsula to the Western Ghats. These are the districts to which the south-west monsoon gives but little rain, blowing over them for the most part as a comparatively dry and warm wind. The north-east monsoon makes up for this deficiency, and in the place of the summer rains which prevail elsewhere gives them a full supply in the autumn.

In April the south-west monsoon currents are slowly forming, and by the end of the month Ceylon and Travancore have received the beginning of their rains. In the diagram for this month, as well as in those for July and October, notice should be taken of the comparatively dry area in central Burma. In July the south-west monsoon is in full force, and it will be seen how greatly the Western Ghats keep the rain from the districts to the east of them.

In October the north-east (or " retreating ") monsoon is beginning. From the direct south-west currents rain is still falling on the south-west coasts of India and Burma, and the retreating current has begun to shed its store along the coast of Madras.

Taking the rainfall of India as a whole, we find that in most parts it is fairly abundant. The northeastern portion of the great Indo-Gangetic plain, the whole of Bengal and Assam, the greater part of Burma, and the West Coast Districts from the Gulf of Cambay to Cape Comorin, have a very copious supply. Next to them come the eastern Districts of the Deccan Plateau. These have as a rule a heavier fall than the western Districts, where the rains are much more uncertain and variable. In the north-west of India the fall is always scanty and insufficient, and much of the land is consequently little better than desert. East of the Indus a long narrow strip is almost rainless.

Though the climate and rainfall of India are thus subject to well ascertained laws, and are on the whole exceedingly regular, they are nevertheless liable, particularly at the change of monsoons, to local disturbances of peculiar violence. Thunder storms are very common in many parts, and, though quickly over, they often deluge large tracts of country over which they pass. They are as a rule very welcome. They bring relief from the oppressive heat, and their rains refresh the whole face of nature. In the Bay of Bengal Cyclones of great severity are also frequently generated, especially at the change of monsoons.

They seem, as a rule, to take their rise in the neighbourhood of the Andaman Islands, and travel at first in a westerly direction gradually changing their course to north and then north-east.

Cyclone storms are approximately circular or elliptical, and their centre is an area of deep depression. The wind blows round the centre, but bends ever inwards and upwards. Cyclones commonly strike the coast to the north of Madras, and, passing northwards, the fury of their winds often does great damage along the coast. They are usually accompanied by exceedingly heavy rains. Owing in part to the rapid decrease in barometric pressure towards the centre (which alone would account for a rise of 3 feet in the level of the water), and in part to the inward and upward motion of the wind, vast storm waves are sometimes formed, and when these strike a confined bay they sweep over the land for many miles, causing great destruction of life and property. About thirty years ago the town of Masulipatam was almost destroyed by such a wave, and a few years later a similar one swept over the Sandarbans and up the estuaries of the Ganges, doing immense damage and destroying over 100,000 lives.

9

THE PEOPLE OF INDIA

ETHNOLOGY

The ethnology of India is still in its infancy, and only its bare outlines can be regarded as in any degree settled. In some respects it is less settled now than it appeared to be a few years ago. By modem ethnologists more reliance is placed on the study of physical types than on that of language, and many conclusions that were believed, on linguistic evidence, to be firmly established are now widely rejected. Twenty years ago language was regarded as yielding by far the most valuable testimony as to the origins of races and tribes and their pre-historic movements. At the present time a minute study of physical type is more relied on and in this direction a large amount of most valuable material has been gathered by the Ethnographic Survey of India, commenced in Bengal twenty years ago and now proceeding in most of the Provinces. The results of this survey up to 190 1 were carefully worked out in the General Report on the Census of that year.

But before summarising these results, it will be well to glance briefly at the theories commonly accepted till within the last ten years. In the main these are supported by recent investigations, but in some important points they must now be greatly modified. The vast majority of the people of India have long been known to belong to two great stocks, the Aryan and the Dravidian. To what extent these two stocks have mingled, where the purest blood of each is now to be found, and over what extent of the country each now predominates —these are questions on which a variety of opinions have been held, and in which a study of type alone can give a decisive answer.

In addition to these great stocks, three others of subordinate importance to India have been distinguished. The Tibeto-Burman, which has influenced the country on the east; the Scythian, of Mongolo-Tartar origin on the west; and the Kolarian, of doubtful origin, but closely related to the Dravidian, and represented in modern days by scattered tribes east and west of Central India. That the Aryans entered India from the northwest, pressing on in successive swarms probably through many centuries, has long been universally agreed. Language, custom, and tradition alike bear testimony to this. Whether the Dravidians and Kolarians had similarly an external origin, and entered India in invading swarms long anterior to the inroads of the Aryans, or whether they should rather be regarded as the true aborigines of the country, has been a disputed point. As regards the Dravidians, the former conclusion has been the one most favoured. There exists in Baluchistan a " linguistic island " of Dravidian speech, the Brahmi language, cut off from the main body of Dravidian tongues by -nearly 1,000 miles. This has been taken as strong proof that the Dravidians, like the Aryans after them, came from the north-west. Sir W. W. Hunter accepted this, and further held that the Kolarians came into India from the east, and, stretching across the north of the peninsula, peopled the highlands from Orissa to the mouth of the Narbada before the influx of the Dravidians; and that the latter, when pressed by the Aryans in the north, broke through the Kolarian line and forced their way into the south of the peninsula. The Dravidians had thus driven " an ethnic wedge " down the centre of the peninsula, dividing the Kolarians into two sections. He thus accounted for the separation of the Bhils, Kolas, etc., of the west from the Santhals, Kols, etc., of the east—all of which tribes he believed to be Kolarian.

To these four stocks a fifth was added almost in historic times. The Scythians appear to have come from Central Asia, and to have forced their way across the northwest frontier. Their influence is to be traced throughout the whole of west India, but Hunter believed that this race had permanently occupied the plains of the Indus, and that the noble race of Rajputs, and the Jats, the most important agricultural tribe of western Punjab, are their modern representatives.

Such were the conclusions drawn mainly from a study of language, with whatever additional light was to be had from a comparison of social systems, from tradition, and from a general agreement of type. modern ethnologists, however, hold that physical type is far more persistent and unchanging than language, and that, when we can decipher it, we shall find the ethnic history of every people more truly recorded in their physical characteristics shape of head, style of features, stature, hair, eyes, etc. than in their speech. They further hold that a minute study of physical type is likely to prove of peculiar value in India, where for centuries tribes and castes have lived apart, with but little intermixture of blood; for in such a case types may be expected to persist with unusual definiteness. It is exceedingly probable that this line of investigation may yield most valuable results in India within the next few years. In the Census Report Mr. H. H. Risley, C.I.E., summarises the results of the Survey as far as it had then proceeded, and on the basis of the data collected divides the people of India into the following seven distinct types :

I. The Turko-Iranian type, in Baluchistan and the Northwest Frontier Province. Stature above wean; complexion fair; eyes mostly dark, but occasionally grey; hair on face plentiful; head broad; nose moderately narrow, prominent, and very long.

II. The Indo-Aryan type, in Punjab, Rajputana and Kashmir. Stature mostly tall; complexion fair; eyes dark : hair on face plentiful; head long; nose narrow and prominent, but not specially long.

III. The Scytho-Dravidian type of Western India. Head broad; complexion fair; hatr on face rather scanty; stature medium; nose moderately fine and not conspicuously long.

IV. The Apyo-Dravidian type in the United Provinces, parts of Rajputana, in Bihar, and Ceylon. Head long or medium; complexion from light brown to black; nose from medium to broad; stature usually below the average.

V. The Mongolo-Dravidian type of lower Bengal and Orissa. Head broad; complexion dark; hair on face usually plentiful; stature medium : nose medium, with a tendency to broad.

VI. The Mongoloid type of the Himalayas, Assam, Nepal, and Burma. Head broad; complexion dark, with a yellowish tinge; hair on face scanty; stature below average; nose fine to broad; face characteristically flat; eyelids often oblique.

VII. The Dravidian type of Madras. Hyderabad, the Central Provinces, most of Central India and Chota Nagpur. Stature short, or below mean; complexion very dark, approaching black; hair plentiful, with an occasional tendency to curl; eyes dark; head long; nose very broad.

It will be seen that the Aryan element is much less prominent than has hitherto been thought, and on the other hand, that the Dravidian element is more widespread. The purest Aryan type is found under Type IV. Among the Rajputs, Khattris, and Jats, and the theory that would assign a Scythic origin to these races may be regarded as finally disposed of.

They have apparently maintained very largely the purity of their blood, while the Indo-Aryans of the United Provinces have commingled with the Dravidians. In explanation of this Mr. Risley surmises that they came into India by slow and peaceful migration, bringing their women with them, while the ancestors of their western neighbours, coming into India at a later date and by a more toilsome and hazardous route, brought few, if any, women with them, and took wives of the daughters of the land. With regard to the Dravidians, Mr. Risley's conclusion is that they are the earliest inhabitants of India of whom we have any knowledge. It must be remembered, however, that each type gradually shades off into the neighbouring one, and that the boundaries are therefore only approximate. The divisions, moreover, only indicate the general type of the bulk of the people. The proportions in which the racial elements combine in different classes of the comiminity arc also very various. Among the Scytho-Dravidians the Scythic element predominates in the Baratha Brahmans, and the Aryan element predominates among the Brahmans of the Aryo-Dravidians. There is also a certain admixture of the Arjan element almost everywhere among the higher castes, and traces Scythic and Mongolian blood are found among Dravidians of the south.

DISTRIBUTION OF THE POPULATION

India is essentially an agricultural country. According to the last Census nearly 200 millions of the people were engaged directly in agricultural or pastoral occupations. These people arc necessarily scattered over the land and not congregated together in towns. Many more are indirectly employed on the land, being engaged in ministering to the needs of the agriculturists proper. These also are scattered over the country. India has no great mineral resources, and even what she has are as yet but little worked. Nor are there any great manufactures to draw the people together in towns. Small manufactures there are in plenty, and some have their centres in particular localities. But in no sense can India, or any Province of India, be called a manufacturing country. The result of this is that the vast majority of the people live in hamlets or villages, and the towns and cities are comparatively few, and for the most part small. This is best seen by comparing.

India with a great manufacturing country like England. While in India, out of a population of 294 millions, only 270 millions—or considerably less than 10 per cent.—live in towns of 5,000 inhabitants and over, in England 77 per cent, of the total population live in such towns. In the one case over 90 per cent, of the people are scattered over the land, but in the other only 23 per cent. India is thus emphatically a land of villages.

In ancient days these villages were generally selfcontained and self-organised communities. They had but little communication with the outside world and needed little. Living upon the soil, the majority of their people were cultivators, but the simple handicrafts, etc.. necessary for the independent life of an agricultural community were represented in every village, and all occupations passed from father to son. In ordinary years, when nature was propitious, such villagers had few inducements to look beyond their own narrow borders. Roads were few; travelling difficult and dangerous; and, except when some religious festival drew them to some famous shrine, they spent their quiet and laborious days among their own people. In many parts of India this is still to a large extent the case, but in others it is rapidly passing away. Better roads, and other means of communication, the spread—even among the illiterate—of some knowledge of the world beyond, the increase of their means, and the opening of outside markets for their produce, are all enlarging the outlook of the people, breaking down their village exclusiveness, and bringing them into touch with a wider world. But these influences do not tend to substitute town life for village life, nor will they ever do so. So long as India remains, as she must remain, an agricultural country, the vast majority of her people must live upon the land they till.

In modern days the growth of towns on particular sites is almost always due to one or more of three reasons. This last is an essentially modern cause of towns, and is due to the increase in the facilities of travel, and of the wealth and leisure of the people. It is naturally, therefore, most operative in Europe and America, where a multitude of towns trace their growth and prosperity to no other cause. But it has also been operative in India, and such hill stations as Simla, Darjeeling, Ootacamund, etc., owe their existence to it alone. Such towns are, however, of less importance than those whose origin is to be ascribed to the other causes named. Though they may grow to considerable size and wealth, and may be, as in India, summer seats of Government, 'they exercise no great influence on the development and destiny of a people.

But while in these modern days most towns are indebted to commerce or manufacture for their prosperity, very different reasons may have led originally to their foundation. In ancient times (i) political and (2) religious considerations had more to do with the founding of towns in India than had commerce. At various periods the country has been overrun by foreign invaders, and at others has been broken up into a multitude of States almost ceaselessly at war with one another. In such times, wherever a powerful chief settled, people flocked to him, partly for defence and partly for trade; and a town soon grew up, which became his capital and the seat of his government. The site of such a town was chosen not so much for commercial as for military reasons. It had, indeed, to be situated, if possible, in some place to which the supplies needed by his retainers and army could be easily brought; but it was still more needful that it should be in a good strategic position, well adapted both for defence and as a base for attack. A large number of Indian towns had this origin. Many others owed their origin to religion. The presence of a famous shrine, or the proximity of a sacred river, attracted annually multitudes of pilgrims, whose requirements in the way of accommodation and provisions afforded lucrative employment for a large resident population.

When once a town has been founded, no matter what its origin may have been, tends to build up for itself a trade and thus to maintain itself in prosperity, even though the circumstances in which it had its rise should quite pass away. Religious change in India is so exceedingly slow, that towns which grew up at first for the convenience of pilgrims are often preserved in prosperity for many centuries by the conditions which gave them birth. We have illustrations of this in Benares and Puri. Puri exists solely for the sake of pilgrims, and though Benares has now an additional importance, due to other and modern causes, yet its shrines and pilgrims are still the chief sources of its fame and wealth.

Political changes in India have, however, been as rapid as religious changes have been slow, but British rule has now given peace to the whole country. Many towns, therefore, that had a strategical origin are now flourishing trade centres. In most cases they possessed from the first, as we have seen, a certain suitability of position for trading purposes. When they became centres of environment, and seats of a large population, roads were pushed out in every direction, and other means of communication opened up, till in course of time they became the recognised emporia for large districts. When their political importance declined, their trade still maintained them and became a more enduring cause of prosperity and wealth. Under British rule such towns have frequently become centres of civil or military administration, and have regained much of their old greatness. Delhi, Lucknow, Allahabad, Poona, and a host of others are examples. When, however, such ancient military towns were not well situated for trade, and did not become the natural and accepted commercial centres of considerable districts, any change in the political circumstances which gave them birth generally led to their decline, and sometimes to their complete extinction. Kanauj, Ajodhya, and Seringapatam are illustrations of this.

Of the ancient towns in India which owe their origin to commerce, comparatively few are of any size or great importance. India has always had a considerable foreign trade, and though even in ancient times the bulk of it was, no doubt, carried by sea, it gave rise to no sea-port of any magnitude that has survived to modern days. This was mainly due to the fact that the trade was carried in foreign ships, and the people of India themselves never took largely to navigation. Further, the trade being chiefly on the West Coast, where the accumulation of sand washed up by the sea is greatest, such ancient ports as there were have either been obliterated or have become inland towns. Even the later ports of Surat, Cambay, and Goa, which enjoyed the earlier trade round the Cape of Good Hope, have greatly suffered from this cause, and the bulk of their trade has now passed to Bombay. Overland commerce has, however, left more permanent marks on many of the towns of the north and north-west. Shikarpur has for ages controlled the trade across the Bolan Pass; Dera Ismail Khan, and, further inland, Shahpur and

Multan, that by the Gonial; Peshawar, than by the Khyber; and Jullundur and Amritsar, that through Kashmir to Tibet. All these towns owe much to the fact that for centuries they have been the natural and recognized centres for the trade carried on across these ancient mountain routes. Inland trading towns grew up in early times, chiefly along the great water-ways of the Ganges and Indus, or where trade routes crossed one another.

THE DENSITY OF POPULATION

In an agricultural country like India, which does not import its food but grows it, the population of every considerable area tends to increase till it approaches the maximum that the produce of the land can feed.

But the abundance of the harvests depends upon the nature of the soil and the sufficiency and regularity of the water supply. And, since in most places the water supply is almost entirely due to the rainfall, it follows that, as a general rule and within certain limits, the density of the population varies with the average rainfall. Of course, there are many exceptions to this. The rainfall may be so irregular that, though the country may have a large annual average, it may, nevertheless, be burnt up for the greater part of the year and flooded for a few weeks. Such an irregular rainfall as this would not greatly promote agriculture. Or, though the rainfall is large and regular, the land itself may consist of rocky and barren hills. Both the produce and the population will then be low. On the other hand, a country which has a scanty rainfall may be well watered by irrigation, and therefore fertile. But if sufficiently large areas be taken, it will be found that regions of ampler rainfall are also regions of denser population.

It should be noted, however, that this connection only holds good in agricultural countries. Wherever other industries are largely developed, whether mining or manufacture, a population is often found far larger than any that the land itself could support. The wealth made by these industries enables such countries to import much of their food from other lands. The following map, which shows the density of the population in the several States and Provinces of the Empire, illustrates in part this relation between rainfall and population.

At one time Dravidian forms of speech probabfy occupied the whole country. That is at least suggested by the fact that scattered tribes, speaking Dravidian tongues, are still found as far north as Baluchistan in the west and Chota Nagpur in" the east. Now, however, the vernacular languages of at least four-fifths of the Indian people belong to the Aryan family. This is precisely what might have been expected. Whenever a stronger people, more advanced in all the arts, and with a more developed language, dispossess a weaker race, the latter will in course of time adopt the language of their conquerors, even though, through intermarriage, the races themselves may coalesce. The superseded tongue may contribute any number of words to the new language which the conquered must adopt, but ultimately the language which survives will be, in idiom, form and structure, the language of the conquerors. This process has gone on largely in India. Though Dravidian blood still prevails in some degree almost up to the Himalayas, and in comparative purity as far north as Central India, Dravidian languages are, with the exception of a few scattered remnants, confined to those parts of South India over which the waves of Aryan immigration never swept in force.

The principal Dravidian languages are Telugu, Tamil, Kanarese, and Malayalam, which are spoken respectively by about 2, 3,4, and 6 millions of people, inhabiting an area which forms a solid linguistic block in south-east India. Gond is spoken by over a million people, chiefly in the Central Provinces; Tulu by over half a million in South Kanara; Kurukh, or Oraon, by about the same number on the hills of Chota Nagpur. And Kandh by nearly as many on the hills of Orissa. There are many other Dravidian languages spoken by smaller numbers, the most interesting of which is Brahi, spoken by an isolated group in eastern Baluchistan.

Santali and Kol, the languages of the Santhals and Kols, who number nearly three millions and are found in Bihar, Chota Nagpur and Orissa, arc the chief languages of the Munda Sub-Family. There are several other members of this group, but less known, and spoken by smaller numbers. These languages used to be called Kolarian, and the Kolarians were believed by some to have entered India from the north-east. The group is, however, essentially Dravidian, and is probably identical in origin with the Dravidian languages of the South.

The Aryan languages spoken in India fall into two classes, the Irano-Aryan, or Iranian, which prevail west of the Indus, and of which Baloch, Pashto, and Persian are the chief examples, and the Indo-Aryan which prevail from the Indus to the confines of Burma, and southwards till they meet the Dravidian languages of the peninsula

All the chief Indo-Aryan languages are Sanscritic in their character, Sanscrit, the great classical language of India, having in all probability been developed into the form in which it is found in the Vedas long after the final Aryan immigrants had settled in the " Middle Land." A comparison of these languages suggests that they were introduced into India at two different periods, probably separated by several centuries; that the earliest wave of immigrants, coming, most likely, from the west, spread over the greater part of western and northern India before the arrival of the second wave; and that these latter, coming most probably across the northern frontier, forced their way into the middle of the previous settlers, and, as they grew in numbers, drove them gradually to the east, south and west, and to some extent also to the north. Dr. Grierson, the head of the Linguistic Survey of India, calls the languages whose origin is to be traced to these later settlers, the Inner Indo-Aryan languages, and those that appear to have sjirung from the language of the earlier settlers, the Outer Indo-Aryan languages. To the east of the Inner gnnip tlicre is also a smaller Intermediate class formed probably by a fusion of the two. The localities in which these various languages are spoken are shown on the map on the following page. It should be remembered, however, that neighbouring languages shade off into one another by almost imperceptible gradations, and though the boundaries are of necessity sharply defined on a map, they are not so in reality.

Most of these languages have numerous dialects, sometimes exhibiting a very wide degree of divergence. The only one of these that we need notice is Hindustani, the chief dialect of Western

Hindi. Hindustani is spoken more or less all over India, and particularly by the Muhammadans, and is often spoken of as the lingua franca of India. Urdu is literary Hindustani, written in the Persian character, and often greatly modified by the introduction of Persian words. The prevalence of Hindustani throughout India is due to the widespread influence of the Mughal Empire, and to the fact that Muhammadans are numerous in every' Province.

In the extreme north of India are tribes speaking Non-Sanscritic Indo-Aryan languages. They are few in number, however, and none of their dialects have native characters. The Indo-Chinese languages spoken in India, of which by far the most important group is the Tibeto- Burman, are very numerous, including no fewer than 92 of the 147 languages enumerated in the Census Report. They are spoken, however, by a comparatively small fraction of the people, less than twelve millions in all, including the people of Burma and the border mountains, the Khasi and Garo Hills, and the slopes of the Himalayas. Burmese, the most cultivated of these languages, is spoken by about 11 millions. Karen and Shan, spoken by tribes bearing the same names, are closely related to Chinese, and are each spoken by about a million people. The rest of the languages of this group are spoken by mere handfuls of people. Comparatively little is known as yet about many of the Indo-Chinese languages.

RELIGION

Of the 294 millions of people in India in 1901, 207 millions were classed as Hindus. But the term Hinduism, as now used, includes such a wide variety of beliefs and customs that definition becomes impossible. The early Dravidians were Animists, i.e., believers in spirits, mostly malign, that had constantly to be propitiated by sacrifice and offering. The non-Caste population of south India are little more than this to-day. The Aryans, on the other hand, early developed a philosophic cult, chiefly pantheistic in character, which was overgrown in later ages by a vast mass of Brahmanical ceremonial and custom. The Aryans in India greatly influenced the earlier races with which they came in contact, imposing their authority and imparting their religious rites, but at the same time adopting and sanctioning many elements of their primitive animistic beliefs. Every type of religion in which a Hindu element is discoverable in any degree is now classed as Hinduism, and that term therefore covers every variety of belief and ceremonial custom, from almost the crudest animism to philosophic pantheism. Between the various sects of Hinduism, or between the multitudinous castes, there are to-day hardly any common bonds save reverence for Brahmans, the observance of caste rules., and belief in the sacredness of the cow. Only a few primitive tribes inhabiting hilly tracts in the peninsula are now classed as Animists. Their number, which is decreasing, is about 84 millions.

Muhammadanism has more than 7 millions of adherents in India. They form the majority of the population in the Punjab, the North-West Frontier Province, Bengal, and Assam, as well as in the State of Kashmir, and are numerous all over India. Muhammadanism was introduced into India in comparatively recent times by the incursions of the Afghans, the Mughals, and others, and its prevalence throughout India is to be traced mainly to the influence of the Mughal supremacy. Its doctrines, based on the Quran, make Muhammadanism an essentially aggressive faith. Over India, as over many other lands, it was spread chiefly through the influence of civil and military power. It is still aggressive in many parts of India, though its growth now is mainly due to social influences.

Buddhism was in its origin a revolt against Brahmanism, and was founded by Gautama, who was born about five and a half centuries before the Christian era. Though it flourished greatly in India for several centuries, Benares itself being for long a Buddhist city, it has not taken permanent root in the land of its birth. It has spread, however, over the greater part of eastern Asia, and now numbers over 100 million votaries. At the date of the last Census there were nearly 6 million Buddhists in the Indian Empire, but they were almost entirely confined to Burma. Jainism arose about the same time as Buddhism, or perhaps a little earlier, and has much in common with it. It does not, however, make nirvana the great goal of aspiration, but believes that the soul, when delivered from the bondage of matter, will enjoy a separate and conscious spiritual life. The modern Jains number about 1,300,000, and are found chiefly in Rajputana, Bombay and Central India. They observe caste, have an inordinate number of temples, and are remarkable for their reverence for every form of animal life.

Sikhism is of much more modern origin. Its founder, Baba Nanak, was a vigorous preacher born near Lahore a little more than 400 years ago. His followers formed a religious society, which his successors in power bound together by strict political organisation and military discipline. In the history of India the Sikhs have been rather a military than a religious force. As a religion Sikhism acknowledges one God, inculcates reverence for its sacred writings, or Granth, and rejects all caste distinctions and ceremonies. The Sikhs number now about 2 millions, and have their headquarters at Amritsar in the Panjab.

Christianity, in one form or another, has existed in India for many centuries, chiefly on the south-west coast, where the Syrian Christians have long been settled. Both Roman and Protestant Christianity have increased rapidly in India of recent years, and the number of Christians returned at the last Census was nearly 3 millions.

Among the minor religious bodies found in India are the Parsis and the Jews. The Parsis are fire-worshippers, whose ancestors came from Persia. Their sacred book is the Zend-avesta of Zoroaster. They are settled chiefly in Bombay, where they constitute a thriving commercial community numbering about 95,000. There are over 18,000 Jews in India, two-thirds of whom are in Bombay and along the west coast. How or when they came is a disputed point, but in some places they enjoy very ancient rights. As in all other countries the Jews in India keep themselves rigidly separate from the people among whom they dwell.

10

NATURAL PRODUCTS

As is necessary preliminary to any useful study of the natural products of India, and especially of the cultivated vegetable products, we must first consider the nature of the soil and the supply of water for agricultural purposes. We have glanced at both these subjects in other connections, but they claim now a more detailed and careful examination if we would understand the natural distribution of vegetable products, and the reasons why different crops, or different methods of cultivation, prevail in different districts.

THE SOIL

The soil is the weathered product of the rocks of which the earth's crust is composed. Whenever rocks, however hard, are exposed to the influence of air and water, heat and cold, they slowly crumble. This process, which is partly chemical and partly mechanical, is termed "weathering." It is accelerated by the presence of vegetation, for not only do plants promote chemical action, but their roots, penetrating into the minutest crevices, soon split the hardest rocks. The soil is the product of long ages of such weathering, increased and enriched by the decay of plants and animals. Whatever other substances may have mingled with it and modified it, it is plain that the character of the soil must everywhere depend primarily upon the character of the rock from which it is derived. In a great alluvial plain like that of the Ganges the soil is a mixture of the crumblings of many kinds of rock which the rivers have brought from great distances, and which have been ground down by attrition to a fine impalpable mud. But in othercases there may be little mixture, and especially is this the case where particular geological formations cover large areas, when the difference between different soils is almost as marked as the difference between the rocks from which they are derived. Nowhere is this more clearly seen than in the Deccan, where the soil that prevails in the north-west offers a striking contrast to that of the cast and south.

We have seen that the Aravallis and the Eastern Ghats are the most ancient hills in India. The geological formation of which they are in the main composed extends right across the peninsula south of a line drawn from Goa to Masulipatam, and across the eastern half of that part of the peninsula which lies north of that line. Over the greater part of this area, and again in the west from the northern slurs of the Aravallis to the falls of kutch and Cambay, Jiard crystalline archican rocks prevail. Such rocks weather very slowly, and although the process of disintegration has been going on for countless ages, the soil is of no great depth excess where it has been washed down from the hill sides into the valleys. The soil from such rock is porous and light, and the rain sinks into it readily. But as the rock itself is comparatively near the surface and is impervious to water, the moisture that the soil receives drains away with rapidity, or is collected in deep hollows of the rock.

Between the Archaean region of the Aravallis and that of the south-west there is a vast area of basaltic rock, known as Deccan Trap, which is volcanic in its origin. Through long geological ages that part of India was the scene of vast and recurrent volcanic disturbances, the outflow of which ultimately covered an area of upwards of 200,000 square miles. It forms the entire north-western part of the Deccan and two-thirds of Kathiawar, and in successive layers extends to a very great depth, in some places exceeding 6,000 feet. Deccan Trap weathers comparatively quickly, and the resulting soil is dark in colour and very fertile, and is known as the black cotton soil. Unlike the soil from the crystalline rocks of the east it retains its water, so much so that it is often described as " water-holding soil." And since, owing to the rapid disintegration of the trap, the soil is generally fairly deep, there is usually a good supply of water a little way below the surface which can easily be tapped by wells.

The water-holding power of any soil is of the greatest possible value to the agriculturist. Where the soil has but little such power the effects of drought are very speedily felt, the fields are burnt up and the wells run dry. A water-holding soil, however, may be caked on the surface, but still vegetation flourishes, for as the surface dries the water rises from below. With such a soil it is only after many rainless months that the effects of drought begin to be seen. The cotton soil possesses this power to a remarkable degree. To a less degree it is also characteristic of most of the alluvial soil of India. This is particularly the case in the valley and delta of the Ganges, where the soil is a mixture of clay and mud, and to a less extent also in the northern part of the great plain between the Jumna and the Indus, where the soil is a light, but not sandy, loam. Passing south-west, however, down the Indus valley, the soil becomes more and more mixed with sand, till in Sind it is little else. The scanty rains which that region receives are quickly absorbed by the light and porous earth; but they evaporate almost as quickly, and the ground is soon perfectly dry for many feet below the surface.

IRRIGATION

By irrigation we commonly mean the watering of the land for the purposes of agriculture by water brought from a distance by means of canals from rivers, or from storage tanks. In many parts of India a sufficient supply of water can be obtained in ordinary years from wells alone. This is the case wherever water-holding soil prevails. Where wells can be depended on there is less need for other sources of supply, though even there a perennial supply of river water may be both cheaper and better for the land. Well-irrigation exists all over India, sometimes alone, and sometimes side by side with other systems, and, taking India as a whole, probably a greater area is watered by wells than by all other systems of irrigation put together. But well-irrigation is chiefly a private work, and land so watered is seldom, in the technical sense, irrigated land. It is probable that irrigation from wells may in some places be taken up by Government, experiments with power-pumps having been made in several taluks in the south. But so far little has been done.

The rivers and plains of North India are peculiarly suitable for the development of great systems of canal irrigation. The rivers being snow-fed afford even in their upper courses and in the digest seasons a fairly abundant supply of water. This can be drawn off into canals at the highest part of the almost level plain, and the gentle slope of the plain then gives the fall necessary for steady flow.
144. As an illustration of this system, and as showing the magnitude of the works that have sometimes to be undertaken, we may take the Upper Ganges Canal which has been in operation for upwards of half a century. The Canal head is near Hardwar, a few miles below the junction of the Bhagirathi and Alaknanda. At this point the Ganges is a fair-sized river, having a flow of about 7,000 cubic feet per second in the driest season, and much more in the rains, or when the snow has begun to melt. The vast head-works of the Canal are of solid masonry and are so arranged as to draw off about 6,500 cubic feet of water per second. This great volume of water is taken in a south-westerly direction across the course of other mountain streams which it does not disturb. It passes under one by means of a tunnel, and is carried over another by an aqueduct two miles in length. Then it bends to the south, and by means of main channels over 450 miles in length, and smaller distributaries with a total length of almost 4,500 miles, waters an area of 1,500 square miles of land between the Ganges and the Jumna. A little lower down, when the Ganges has again become a river of considerable volume, another canal takes off an almost equal quantity of water.

Similar canals are taken from almost all the main tributaries of the Ganges and Indus, and some are of even greater magnitude. The Sirhind Canal from the Sutlej waters more than 1,200 sq. miles of the Panjab, as well as large tracts in the Native States of Patiala, Nabha and Jind. Its main channel exceeds 500 miles in length, and has over ten times that length of distributaries. The Lower Chenab Canal has a main channel of 427 miles, and waters the large area of 3,040 square miles. The Jumna, the Ravi, the Jhelum and the Gandak, provide water for other canal systems which give a perennial supply to many millions of acres. In the Punjab alone 250 square miles of laud are thus watered. 146. In the canals already mentioned the supply of water is constant, the head-works being so constructed as to draw off a sufficient volume even when the river is at its lowest. In the lower course of the Indus a different system is adopted, the canals being tilled only during the lime with the river is in flood. Such canals are distinguished as Inundation Canals, the Indus, owing to the high level of its bed, offers special facilities for this system, which, though not affording so perfect a protection, has the advantage of cheapness. The solid masonry canal heads necessary for the perennial canals give place to simpler earthworks, and a much smaller capital expenditure is required. While the Upper Ganges Canal has cost over;£2, 000,000, and. the Sirhind and Lower Chenab Canals each not very much less, the Indus Inundation Canals, with over 650 miles of main channels, have cost less than;100,000. Sind is almost entirely dependent upon irrigation of this kind.

In the peninsula canal irrigation from the rivers is much more restricted than in the northern plains, since the rivers, not being snow-fed, do not offer a continuous supply of any great volume until they are comparatively near the sea. Small canals, however, draw their supplies from the upper reaches of the Godavari and Kistna; and the Son, shortly before its confluence with the Ganges, supplies canals which irrigate a considerable area in Bihar. But it is in the deltas of the rivers that the great irrigation works of the peninsula are found. The waters of the Mahanadi, the Godavari, the Kistna and the Cauvery are all thus utilised, as well as those of some of the smaller rivers. An anicat, or masonry dam, is thrown across the river near the apex of its delta, which prevents the water draining away too rapidly to the sea. The level of the water above the anicat is thus considerably raised, and a slight fall secured that enables it to be easily distributed throughout the delta and to some extent further inland. The irrigation systems that water the deltas of the four great rivers that discharge into the Bay of Bengal have over 2,000 miles of main canals and 5,300 miles of distributaries, and give an unfailing supply of water to over 4,000 square miles of exceedingly fertile land.

Irrigation in the interior of the peninsula is, however, chiefly from tanks. We have seen that the rivers are in flood for only a short time, and that over the whole of the eastern and southern half of the peninsula the ground is such that the water speedily drains away. The problem to be solved is, therefore, how to hinder the water that Hoods the land during the rainy season from running to waste. This is solved by storing it in " tanks " where it is available for future use. These tanks are of all sizes, from mere ponds to lakes five or six miles in length. They are usually constructed by throwing a dam or bund of masonry or earthwork across a narrow valley through which a stream passes, thus confining the natural drainage. Or sometimes these tanks, or lakes, are constructed at some distance from a river whose waters are artificially turned into them. The water is then distributed over the surrounding country by a network of channels.

In the Madras Presidency alone there are 60,000 such tanks of all sizes. Many of them are ancient works, but most of the greatest have been constructed in recent years. One notable illustration may be mentioned—the Periyar Project, as it is called. The Periyar is a river on the western side of the Western Ghats, whose waters used to be lost in the Arabian Sea. They are now diverted and carried through a tunnel under the Ghats to the eastern side of the hills where water was greatly needed. They supply a vast artificial lake capable of watering more than 300 square miles of land.

Indian irrigation works surpass in extent and utility anything else of the kind in the whole world. The total capital outlay upon them up to the end of 1906 exceeded £3 1,000,000. The payment received from the cultivators for the water supplied meets all the working expenses and returns a fair interest on this large sum. The extent to which such works increase the wealth of the country, and especially of the ryots, is best seen from the fact that in seasons of only slight scarcity the value of the crops raised on irrigated land, and which, but for irrigation, could not have been raised at all, exceeds the whole capital outlay on the works themselves.

FORESTS

The forests of India constitute a valuable part of the natural resources of the country, because of the limber they provide, and they arc of further importance because of their influence on climate and rainfall. Forests protect the hill-sides, the roots of the trees binding the soil and hindering it being washed away. They also check evaporation, and so preserve the moisture of the soil. And, what is of still greater moment, wherever a large extent of forest occurs its comparatively cool area is frequently sufficient to attract the clouds and determine a downpour of rain, which, when once started, spreads far beyond the actual forest area. Forests are of importance for another reason. They encourage and protect the undergrowth of grass and small shrubs, which constitute an invaluable grazing ground when vegetation on the more exposed land is burnt up.

If tradition is to be believed the forests of India covered at one time the face of the whole land. But for centuries they have been exposed to indiscriminate destruction. No steps were taken for their preservation till 1846 when conservancy operations were begun in Bombay. Ten years later this example was followed in Madras. In 1861 the Forest Department of the Government was created, and the work thus begun was completed by the Forest Act of 1878, which gave to India a complete, scientific, and efficient system of forest administration. In all the Provinces there are now large areas of " reserved " forests, which are entirely under the control of the Department, as well as other, and in some provinces considerably larger, areas which are demarcated and efficiently protected. The objects which the Department has in view are (1) the protection of such forests as now exist from damage through unscientific felling of timber, or from fires; (2) the extension of the forests by planting suitable and useful trees over areas reserved for the purpose; (3) the production of as much good timber and firewood as the forest can yield without injury; and (4) the provision of grazing areas which can be relied on in times of drought. The total demarcated forest in British India is over a quarter of a million square miles, or about twice the area of the British Isles.

Numerous valuable timber trees are native to the forests of India. Of these by far the most important is teak. The tree is found chiefly in the forests of Burma and the Western Ghats, in both of which regions much attention has been given to its cultivation. About 150,000 tons of teak, are exported from Burma yearly. It is floated in vast rafts down the rivers, particularly the Salwin. Teak is a hard and durable wood, and until it is very old is not attacked by white ants. It is, therefore, specially useful for building purposes and for furniture. The sal is found in great abundance in the forests of the Himalayas and the Central Provinces. Its wood is hard and heavy, and is used for building purposes and railway sleepers. The sissoo is also characteristic of the Himalayan forests. Its wood is of a rich dark brown colour, hard and capable of a fine polish, and is used for furniture. The blackwood is found chiefly on the Western Ghats. Its heart-wood is a deep reddish-black, hard and firm.

The sandal grows in the drier parts of the peninsula, especially in Mysore. It is cultivated by Government in the Central Provinces. The heart-wood, has a lasting fragrance, and is much used for carving, and as a perfume. It is also employed in the manufacture of incense, and is exported for this purpose. The khair and the toon, both of which are common in the N.W. Himalayas and Burma, yield red woods used for furniture. The heart- wood of the former is dark in colour and very hard and durable, and is valuable for building. The deodar, a kind of cedar, along with various species of pines, are the chief trees in the higher forests of the Western Himalayas. The ebony tree grows on the Western Ghats, and in Burma the ironwood tree is next in importance to the teak.

The forests yield other important products besides timber. From the heart-wood of the khair cutch, or catechu, an astringent gum-resin used both in tanning and as a medicine, is obtained. Myrobalans, the dried fruit of several species of terminalia, are also a valuable tanning material. They are exported in considerable quantities. Caoutchouc, or India rubber, is obtained from the milk which exudes from incisions in the stem of the rubber tree, a species of fig, which is found in the eastern provinces of the Empire. Great attention has been paid of late to the cultivation of this tree, and Government plantations have been started in Bengal, Assam, and Burma. Two other species of the same genus, the banyan and the peepul are common in most parts of India. They, are large and handsome trees, but are not of any great economic value. The peepul is a sacred tree among the Hindus. The bamboo, a giant grass, is common in almost all parts of India where water is plentiful, up to an elevation of 3,000 feet. It is an important forest product, the reserved forests yielding in a single year nearly 100 million canes.

Many trees not indigenous to India have been introduced of recent years. The most notable of these are various species of eucalyptus which have been introduced from Australia and of which there are now extensive plantattons on the Himalayas, Nilgiris, ami Palnis, where they flourish greatly. The leaves of these trees contain an aromatic resin, and their cultivation is said to counteract malaria. The tree grows to an immense height, but develops so quickly that its wood is of little use except for fuel. The pain tree is also spreading in the hotter plains. It grows with great rapidity, spreading its branches over a wide area, and giving a thick and welcome shade. The casuapina is another quick-growing tree, which is cultivated in many places along the coasts of the peninsula. Large Government casuarina plantations have been established on the east coast. The straight poles of the trees are used for scaffolding, but the chief value of the casuarina is as a source of excellent firewood.

FOOD GRAINS

Rice

Of all the food grains of India rice is the most important. It is the staple food of more than a fourth of the people, and a common article of diet of at least as many more. Rice requires for its cultivation an abundant supply of water and warmth, and is therefore chiefly grown in those districts on the plains which have a copious rainfall or are well irrigated. The rich wet plains of Bengal form one of the largest and most productive rice-fields in great rice-producing province, but its total output is less than one-fourth that of Bengal. In both these provinces rice is the main food of the people, but while the vast population of Bengal consumes almost the whole of the rice grown in the province, three-fifths of the crop of Lower Burma is available for export. Rice is also extensively grown in the deltas of the peninsular rivers, and wherever the conditions of the country are favourable. Wheat is cultivated largely in North and Central India, and is a cereal of increasing importance, both as a staple food of the people and as an article of export. It requires for its cultivation much less water than rice. When young it can stand keen frosts, but after the ear is formed it needs a dry air and bright sunshine to bring it to perfection. The plains of Northern and Central India, especially towards the west, are thus well adapted for its growth. Indian wheat is hard and of excellent quality, and is growing in favour in Europe. Its cultivation is, therefore, spreading, and its export rapidly increasing. In the year 1907 the extent of land devoted to wheat culture in British India was 25 million acres, against 73 million acres devoted to rice. The total rice crop was about 21 million tons, and the wheat crop exceeded 8 million tons.

Millets

The chief millets grown in India are cholum (or jowar), cumbu (or bajra), and ragi. They require much less water than rice and take the place of that grain in most of the drier provinces of India. In all but the great rice-producing districts of the peninsula millets form the staple food of the poorer people, rice being a luxury of the wealthy. In Bombay, Sind, and Berar more than half of the total area devoted to food grains is given up to millets, and more than one-third in Madras and in at least half the Districts of the Punjab,

Agra, and Upper Burma. Taking British India alone the millets are not so important a food crop as rice, but if the Native States be added, the majority of which are less abundantly watered than the British Provinces, they are more important, and form the staff of life to a larger number of people.

Pulses

Various pulses, the chief of which are gram and dal, are widely grown in the United Provinces and the Punjab, and less extensively in other provinces. They are valuable as foods, being more nutritious than either rice or millets, because of the larger proportion of nitrogenous matter they contain. They are eaten in combination with less nutritious grains almost all over India.

Barley is grown in the United Provinces, and to a less extent in the Punjab and Bengal, It is less nutritious than the millets, but is cheaper, and is, therefore, largely used by the poorer classes. Barley is also extensively used for brewing.

Maize, or Indian corn, is also cultivated in these provinces, and to a less extent in many other parts of India. It is nowhere, however, a crop of first importance.

OTHER VEGETABLE PRODUCTS

Palms

Various species of Palms are common throughout the plains of India, and on the hill sides, though being an essentially tropical order they do not flourish at any great height. By far the most useful of these is the cocoanut. It loves a well-watered, sandy soil, and flourishes all round the coasts of the peninsula, and particularly around the backwaters of Cochin and Travancore. It is also largely cultivated in the interior. The chief products of the cocoanut are copra and coir. Copra is the dried kernel of the nut from which coconut oil is expressed. Coir is the fibrous husk of the nut, which is woven into coarse matting and rope. There is a considerable export of both copra and coir from the ports of the West Coast.

The palmyra palm which is common all over the peninsula, but cannot stand the cold nights of the north-west, is chiefly of value as a source of " toddy," which is the sap drawn from the flower stalk and slightly fermented.

The areca palm, cultivated chiefly in Bengal but found almost wherever the cocoanut grows, yields a nut which is chewed all over India along with the leaf of the betel, or pepper vine. A species of date palm, known as the bastard date, is found all over India, particularly in Bengal, and is one of the chief sources of jaggery, or native sugar. The true date, the fruit of which is of great value in Arabia and North Africa, needs a dry, hot climate; and brings its fruit to perfection only in Sind. The wood of all the palms is used for temporary buildings, and the leaves make an excellent and durable thatch.

FRUITS AND VEGETABLES

Many kinds of fruit are grown in India, the most universal and useful of which is the plantain or banana. The mango, one of the most luscious fruits in the world, is abundant, and much attention has in some places been given to its culture. Oranges of excellent quality, limes and figs are cultivated in many parts. The jack fruit, the papaw, custard apples, guavas, pomegranates, melons, and pineapples are also common. On the hills many kinds of European fruit have been introduced — apples, pears, plums, strawberries, etc.—and in some places with fair success.

The same is also true of European vegetables. Peas, beans, cabbage, cauliflower, etc., are grown on the hills and on the Deccan plateaux, and potatoes have taken kindly to the country and are now grown even on the plains. The vegetables native to India are very numerous, but of little importance. The most useful are the sweet potato, a species of convolvulus and the brinjal, or egg plant. But a tropical country, especially where the rainfall is precarious and confined to particular seasons, is not well adapted to the cultivation of succulent fruits or vegetables. The temperate regions are richer both in the variety and quality of these products.

Oil Seeds

About 10 million acres in British India are devoted to the cultivation of various seeds which are valuable chiefly for the oil which they contain. The largest areas of cultivation are in Bengal, the Central Provinces, Bombay, and Madras. The greater part of the crop is annually exported, the shipments in 1904-5 representing a value of nearly 10 millions sterling. Linseed is the most important of these seeds, and accounts for nearly half their total value. Linseed oil is a drying oil, and is used for mixing paints. Rapeseed yields rape, or colza oil, which is used for lamps and for lubricating. Sesamum (til or jinjili) seed yields an oil much used in India for bathing purposes. Cotton seed, mustard seed, and ground nuts yield oils which are used in the manufacture of soaps. The last two are also used in the manufacture of sweetmeats, chiefly in France. There is a considerable export of ground nuts from Pondicherry to French ports for this purpose. Castor seed yields an oil valuable as a medicine. The dry residue of these seeds, after the oil has been expressed, forms oil cake, a useful food for cattle. Linseed cake, rape cake, and cotton cake are especially valuable.

Sugar

The sugar cane is largely grown in the United Provinces. Bengal, the Punjab, and the North Western Frontier Province, and to a less extent in other parts of India. In the whole of British India, nearly 2 million acres are devoted to its cultivation. It needs abundant water, and is therefore grown on irrigated land. The total crop in an ordinary' year yields about 2,000,000 tons of sugar, or about four-fifths of the entire amount consumed in the country.

Tea is the fermented and dried leaves of a shrub native to the forests of Assam. The production of tea in India has increased enormously of recent years. Its cultivation on any large scale is, indeed, entirely a development of the last half-century. In 1S30 the Government established a small plantation of the China shrub on the slopes of the Garhwal Himalayas, and China tea is still grown there, chiefly for export by land to Tibet and Central Asia. About the same time the shrub was discovered in the forests of Assam. During the next quarter of a century experimental cultivation, gradually increasing in extent, was carried on in many places, but it was not until about forty years ago that the Indian Tea industries really began; and in Ceylon it was ten years later. In 1865 only 2 per cent, of the tea used in Great Britain came from India, and none from Ceylon; in 1907 India supplied 54 per cent., and Ceylon 36 per cent. In the last twenty years the output of Indian tea has increased threefold. The area devoted to tea in British India is over half a million acres, more than nine-tenths of which are in Bengal and Assam. The rest is on the hills of the Punjab and the United Provinces, and the Nilgiris and Palnis in Madras. There are also about 24,000 acres of tea in the State of Travancore. The value of the tea annually exported is from five to six millions sterling.

Coffee is the dried berry of a shrub said to have been introduced into India from Arabia, where it grows in great perfection. For some years coffee culture has been declining in India. Bad seasons and the ravages of insects have done much to discourage planters. The darker shading shows more e.xtensive cultivation.

Decline in prices has made the cultivation unremunerative. Indian coffee at the best can hardly compete with Brazilian. The area devoted to coffee at present is under 100,000 acres, of which more than three-quarters are in Mysore and Coorg, and the rest on the Nilgiri Hills and the Western Ghats. Comparatively little coffee is used in India, and the bulk of that grown is exported to Great Britain. The total export for 1907 was about 25,000,000 lbs., and its value 660,000.

Spices and Condiments. Of these India has no great variety. Chillies and turmeric arc grown in most parts and arc universally used. Coriander, aniseed, ginger, and cummin are also cultivated. Several species of pepper are grown along the Malabar coast strip, and in Travancore cardamoms are a valuable Government monopoly.

Opium is a powerful narcotic drug obtained from a species of poppy. Shortly after the plant has flowered incisions are made in the green capsule. The juice which exudes solidifies on the outside of the capsule, from which it is daily collected. Cleaned and further dried this exudation constitutes the crude opium of commerce. Opium is an exceedingly valuable medicine. It is also widely used as an article of vicious indulgence. For this purpose it is commonly smoked, or small quantities of it are swallowed, or an infusion is made and drunk. In whatever form it is used it acts first as a stimulant and then as a powerful narcotic and soporific. It has long been widely used as a luxury by many classes in India, notably the Sikhs and Rajputs; and, in parts of Bengal, Assam, and Burma, it is relied on as an antidote to malaria.

Following the example of the Mughal Emperors the British Rulers of India early made opium a Government monopoly. In British India it is produced chiefly in Bihar and the United Provinces, where the cultivators grow it under official inspection, the Government making advances on the crop, the whole produce of which is handed over to their agents.

The central Government Opium Depots are at Patna and Ghazipur. There the opium is packed in chests and forwarded to Calcutta, where it is sold by auction for export. Opium is also grown in the Native States of Central India and Rajputana. From some of these States large quantities of the drug are despatched to Bombay for export. This is known as Malwa Opium, and is subject to a very heavy tax as it passes through British territory. The area devoted to the culture of opium in the Ganges valley is about 600,000 acres, and the value of the crop is usually nearly 5 millions sterling. About 93 per cent, of the entire produce is exported, chiefly to China.

Tobacco is not a native of India, but was introduced by the Portuguese. It is now grown and used in every province, but most extensively in Bengal, Madras, and Burma. The area under tobacco in British India in 1907 was over a million acres, more than half of which was in Bengal. Much of the Bengal tobacco goes to Burma, where smoking is a universal habit. A small quantity of manufactured tobacco is exported to Europe.

Cinchona

The Cinchona tree is grown for its bark, which is the source of quinine, the most useful of all febrifuges. Cinchona was introduced into India in i860, prior to which time it was almost confined to South America. There are now large Government Cinchona Plantations on the Nilgiris and at Darjeeling, and numerous private ones. The tree is also grown on many coffee estates, being planted between the coffee bushes. At the factories on the Government plantations quinine and a mixed febrifuge are manufactured and are supplied to the public at a cheap rate. Quinine is also supplied to the public through the Post Offices, where it is sold in small pice packets. An abundant supply of a cheap and effective febrifuge is of the greatest importance where fever is so prevalent as in India.

Indigo is a dark blue dye extracted from the leaves of a small annual plant by maceration in water. The indigo crop used to be of great value, but the dye is being rapidly superseded by a chemical product which is much cheaper though not so good. Indigo culture is consequently rapidly declining. Between 1880 and 1890 the value of the indigo exported from India averaged over 2 J millions sterling. It has now fallen to about one-fifth of that amount. Indigo is chiefly grown in Bengal, Madras, the United lrovinces and the Punjab, four-ninths of the entire amount produced being grown in Bengal, and half the remainder in Madras.

Cotton is the soft fibre which enfolds the seeds of a small annual plant which has been cultivated in India for many centuries. It grows with great luxuriance on the rich black soil of the Deccan Trap, which has thus earned the name of " cotton soil." Cotton is one of the most important agricultural products of India, for it is not only one of the main articles of export, but, what is of still greater moment, is the raw material of a considerable and growing local manufacture. Great efforts have been, and are still being made to improve the quality of Indian cotton. At present it is not equal to the American variety, which has a longer fibre and is therefore more easily worked, and of greater strength. Careful cultivation, and the introduction of the American species, will probably overcome this difficulty and make Indian cotton equal to any in the world. Cotton cultivation is steadily increasing in India. At present, about 10 million acres are devoted to it, 14 millions of which arc in British India and 5 millions in the Native States. The value of raw cotton exported in 1907 was over /14, 600, 000. The greatest cotton-growing Provinces are Bombay (including the Native States), Berar, and the Nizam's Dominions, but it is extensively grown also in Madras, the United Provinces, the Punjab, and the Central Provinces.

Jute is the fibre of a quick-growing herbaceous mallow, which usually attains a height of eight to ten feet within four months of sowing, and often reaches twelve feet. It is then cut and the stalks are left for some weeks to soak in water when the fibre is easily extracted and cleaned. Jute is grown almost exclusively in the Gangetic delta, where over 3 million acres are devoted to it. Although it exhausts the soil upon which it grows to such an extent that it is usually allowed to lie fallow one year in four, it is nevertheless a most valuable crop. Not only does the fibre realise remunerative prices, but the plant can be grown on land exposed to such severe floods that any other form of cultivation would be extremely precarious. The value of the export of raw and manufactured jute in 1907 was over 25,000,000.

MINERAL PRODUCE AND RESOURCES

Coal

There are several valuable coal fields in India, some of which are being successfully worked. The most important of these is in Bengal, south of the Rajmahal Hills, from which point it extends westwards to the valley of the Son, and from thence south-eastwards through Chota Nagpur to Orissa. Another large field is in the valley of the Godavari stretching north-west from the Ghats to beyond Warora, and extending westwards into the Nizam's Dominions. A smaller field is in the basin of the Narbada, south of Jubbulpore. In Assam there are several coal fields in the valley of the Brahmaputra, where coal of a better quality is found. In the Native State of Rewah is another field which is being successfully worked. In Burma there are some promising fields, but little mining has as yet been attempted.

At present by far the largest output of coal is from the Bengal mines. The chief collieries are near Raniganj, and at Jherria and Giridih. In the Central Provinces there are mines at Warora (worked by Government) in the Godavari coal field, and at Mohpani in the Narbada field. In Hyderabad the Singareni mines are very successful and productive. So, also, though on a smaller scale, arc the Umarift mine in Rcwah (which, like the Warora mine is worked by Government) and the Makum mine in Assam. The total output of coal from Indian mines in 1907 was over 11 million tons, of which nearly 10 million tons came from Bengal alone. This was sufficient to supply the chief needs of the country, and to leave a million tons for export to Ceylon and the Straits Settlements. The import of coal from England has fallen during the last twelve years from three quarters of a million to a quarter of a million tons.

Iron

There is an abundance of iron ore in India, and much of it is of excellent quality. Especially rich ores are found round Salem in the Madras Presidency, in the Raipur District of the Central Provinces, and in Orissa. At one time large quantities of iron were produced in India. But the native system of smelting needed an abundant supply of charcoal, and the decay of the industry was due in part to the decline in the fuel supply, owing to the wholesale destruction of forests. Native smelting is still carried on by isolated groups of metal workers, but the quantity of iron produced is very small, and there is now no possibility of a revival of the industry, as imported iron is much cheaper.

Iron can only be profitably worked in India where, along with the ore, coal and some form of limestone are found, the latter being needed as a flux. If either of these has to be brought from a distance the cost of carriage makes the work unremunerative. At Raniganj, in Bengal, these conditions exist, and iron-works have been established there which smelt about 70,000 tons of ore a year. But the great bulk of the iron used in India is imported from Great Britain and Belgium.

Gold

This precious metal has for ages been found in India. Gold commonly occurs embedded in quartz, a hard crystalline rock of the most ancient geological formation. Rivers which cut their way through such rock almost always bring down more or less gold, which is deposited along with the other detritus which forms their alluvium. Often, through the greater weight of the particles of gold and the variation in the speed of the current, the metal is deposited in particular parts of the river bed. All the greater rivers of India cut through archaean rock, and almost all of them have in the past yielded gold. This is particularly the case with the Brahmaputra, the Irrawaddy, the Godavari, and the Himalayan rivers just as they emerge from the hills. Washing the river sands for gold is still a favourite occupation of many of the hill tribes, and small quantities of the metal are thus obtained.

In Mysore, the Wynaad, and Hyderabad, the rich gold-bearing quartz is mined. It is then crushed and washed. The process is costly, and many mines sunk during the last quarter of a century have not found quartz sufficiently rich in gold to pay for working. Large numbers of ancient, disused, mines exist, which were doubtless the main source of the gold for which India was famous many centuries ago. Almost all the gold now produced in India comes from the Kolar mines in the Mysore State, which for some years have yielded about 2,000,000 worth per annum.

Salt

Of all the mineral products of India salt is in many respects the most important. Native salt supplies the needs of the entire empire, save the Provinces of Bengal and Burma, and forms considerably more than two-thirds of the whole amount consumed. Of imported salt more than half comes from England, more than a third from Arabia, and most of the rest from Germany. The Indian supplies are from three main sources : (1) the sea coast, (2) the salt lakes and pits of Rajputana, of which by far the most important is the Sambhar Lake, and (3) the salt hills of the Punjab and the North -Western Frontier Province.

Along the sea coast salt is manufactured from the sea water by solar evaporation. Both in the Madras and Bombay Presidencies the manufacture is carried on partly at Government factories, but chiefly at private ones under Government license. The Madras salt supplies the whole of South India, the east coast including Orissa, and the eastern part of the Central Provinces. The coast factories of Bombay supply the chief needs of Bombay and Sind, and a part of the Deccan. On the Rann of Cutch the Government own the Pritchard lirine Works which yield a large quantity of excellent salt, most of which goes to the United Provinces, Central India, and the Central Provinces.

The Sambhar Lake—a lake about 20 miles long, lying a little to the north-east of Ajmere—has water so salt that in dry seasons the crystals gather on the surface to a thickness of six or eight inches. Vast quantities (about one-seventh of the whole produce of India) are taken from it without appreciably diminishing the salinity of its water. What the source of its salt may be is a matter of conjecture. The Sambhar Lake, together with brine springs at Pachbhadrii in the Jodhpur State, 180 miles to the south-west, supply Rajputana, and a great part of the United Provinces, Central India, and the Central Provinces.

In the north-west corner of India ranges of hills containing vast quantities of rock salt stretch east and west on both sides of the Indus. The name Salt Range is, however, confined to those on the east side of the river. There are numerous mines both in the Salt Range proper and in the hills of Kohat west of the river, and in the latter district, where the salt crops out. it is quarried like stone. From these mines and quarries a cheap and plentiful supply is obtained for the Punjab, the Northwestern Frontier Province and Kashmir.

Petroleum

There are three valuable petroleum fields in Burma, the produce of which is rapidly increasing. These are, in the order of their yield, the Yenang Haung, the Singu, and the Yenang at fields. The crude oil is obtained in wells and has then to be purified. The yield of petroleum in 1907 was over i so million gallons, which is more than three-fifths of the entire quantity consumed in India. The imports of petroleum in the same year fell to 60 million gallons. Not many years ago three-quarters of the petroleum used in India was imported, now little more than a quarter. The Burma fields thus promise at no very distant date to supply the entire needs of India. A considerable quantity of petroleum is also obtained at Mlkuni in Assam.

Manganese ore is found in Madras, near Vizagapatam, and, in unusual richness and purity, in the Central Provinces and Central India. The amount raised has increased twelve-fold during the last eight years, and in 1906 nearly half a million tons were exported. Manganese is used chiefly in the manufacture of steel.

Mica of excellent quality is found in Bengal, and in smaller quantity in Madras. About 2,000 tons are shipped to Europe yearly. Saltpetre is found in Bengal, as well as in some of the ether northern Provinces, and about £-20,000 worth is exported yearly. Copper also exists in Bengal, but is not as yet worked. Plumbago is found in Travancore. Tin exists abundantly in the southern parts of Tenasserim, but is not worked to any large degree.

Precious Stones

Burma has valuable puby mines. Indeed, of the best stones it has a monopoly, and supplies the world. Mong with the rubies a few sapphires are also found. The Mines are worked by a Company who hold them on lease from the Government. The Company also grants mining license to private individuals who make no return of their finds. The total output is, therefore, difficult to discover. Jade, a green stone greatly valued by the Chinese, is also found in Burma. Valuable diamonds have been found in the past in the Godavari basin, and are occasionally found now. But there is no systematic mining for them.

Wild Animals

The liǫn is now found only in Kathiawar, and though for many years it has been rigidly preserved, it is almost extinct even there. The tiger is found in most parts of India wherever extensive forests or jungles exist. Tigers abound in the Terai, the jungles of the Sandarbans, and the forests of Central India and the Western Ghats. The panther, or leopard, is still more common. The cheetah, or hunting leopard, is a different species, and is native only to the Deccan. It is trained for hunting the antelope, but though swift and sure in attack has no staying power. Wolves abound still in the open country but shun the forests. The common black bear is met with in the forests of rocky hills, and the Tibetan sun bear is found throughout the whole length of the Himalayas, but only at heights of over 5,000 feet. Hyaenas;ire nunicrous, but only where the wolf is not. Jackals are common everywhere and are useful scavengers.

The wild dog, which hunts in jiacks, is found in the forests of Burma and Assam.

The wild elephant exists chiefly in the forests of Eastern Bengal and Assam; less commonly in those of Burma and the Indian peninsula. Under a special Act of the Indian Legislature the elephant is strictly preserved, and can only be captured by license. Considerable numbers are caught and trained for the Government service and for sale. The elephant is not found at all in the north-west of India, where the climate is too dry and the temperature too variable for him. Several species of rhinoceros haunt the swamps of the Brahmaputra valley, the Sandarbans, and Chittagong; and their horns are valued by certain classes of the natives. The wild hog is common in most Provinces in the vicinity of cultivation, and hunting him is a dangerous and exciting sport. The wild ass roams in herds of 20 to 30 in the deserts of Sind and Cutch, and several species of wild sheep and goats have their home on the Himalayas, the mountains of the north-west, and the Sulaiman range. The ibex, a species of goat, is found on the mountains of the peninsula and Kashmir. Antelope arc fairly common in Central India and in the coast flats of Gujarat and Orissa. Bison are mot with in the hill jungles of South India and Burma, and the wild buffalo in Burma and Assam. Of deep there are many species, the chief being the sambup. Monkeys of many kinds are exceedingly numerous almost everywhere. Rats and mice abound throughout the land, and the bandicoot, the most gigantic member of the tribe, is exceedingly destructive.

Of reptiles, snakes and scorpions of many kinds are everywhere found. The largest Indian snake is the python, which sometimes attains a length of 30 feet. Most of the snakes found in India are harmless, but there are three or four whose bite is deadly, and for who.se poison no effective antidote is known. One of the worst of these, and at the same time one of the commonest, is the cobra dicapello. Numerous poisonous water snakes are also found. The blunt-no.scd crocodile infests swampy rivers and backwaters, and the sharp-nosed species, the ghavail, which preys only on fish, is numerous in some of the greater rivers, especially the Ganges, Brahmaputra, and Mahanadi.

The destruction of life and property by wild animals and snakes is very great, and shows little tendency to decline. The total number of persons killed by wild animals (chiefly tigers and leopards) in 1904 was 2,157, 000 of cattle 88,206. Poisonous snakes are ten times as destructive of human life, but not so fatal to cattle. Deaths from snake bite in 1904 numbered 21,880, and the number of cattle killed by snakes was 10,376. Rewards are given by the Government for the slaughter of poisonous snakes and many species of dangerous wild beasts.

The birds of India are very numerous and beautiful, but are more esteemed for the gaiety of their plumage than for the sweetness of their song. Parrots abound, and many kinds are made household pets, as also is the maina, a species of starling which can be taught to talk. Small winged game exists in great variety, including snipe, partridge, quail, plover, teal, and wild duck. The peacock is found in the forests of the Deccan, Assam and Burma; the pheasant in the Himalayas; and the red jungle-fowl, from which domestic poultry are said to have been derived, is met with in most parts. The common crow is familiar everywhere.

Of birds of prey the vulture and the kite are the best known. They are everywhere useful scavengers. Eagles are numerous in the Himalayas. Several species of falcon are trained by the natives for hawking purposes. Hawks, herons, and kingfishers of many kinds abound, and the last is much sought after for its beautiful plumage.

Fish of many excellent varieties abound in all the rivers and most of the tanks. The best river fish belong to the carp and barbel families. The mahsir, sometimes called the Indian salmon, is found in the hill streams both of the Himalayas and the peninsula, and grows to a great size. The hilsa is a similar fish, though smaller in size, which abounds in the streams of the Gangetic delta. All round the coasts salt water fish is caught in great abundance, and the fisheries are a source of wealth to many thousands of people.

As in every tropical country insect life is abundant in India. Ants of many species are found everywhere, and though destructive, they are of immense use as scavengers, for they quickly remove every particle of decaying animal matter. The most destructive of all insects, and one that has to be constantly guarded against, is the white ant. The mosquito is, the greatest of insect plagues, and where it alioimds renders life almost unendurable. Fierce war is waged against the mosquito now, as one species has been proved to be the chief distributer of malarial poison. Of useful insects the bee, the silk-worm, and the lac insect arc cultivated.

Domestic Animals

Horses and ponies are common in lower Province of India, but in relation to the population are most numerous in the Punjab, the United Provinces, and the Central Provinces. Indian bred horses are not,- however, so good as those imported from Arabia, Persia, and Australia. Pegu ponies liavc long been famous. Asses and mules are most numerous in the Punjab. The Indian Government breeds mules for use in army transport. They are strong and hardy, and especially useful in hilly districts and rough roads, being more sure-footed than the horse. 200. Cattle, i.e., bulls, bullocks, and cows, are everywhere reared and greatly valued. They are almost equally common in every Province, and their number is everywhere found to be roughly proportionate to the population. The Government has of late years paid great attention to the improvement of the breeds of cattle, and their protection from disease, as well as to the provision of fodder. Sheep and goats also are pretty generally distributed, except in Burma, where they are rare. Sheep are most numerous in

Madras, and next in the Punjab. Goats are most numerous in the United Provinces, next in the Punjab and Madras.

The elephant is used for state display by the Native Princes, and for heavy transport by the Government. In Burma elephants are trained to work in the timber yards and may be seen hauling and stacking the heavy logs. For sagacity the elephant is hardily equaled even by the dog. The camel, the most useful of all beasts of burden in a hot and dry climate, is commoner than the horse in Sind, and almost as common in the Punjab and the North-Western Frontier Province. Camels are used also to some extent in the United Provinces, but in other parts of India they are hardly known. The buffalo is common throughout India, and, like the bullock, is used for draught purposes both on the road and in the fields. As in every other country, dogs of various breeds are universal. The most notable are the mastiff of the Himalayas, and the polegar hound of South India.

Economic Animal Products

The ordinary animal products which are everywhere used as food, and, as such, are common objects of local production, trade and consumption, need only be mentioned. Such are milk, butter, ghee, eggs, fish, poultry, game, flesh, etc. Flesh, either of beasts or birds, is a less common article of diet in tropical regions than in colder latitudes, and in India a vegetable diet has the added sanction of religion. Of the natives of India few beyond the Muhammadans and the lowest castes of Hindus are habitual flesh eaters. Milk, butter, and ghee, and all forms of dairy produce, are, however, universally used. So also are eggs. Fish, wherever it can be had, is a welcome food to full two-thirds of the people, and in the deltas of the rivers and along the coasts it forms a staple article of diet.

Fish curing is being developed in India as an economic industry, and it is possible that at no very distant date salt fish may become an article of export. Already there is a small quantity exported from Sind. Fish in India is commonly eaten fresh, and until very recently the process of fish curing was hardly known, or was rendered impossible by the prohibitive price of salt. For some years now the curing industry has been fostered by Government on the coasts of

Madras and Bombay. Fish curing yards have been opened, and salt for the purpose has been supplied at a nominal figure.

There is a considerable production of wool in India, though of an inferior quality. Much of it is u.sed locally in the manufacture of carpets, and almost all the rest is exported to Great Britain. The value of the raw wool exported in 1907 was 1, 600,000. For the best class of woollen manufacture in India raw wool is imported.

Hides of various kinds are a valuable article of commerce. They are collected in every Province both for the local leather industry and for shipment to Germany, Italy, and Austria. The value of the hides exported in 1907 was over 10,000,000. There are also small exports of horn, bone manure, and bristles.

Silk is the produce of the silk-worm, which is cultivated largely in Bengal and Assam, and to a less extent in several other provinces. It lives only on the leaves of the mulberry tree. Of late years great attention has been given to the culture both of the silk-worm and of the mulberiy, and the silk industry is increasing. A wild silk is obtained in large quantities in Assam, which is known as tusser silk. It is locally manufactured, and silk fabrics are much used by the Assamese. A good deal of the cultivated silk is also manufactured locally. The value of silk exports in 1907 was over ,500,000. Lac is deposited by the lac insect, and is collected by the hill tribes in the Central Provinces and Chota Nagpur. It is the source of shellac, a material used in the manufacture of varnishes and sealing-wax, and of lac-dye. The lac insect lives on many kinds of forest trees, and its artificial culture has been attempted by the Forest Officers in the Central Provinces. The lac industry is a remunerative and a growing one, and the exports of lac and lac-dye in 1907 were over 2,300,000 in value.

BIBLIOGRAPHY

Clark, Michael J., Kenneth J. Gregory, and Angela M. Gurnell: *Horizons in Physical Geography.* Basingstoke and London: Macmillan Education, 1987.

E. Dereniak and D. Crowe, *Optical Radiation Deiectord,* John Wiley and Sons, 1984.

Haggett, Peter: *Geography: A Modern Synthesis.* 2nd ed. New York: Harper and Row, 1975.

Hartshorne, Richard: *Perspective on the Nature of Geography.* Chicago: Published by Rand McNally and Company as Monograph No. 1, 1959.

Harvey, David: *Spaces of the Capital: Towards a Critical Geography.* Edinburgh: Edinburgh University Press, 2001.

Katz, Cindi, and Janis Monk: *Full Circles: Geographies of Women over the Life Course.* London and New York: Routledge, 1993.

Livingston, David N., and Charles W. J. Withers: *Geography and Enlightenment.* Chicago: University of Chicago Press, 1999.

Quaino, Massimo: *Geography and Marxism.* Translated by Alan Braley. Totowa, N.J.: Barnes and Noble, 1982.

Thrower, Norman J. W.: *Maps and Civilization: Cartography in Culture and Society.* Chicago and London: University of Chicago Press, 1999.

Wood, E.J. Ferguson: *Marine Microbial Ecology,* London, Chapman and Hall, 1965.

INDEX

□□□